This is the first comprehensive treatment of Nietzsche's philosophy of art to appear in English. Julian Young argues that Nietzsche's thought about art can be understood only in the context of his wider philosophy. In particular, he discusses the dramatic changes in Nietzschean aesthetics against the background of the celebrated themes of the death of God, eternal recurrence and the idea of the *Übermensch*. Young divides Nietzsche's career, and his philosophy of art, into four distinct phases, but suggests that these phases describe a circle. An attempt at world-affirmation is made in the central phases, but Nietzsche is predominantly influenced at the beginning and end of his career by a Schopenhauerian pessimism. At the beginning and end art is important because it "redeems" us from life.

This is a clear and lucid account of Nietzsche's philosophy of art. It combines exegesis, interpretation, and criticism in a judicious balance, and will be essential reading for all scholars of philosophy and German studies with an interest in Nietzsche or aesthetics.

NIETZSCHE'S PHILOSOPHY OF ART

NIETZSCHE'S
PHILOSOPHY OF ART

JULIAN YOUNG

Department of Philosophy,
University of Auckland

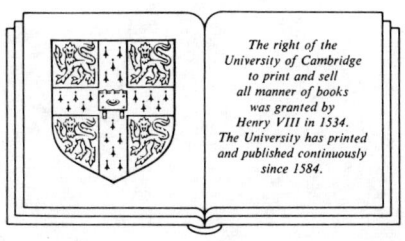

CAMBRIDGE UNIVERSITY PRESS

Cambridge
New York   Port Chester
Melbourne   Sydney

Published by the Press Syndicate of the University of Cambridge
The Pitt Building, Trumpington Street, Cambridge CB2 IRP
40 West 20th Street, New York, NY 10011-4211, USA
10 Stamford Road, Oakleigh, Victoria 3166, Australia

First published 1992

Printed in Great Britain at the University Press, Cambridge

A catalogue record for this book is available from the British Library

Library of Congress cataloguing in publication data applied for

ISBN 0 521 41124 6 hardback

For
Michael Cherniavsky

Contents

Acknowledgments

I am grateful to the University of Mainz and the German Academic Exchange Service for providing, respectively, the hospitality and the finance that made possible the birth of the thoughts here recorded, also to the students, too many to be named, at the Universities of Auckland and Calgary who contributed to graduate seminars in which these thoughts were tested and molded into shape. I should like to thank friends and colleagues who have read the manuscript or in other ways helped make this a better work than it would otherwise have been: Rudolph Malter, Bob Solomon, Kathleen Higgins, Stephen Davies, Chris Goj, Heath Lees, Peter Kraus, and the (anonymous) readers for Cambridge University Press. And finally I thank Jenny Diepraam and Maggie Kohl for laboring long and hard with my appalling handwriting.

Abbreviations

Nietzsche's works are abbreviated as follows (textual references are to section numbers):

A	*The Anti-Christ*
BGE	*Beyond Good and Evil*
BT	*The Birth of Tragedy*
CW	*The Case of Wagner*
D	*Dawn (Daybreak)*
EH	*Ecce Homo*
GM	*On the Genealogy of Morals*
GS	*The Gay Science*
HH ɪ	*Human, All-too-human*
HH ɪɪa	*Assorted Opinions and Maxims*
HH ɪɪb	*The Wanderer and his Shadow*
NCW	*Nietzsche Contra Wagner*
TI	*Twilight of the Idols*
WB	*Richard Wagner at Bayreuth*
WP	*The Will to Power*
Z	*Thus Spoke Zarathustra*
KG	*Werke: Kritische Gesamtausgabe*, ed. G. Colli and M. Montinari in 30 vols.

And Schopenhauer's works as follows (textual references are to page numbers):

WR ɪ, *WR* ɪɪ	*The World as Will and Representation* vols. ɪ and ɪɪ
PP ɪ, *PP* ɪɪ	*Parerga and Paralipomena* vols. ɪ and ɪɪ

Full bibliographical information can be found under "Texts and translations" (p. 166).

Introduction

1 This, first of all, is a book about Nietzsche's philosophy of art, about his view of the genesis of art, of what makes good art good and bad art bad; about, above all, the relationship between art and life. Or rather, it is a book about Nietzsche's philosoph*ies* of art for, so runs a central thesis of the book, there is, in Nietzsche, no single view of art (or of very much else). Rather, his career divides up into different periods distinguished from each other by sharply contrasting attitudes to and about art. More specifically, I hold that Nietzsche's thought about art divides into *four* main periods. I also hold, however, that the fourth constitutes a return to the first. In the end, so I argue, the path described by Nietzsche's thought is a circular one.

Philosophy is distinguished by the fact that everything is connected with everything else. Of Nietzsche's philosophy this is even more true than usual. Thus this is not *just* a book about art. It is not just an essay in "aesthetics," for it turns out that it is not possible to discuss the development of Nietzsche's aesthetics without trying to understand his metaphysics, his fluctuating beliefs concerning the scope of human knowledge, concerning the nature and value of science (roughly, the higher his valuation of science the lower his valuation of art and vice versa) and concerning pessimism (roughly, the more seriously he takes pessimism the more seriously he takes art and vice versa). And when it comes to Nietzsche's later philosophy of art, it turns out that that cannot be understood without confronting the celebrated Nietzschean themes: the death of God, the eternal recurrence, and the idea of the *Übermensch* ("overman"). (Interestingly, though, the "will to power" turns out to be relatively *un*important – but that, it has always seemed to me, is a notion which figures much more prominently in commentaries than in the

I

texts themselves.) Hence what the book offers is a particular perspective on the development of Nietzsche's philosophy as a whole.

The work is organized chronologically. (Chapters 2 to 5 correspond to the four periods into which I claim Nietzsche's career falls.) It thus constitutes a kind of biography: not a biography in the usual sense but rather a *philosophical* biography, a record of the twists and turns taken by Nietzsche's philosophy viewed through the prism of his philosophy of art. The model it follows is supplied by Nietzsche himself; by his last book, *Ecce Homo*, the work which purports to be his philosophical autobiography. As in *Ecce Homo* the matter of this study is the life lived by Nietzsche *in* rather than outside of his writings, and as in *Ecce Homo* that life is viewed as falling into sharply separate phases, phases which nonetheless add up to a kind of unity, an *aesthetic* unity. Unlike *Ecce Homo*, however – in many ways a mendacious, deluded book – this study aims at *truthfulness*. In this respect it aims to be an improvement over its often questionable model.

Unlike *Ecce Homo*, too, this is a *critical* study of Nietzsche's thought. This sets it apart from what seems to me a regrettable trend in recent discussion of Nietzsche (at least in English), a trend to mere interpretation. There are, it seems to me, at least two, more or less conscious modes of thinking which underlie this trend. The first consists in thinking that since, according to Nietzsche's "perspectivism" (in chapter 4 I *reject* this interpretation of the doctrine), there are no truths but only interpretations, it follows that there is no definitive text to criticize and that all one can do is to offer interpretations that one finds appealing. The second and opposite tendency (one which would have delighted the author of *Thus Spake Zarathustra*) consists in elevating the texts to quasi-biblical status, in treating them as unquestionable repositories of profound and wonderful truth, the only task being that of recovering and articulating this truth.

Both of these ways of thinking are, I believe, to be avoided. The first because it is self-undermining – if there is no definitive text because of perspectivism then perspectivism is true (and a definitive part of the text) and there are, after all, some truths – and the second because it is blind. Whatever Nietzsche may have come to believe, ultimately, about his own infallibility (see the Epilogue below), the fact is that the texts are by no means that but are, along with their brilliance and insight, full of prejudice dressed up as philosophy,

manipulative rhetoric, and, on occasion, atrociously poor argu-
mentation.

Criticism of Nietzsche is legitimate. There *is* definitive text, or
rather texts, and their character is not as difficult to discover as is
often pretended. And it is vital. Otherwise, having entered that
Nietzschean maze, one never finds one's way out again.

2 My first chapter is about Schopenhauer. It is well known that as
a young man Nietzsche was deeply impressed by the great pessimist
and that his first book, *The Birth of Tragedy*, was written under his
influence. The general view is that after this relatively brief, youthful
infatuation Nietzsche turned in the direction of "health" and away
from Schopenhauer's philosophy of "sickness": that thereafter
Schopenhauer figures in Nietzsche's thought only as the "antipode"
of himself and his philosophy. And this, certainly, is the view put
about by Nietzsche himself: whereas the early writings refer to
Schopenhauer in terms of almost religious veneration, the later
writings refer to him almost always as an epitome of sickness,
"decadence," and error.

I oppose this view of things. *The Birth of Tragedy*, I shall argue (in
ch. 2), was (not just cosmetically but fundamentally) influenced by,
in particular, Schopenhauer's metaphysics and his philosophy of art.
And on the crucial question of pessimism, the Schopenhauerian
assessment of the worth of human existence is, I shall suggest,
endorsed. In the middle of his life Nietzsche turned against pessimism
and against Schopenhauer. But in the end, reluctantly and making
every rhetorical effort to disguise this from us and, more importantly,
from himself, he came back, I shall argue, to pessimism. Though
Schopenhauer's *name* is never rehabilitated – to do so would have
been to admit to that which Nietzsche was trying so hard to
conceal – his essential spirit, his pessimism, lives as strongly in
Nietzsche's final works as in his first.

But even on the view that Schopenhauer really *is* the antipode of
Nietzsche's later philosophy he remains the crucial figure to an
understanding of Nietzsche (crucial, on *this* view, somewhat in the
way that Catholicism is crucial to the psychology of the lapsed
Catholic). From any point of view Schopenhauer is vital to the
understanding of Nietzsche. Except for the Greeks, there is no other
philosopher he knew with anything like the same intimacy. His
writings, all of them, are full not just of quotations and paraphrases

from Schopenhauer, but of phrases, allusions and rhythms both conscious and unconscious. Nietzsche *breathed* Schopenhauer and cannot be understood without him.

3 Any work on Nietzsche has to express a policy with respect to the *Nachlass*, in particular with respect to that portion of it published posthumously as *The Will to Power*. It has now been established[1] that far from *The Will to Power* constituting, as Heidegger and many others have held, his "philosophy proper," a philosophy he would have eventually published had not madness and death intervened, over three-quarters of the entries were, in fact, never intended for publication at all. What follows is that (1) no interpretative thesis must be based on *The Will to Power* alone, and (2) passages from that work must never be given interpretative precedence over passages from published works. Their sole legitimate use is as clarifications of, and expansions upon, that which Nietzsche published. In general, it seems to me, the distinction between the public and private is very important with respect to Nietzsche. Like many people, he used private notes to *entertain* (not affirm) a variety of positions with respect to a given issue. The act of affirmation was the act of publication. Nietzsche's celebrated self-contradictions are greatly diminished if this is borne in mind (together with the fact that to change one's mind over time is not to contradict oneself).

Schopenhauer

1 Nietzsche's thought about art is, I suggested in the Introduction, deeply rooted in the philosophy of Schopenhauer; in Schopenhauer's philosophy of art but in his general philosophy too. Accordingly, in this chapter, I provide a brief sketch of Schopenhauer's philosophy as a whole, first a highly impressionistic account of his general philosophy and then, in somewhat greater detail, an account of his philosophy of art. In doing so I shall try to present him as Nietzsche saw him, through his eyes and sometimes in his words. Of the several images which might be offered of that clear yet ultimately ambiguous structure which is Schopenhauer's philosophy, this chapter tries to present the Nietzschean image.

2 Schopenhauer's metaphysics, propounded mainly in the first two books of his main work, *The World as Will and Representation* (1819), is a version of Kantian idealism. The everyday world, the world given in sense-perception, is ideal, mere "representation," "pheno-menon," or "appearance," a creation of the human mind quite different in character from the reality, the world "in itself" that underlies it.

In the main, Schopenhauer takes this, as simply a *datum*, as something established beyond all doubt by Kant's great *Critique of Pure Reason* (1781). Yet he does provide one original and quite un-Kantian argument for (a kind of) idealism. This consists in an elaboration of the observation that, as a survival mechanism, the human brain can be expected to present the world to us in a useful rather than – a by no means coincident notion – truthful manner (see especially, *WR* II, ch. XXII).[1] (Biological idealism, the idea that we perceive the world in terms of "life-preserving errors" [*GS* 110], is central to Nietzsche's philosophy in all its phases, and even at his most anti-Schopenhauerian he is prepared to acknowledge his debt

5

in this regard. In *The Gay Science*, for instance, he refers to Schopenhauer's "immortal doctrine" of the "instrumental [i.e. practical] character" of human thought and perception [*GS* 99]).

Notice that the biological route to idealism modifies the character of Kantian, strictly "transcendental," idealism. For, according to Kant, it is not merely the world of common sense but, more comprehensively, "nature," the entire world of space and time, that is ideal. Yet an argument to the ideality of the common-sense image of the world that is grounded in an appeal to proto-Darwinian facts concerning the biological function of the brain seems to presuppose that a scientific, and hence natural, image of the world presents it as it really, in itself, is. The non-natural *an sich* of Kant's metaphysics is transposed into a natural, albeit esoteric, domain.[2]

3 What is this metaphysical yet natural substratum upon which we impose our near and orderly story of common-sense objects and events? Schopenhauer calls it "will"; it is "The World as Will." He arrives at this description on account of the conjunction of two main lines of thought. The first consists in reflections upon the foundations of natural science ("there is much science in Schopenhauer," Nietzsche remarks in *Human, All-too-human*), reflections concerning, in particular, the inadequacy of the atomistic conception of matter. This he describes as a "revolting absurdity" subscribed to mainly by the French on account of "the backward state of [their]... metaphysics" (*WR* II, p. 302). Ultimate nature, he holds, cannot be conceived as a collection of tiny, indestructible chunks of matter but must, rather, be conceived as a flux of immaterial force or energy. The only coherent conception of ultimate nature is a dynamic rather than mechanistic one.[3]

The second factor that leads Schopenhauer to use "will" to characterize the ultimate reality of nature is a particular version of meaning-empiricism: his doctrine, taken over from Kant and ultimately from Locke, that terms are meaningful only if their meaning can be elucidated in terms of sense-experience. Schopenhauer chooses to satisfy his own metatheoretical constraint by identifying the force that nature ultimately is with "will."[4] He defends this extension of the concept beyond its normal restriction to the human or at least sentient domain by inviting us to reflect upon the analogies between the behavior of objects throughout nature – the turning of the magnet towards the pole, the "striving" of the stone for ever-closer union with the earth – and that behavior, human behavior, which we *know* to be a manifestation of will (of desiring, hoping, suffering, fearing, and so on). Satisfying the constraints of concept-empiricism in the Schopenhauerian manner is to be seen not as arbitrary but as provided with an epistemological, that is analogical, warrant.

Schopenhauer conceives of the force, that is to say will, that nature fundamentally is as a single quantum. This introduces into his metaphysics a distinctive – and distinctly un-Kantian – contrast between the one and the many.[5] The everyday, phenomenal world is a world of individuals; it is subject, as Schopenhauer puts it, to the *principium individuationis*. But the metaphysical reality beneath it is "beyond plurality," is, that is to say, "One." Plurality is therefore an "illusion." (As we will see, Nietzsche's first book, *The Birth of Tragedy*, combines both the substance and the terminology of Schopenhauer's one–many contrast. He even emphasizes it by referring to metaphysical reality not only as "the will" but also as "the primal unity.")

4 The best-known fact about Schopenhauer is that he was a pessimist. The world of the *principium individuationis* is a world of terror and suffering, from which it follows, he holds, that its membership is a curse not a blessing. And the will that is responsible for, and expresses itself in, such a world – as it were, the "inner character" that materializes itself in the horrors of nature – must be concluded to be evil, morally repugnant, something that ought not exist. Hence his vigorous insistence that, notwithstanding certain similarities to the doctrine, he is no pantheist: nature he says, fitting his own meaning to Aristotle's words, is not divine but demonic (*WR* II, p. 349). (Nietzsche accurately comments: "Against the theory that the 'in-itself' of things must necessarily be good, blessed, true, and one, Schopenhauer's interpretation of the 'in-itself' as will was an essential step; but he did not understand how to *deify* this will; he remained entangled in the moral–Christian ideal...see[ing] it as bad, stupid, and absolutely reprehensible" [*WP* 1005].)

What reason is there to regard the world of individuals as a world of such horror? Schopenhauer has several distinct routes to pessimism (one of these I shall touch on in sec. 5 below) but that which has greatest relevance to our interest in Nietzsche is grounded in the, in some respects, Darwinian character of Schopenhauer's perception of nature.

From his proto-Darwinian perspective Schopenhauer saw that the suffering of individuals is no accidental phenomenon but is, rather, written into the system of nature. The means, that is, that nature, the world-will, adopts to ensure the perpetuation of its system of species is the massive overpopulation of the world by members of one species so that there remains always a surplus to act as food for members of another (*WR* II, p. 351). It follows that the pain and destruction of individuals is part of the order of things decreed by a world-will criminally indifferent to the fate of the individuals.

In the case of human beings, of course, the grosser of the ways in which one individual preys upon another are eradicated by the state (its sole function). Nonetheless, human life, too, is dominated by rival egoisms, the satisfaction of the one necessarily entailing the suffering of another. Thus nature as a whole, whether within or outside of society, is essentially more or less open *bellum omnium contra omnes*, Hobbes' war, all against all. When we add that such "contradiction" is the eternally repeated order of things – there is no goal towards which the world is evolving and hence no possibility of an ultimate redemption or justification of present horrors – we understand the full bleakness of Schopenhauer's view of nature. (And when we add that the ultimate bearer of the world's pain is identical with its ultimate source we see a terrible "eternal justice" in things: the world-will's pain exactly balances its guilt [*WR* I, p. 352].)

5 Human beings, we have seen, are compelled to cause suffering to each other by the competitive character of existence. But, normally, to do so causes them little compunction. The reasons for this are epistemological: only one's own body is presented to one as "inhabited" by will, other human bodies being presented as *mere* bodies. Only, that is, my body is presented to me as capable of desire and frustration, as susceptible to pleasure and pain. Hence it is entirely natural for me to treat other humans as inanimate things, to dispose of them as mere means to the satisfaction of my own ends. "Egoism" is the *natural* stance of one human being to another. Virtue, that is to say altruism (the supreme principle of morality is "hurt no one: on the contrary help everyone as much as you can"), constitutes, therefore, a theoretical problem: how is it possible?

Schopenhauer answers that when it occurs – there are, he believes, rare but genuine exceptions to the egoistic norm of human action – it constitutes an occasion of extraordinary metaphysical insight, a transcendence of the common-sense metaphysics of the *principium individuationis*. The psychological basis of altruism is sympathy – feeling the same kind of concern for the well-being of another that one normally has for one's own – and the basis of that is the altruist's penetration of the "veil of maya"; her inarticulate, "intuitive" realization that the *principium individuationis* is an illusion, that every individual is as much an "objectification" of the primal unity as the one she normally calls "me." The ultimate basis of altruism is, as we may call it, "metaphysical solipsism": the realization that I am the only being that exists but that every other individual is this "I" too: "tat tvam asi," "this art thou," in the formula from the *Upanishads* that Schopenhauer often quotes.

What is the point, the justification, of altruism? A kind of point, and as it were interim justification, is provided by the contrast between the worlds inhabited by, respectively, the altruist and the egoist. The latter inhabits (in terms of Ferdinand Tönnies' later distinction) a *Gesellschaft* of individuals who stand to each other in essentially competitive, hostile relations. Because the heart is "contracted" by egoism, because it "concentrates our interest on the particular phenomenon of our own individuality and then knowledge always presents us with the innumerable perils that continually threaten this phenomenon ... anxiety and care become the keynote of [our] disposition" (*WR* I, p. 373). The altruist, on the other hand, inhabits a warm and friendly *Gemeinschaft*. Because the heart is "enlarged" by altruism, because altruism "extends our interest in all that lives," it follows that "the anxious care for... self is attacked and restricted at the root: hence the calm and confident serenity afforded by a virtuous disposition" (*WR* I, p. 374).

But the real reward for altruism – here Schopenhauer's pessimism comes into play – is knowledge. For as altruistic identification with others becomes increasingly universal in scope, as occurs in the life of the saint, the altruist comes to the increasingly vivid realization that suffering is the dominant character not just of her own but of all life, that life as such is suffering. She comes, that is, to an intuitive realization of the truth of philosophical pessimism. This brings about a "transition from virtue to asceticism" (*WR* I, p. 380), a retreat from action, even moral action, which is seen now to be futile. And it brings about, too, a "denial of the will," a moral nausea at, and consequent retreat from identification with, the will which is now perceived to be the evil source of the world's pain. The ultimate point, then, to altruism is that it is a "stage" on the path to that ultimate enlightenment which constitutes "salvation"; the realization that the will is to be denied.

Why should denial of the will constitute salvation? What does the holy ascetic identify *with* after disassociation from the will? From the rationalistic point of view demanded of philosophy, there is nothing that can be said. The account of the world as will takes us to the limits – limits imposed by concept-empiricism – of language. But we only have to observe the tremendous unanimity in the (literally meaningless) literature of the mystics concerning both the existence and character of a domain beyond the natural – they all report its wonder and oneness – to "banish the dark impression" that an absolute "nothingness" "as the final goal hovers behind all virtue and holiness" (*WR* I, p. 411). There *is* something "beyond the will" (*WR* II, pp. 197–8), something which though, for us, a know-not-what is accessible, present, and wondrous to those in whom the will has turned and denied itself.[6]

6 How, to come finally to the center of our concern, does Schopenhauer's philosophy of art fit into the philosophical landscape we have thus far described? Schopenhauer's discussion of art occupies the third of the four books that constitute his main work and falls into two halves: the first offers a theory of art in general; the second develops out of it a special theory for each of the particular arts.

The heart of the general theory is the idea that there is a special kind of consciousness or perception which is uniquely aesthetic. Anything which is a genuine work of art must be created out of this state, created with the intention of prompting and aiding the re-creation of a similar state in the mind of the spectator (*WR* II, pp. 407–8). It is tempting, particularly given Schopenhauer's identification of the capacity to sustain and communicate the aesthetic state with the rare phenomenon of *genius* (*WR* I, p. 185), to protest that it cannot be art as such but only *good* art that could be required to be inspired by this special state: to suggest, in other words, that Schopenhauer's requirement is not intended to distinguish art from non-art but rather good from bad art. In fact, however, this distinction is not one Schopenhauer acknowledges: to him bad art counts as non-art. There are, that is, on the one hand authentic artists whose works genuinely embody the aesthetic state, and on the other "imitators," "mannerists," pretend-artists who "suck their nourishment" from the work of the genuine artist but produce nothing (save, presumably, expensive handicraft) themselves (*WR* I, p. 235). Schopenhauer, in short, and very often Nietzsche too, refuses to use the term "art" in anything but an evaluative sense.

Like altruism, Schopenhauer regards aesthetic vision as a rare and extraordinary transcendence of our ordinary mode of perceiving the world. This makes it natural for him to define the aesthetic state via a contrast between it and the ordinary state.

Ordinarily, we identify ourselves with an empirical individual, an "object among objects" in the spatio-temporal world. This is the precondition of our ability to locate other objects in the world: I can only locate an object in space or time by relating it, ultimately, to a *here* and *now*, the reference of which is determined by the location of my own body. Epistemologically, I am, in Wittgenstein's phrase, "the centre of my world." Now, because one's essence is to will, the question of what kinds of objects are located where and when is by no means a matter of indifference. On the contrary, we find the objects around us and the question of their relationships to ourselves deeply "interesting." We view them "in relation to the will" (*WR* I, p. 177) either as threats to our well-being or as potential satisfiers of our desires. But this means (here we return to the theme of the "instrumental" character of ordinary consciousness) that much manipulation of perceptual data occurs in the interests of the will: to the traveler in a hurry, for instance, the beautiful Rhine bridge may appear as little more than a dash intersecting with a stroke (*WR* II, p. 381).

The final hallmark of ordinary consciousness (here another of Schopenhauer's routes to pessimism presents itself) is suffering and anxiety. Generally speaking, there is a disjunction between the will and the world: the way the world is is rarely in all respects – and then only briefly and, as we have seen, uncertainly – the way we want it to be. And in those moments when it is we suffer the terrible penalty of "boredom": a frustrated "pressure" of the will which lacks any object upon which to express itself (*WR* I, p. 364). Everyday life, if we are honest, we must admit to be, in the main, an oscillating mixture of pain, anxiety, and boredom.

Ordinary consciousness, then, is marked by epistemological egocentricity, interestedness, the manipulation of perceptual content by the will – Schopenhauer speaks here of "subjectivity" – and by pain and anxiety. Aesthetic consciousness is marked by the disappearance of each of these features. How does this happen? It happens, says Schopenhauer, when, "to use a pregnant expression," we "lose" ourselves in the object of perception so that "we are no longer able to separate the perceiver from the perception but the two have become one since the entire consciousness is filled and occupied by a single image of perception" (*WR* 1, pp. 118–19). When this happens one ceases to be aware of oneself as one spatio-temporal object among many and hence ceases to view objects in relation to an individual will: perception becomes (here Schopenhauer adopts Kant's hallmark of aesthetic awareness) "disinterested." From this it follows that the "subjectivity" of ordinary consciousness disappears – perception becomes "objective" – and that its painful character disappears too: if my consciousness is wholly absorbed by the object of perception, then I can be aware neither of a disjunction between the will and the world nor of the will as being objectless. This blessed disappearance of pain constitutes one of the two forms of aesthetic pleasure (the other we will come to shortly). Often, that is, when we describe an object as beautiful – a landscape lit by evening light, glimpsed on one's first escape from the city, perhaps – we simply express the subjective state the object helps produce in us, "a painless state" in which for a brief moment we are "delivered from the vile [*schnöde*] pressure of the will" and "celebrate the sabbath of the penal servitude of willing; the wheel of Ixion stands still" (*WR* 1, p. 196). Schopenhauer regards this state as pregnant with significance since it is a brief (and partial) indication of the bliss of the ascetic, an intimation of "how blessed must be the life of a man in whom the will is silenced not for a few moments... but for ever" (*WR* 1, p. 390). The aesthetic state, in short, is a signpost to the (permanent) solution to the problem of pain.

7 In aesthetic consciousness there is, we have seen, a radical transformation of its *subject*, a transformation into, as Schopenhauer put it, "the pure will-less, painless, timeless subject of knowledge" (*WR* 1, p. 179). Inseparably connected with this, however, there occurs also a transformation of the object. For since we cease to be aware of ourselves as occupying a *here* and a *now* in the world and since, as we saw, the locating of other objects in the space–time world is dependent on such consciousness, it follows that we cease to be

aware of the object of perception as an inhabitant of that network of relations which constitutes the space–time world. But that means that we cease to perceive it as an individual, for individuality, Schopenhauer holds, is constituted only by membership of that network.

What then do we perceive? Schopenhauer's initially surprising answer is that the objects of aesthetic perception are Plato's Forms, the "Platonic Ideas." The everyday world, we saw, is an appearance of the world as will. But the will appears, manifests, "objectifies" itself at various "grades" which are higher or lower depending on the clarity with which the will reveals its essential nature in them. At the lowest level are natural forces such as gravity and magnetism, above them the various species of inorganic and organic bodies. Finally, at the highest level, there is the human species in which that same will obscurely manifested in gravitational or magnetic phenomena reveals its nature most clearly. These grades are the Ideas, the objects of aesthetic perception. It follows then that aesthetic perception involves a *double* transformation: "at one stroke the particular thing becomes the *Idea* of it species, and the perceiving individual the pure subject of knowing" (*WR* I, p. 179).

8 Before passing to Schopenhauer's treatment of the particular arts, I want to raise, and try to answer, a number of questions concerning the general theory which lies now, in outline, before us.

The first can be introduced by observing that Schopenhauer's insistence on the will-less disinterestedness of aesthetic contemplation provides him with, among other things, a criterion for distinguishing between art and, roughly speaking, pornography. For since art not only arises out of, but also seeks to communicate, the aesthetic state, it follows that genuine art should never represent objects (the female form, for example) in a manner calculated to arouse the appetites. Although, *pace* Nietzsche (see ch. 5, sec. 8 below), this seems a plausible account of the distinction between art and pornography, it also raises a problem. For if art is to be confronted in a will-less state then, since every emotion is classified by Schopenhauer as a state of the will (*WR* II, p. 202), the unacceptable consequence seems to follow that art, properly perceived, never evokes emotion. On a much criticized yet stubbornly vital theory of what it is for a work of art to express emotion, moreover – the theory that the work is cheerful or sad or angry just in case it tends to produce that feeling in the audience – it would further follow that art cannot express emotion.

As we will shortly see, Schopenhauer's central interest lies in emphasizing the cognitive function of art. For this reason he attends only *en passant* to its expressive aspect. Nonetheless, he says enough, I think, to show that he neither supposes, nor is committed to supposing, that the will-lessness of aesthetic perception excludes the propriety of an emotional response to art.

Schopenhauer repeatedly emphasizes that the kind of emotion that is incompatible with aesthetic contemplation is *personal* emotion – "personal participation" (*WR* II, p. 373), the presence of "personal aims" (*PP* II, p. 205), "*individual* [my emphasis] subjectivity" (*WR* I, p. 199). This suggests that he might allow an affective response to art provided that the emotions involved are in some way depersonalized.

The clearest confirmation that this is his position is to be found in his discussion of the sublime. We experience the "feeling of the sublime," he says, when we perceive an object that normally stands in a "hostile" relation to the will without feeling, in the *ordinary* way, fear. (The hostility of the "dynamically" sublime – huge tempests, waterfalls, the wind howling through gullies, bleak, black, over-hanging rocks – consists in their bringing home to one one's powerlessness in the face of the might of nature, of the "math-ematically" sublime – the night sky, the dome of St. Paul's – in making one aware of the vanishing insignificance of one's tenure in space and time.) How is such "fearlessness" in the face of the fearful possible? Why do we not only not flee the sublime but even seek confrontation with it? The crucial phenomenon is simply that disassociation from one's normal identity, that ascension to the standpoint of the "pure subject" which occurs in experiencing the beautiful. What distinguishes the sublime from the beautiful, however – the two may merge into each other – is that in ex-periencing the former one has a split, "two-fold" consciousness so that although one is the pure, non-individual subject one *also* feels oneself as the "feeble phenomenon," "dependent," "threatened," "insignificant," "abandoned to chance" (*WR* I, pp. 204–6). This latter induces a specially intense feeling of joy as one becomes aware of one's separateness from the threatened, insecure, above all *mortal* individual. The feeling of the sublime is for Schopenhauer, as for Kant, whom he follows closely in this matter, an intimation of immortality, a coming alive, in Kant's words, to the "supersensible side of our being" (*Critique of Judgment*, sec. 27). Notice, however, that one also experiences the fearful emotions of the threatened individual. That one does not flee the sublime is explained by one's disassociation from that individual: one, as it were, empathizes with those emotions without regarding them as one's own.

If we now, as I believe we should, infer from this account of the sublime to a general account of the expressiveness of art, the crucial distinction can be seen to lie between ordinary, personal, action-prompting emotion on the one hand, and depersonalized, universal emotion on the other – universal because if the individual who confronts the sublime object is not "me" it is, surely, *everyman*. It is the former, but not the latter, which is excluded from aesthetic contemplation.

9 The second issue I want to raise is that of the nature and significance of the "Platonic Ideas" in Schopenhauer's general theory of art. In *Willing and Unwilling* (ch. VII, sec. 6) I have argued at length against the view that Schopenhauer's use of Platonic terminology is intended to introduce as that which the artist apprehends and makes into the content of the artwork a domain of objects ontologically distinct from the domain of ordinary individuals. That which Cézanne perceives and his work represents is, I have suggested, not the Idea of the apple *rather than* the particular apple; rather, he perceives and represents the particular apple *as Idea*. That which a Rembrandt self-portrait represents is not Humanity *rather than* Rembrandt; it is, rather, Rembrandt but with the focus and emphasis upon not the idiosyncratic in the individual – that way lies the path to caricature (*WR* I, p. 225) – but the universal, that "side of the Idea of mankind specially appearing in this particular individual" (*WR* I, p. 221).

To perceive or represent an object as Idea is, as we may put it, to *idealize* it; to bring out its "significant form" (*WR* I, p. 201), to produce a representation of it in which "everything essential and significant is gathered together and placed in the brightest light, but everything accidental and foreign eliminated" (*WR* I, p. 248). This is what it is to represent an object as beautiful, to beautify it. (Delight in significant form is the second of Schopenhauer's two kinds of aesthetic pleasure [see sec. 6 above].) To some extent beauty already occurs in nature. Every natural object instantiates the Idea of its species and hence, if its form is such as to express that Idea clearly, it is beautiful. In general, however, art is more beautiful than nature since the artist's control over form is greater than that of nature. He is able to provide a "purer repetition" (*WR* II, p. 407) of nature's forms and hence to "express clearly what nature only stammers" (*WR* I, p. 222).

The impetus behind this account of aesthetic representation is the rejection of naturalism. Art does *not* mirror nature, Schopenhauer insists, but rather eliminates, obscures or deemphasizes everything in an object or action that is not to its purpose. That purpose – a purpose, he holds, which art shares with philosophy – is the revelation of ultimate and universal truth; "the true nature of things, of life and of existence" (*WR* I, p. 406). It is the emphasis of this purpose, not the introduction of Plato's ontology, which, I believe, provides the rationale for Schopenhauer's use of Plato's terminology. Plato, that is, pursuing "the ancient quarrel between philosophy and poetry," condemns art for seducing the mind away from the quest for truth with a play of sensuous surfaces. Schopenhauer's aim is to rebut Plato's critique of art, "one of the greatest errors... of that great man" (*WR* I, p. 212), by redescribing art in precisely the terms which Plato reserved for philosophy. Art does not baffle but rather, in its own way, prosecutes the quest for ultimate knowledge.

10 Schopenhauer holds, as has been mentioned, that the Platonic Ideas in which the will, the metaphysical essence of the world manifests itself, constitute a hierarchy in which different "grades" correspond to the different degrees of clarity with which the will reveals itself. Corresponding to this hierarchy is a hierarchy of the arts. For each art has a special appropriateness to a certain grade of the will's self-revelation. Architecture is the "lowest" art, for it has as its central concern the "dullest visibility" of the will, the play between the forces of gravity and rigidity inherent in its material. At the top of the hierarchy are the poetic arts, for in their subject-matter the metaphysical truth about the world reveals itself most clearly. (Notice that Schopenhauer orders the arts solely in terms of their cognitive value: aesthetic value is, for him, identical with cognitive value.) With the exception of his discussions of poetry and, above all, music, Schopenhauer's discussion of the particular arts has only marginal relevance to our interest in Nietzsche. I shall, accordingly, confine my attention to what he has to say about these two arts.

11 One of the hazards of attempting to refute Plato's critique of art by redescribing it in the terms which Plato reserves for philosophy is that of obliterating the distinction between art and philosophy. Schopenhauer is aware of the need to accommodate the distinction. He does so by insisting that although the *topic* of art and philosophy is the same – both are concerned to reveal the nature of ultimate reality – their modes of communication are different. For while philosophy is essentially *conceptual*, art is *perceptual* (*WR* ii, p. 406). The heart of this contrast is the idea that whereas philosophy presents its universal truth abstracted and isolated in the form of a proposition, art presents its truth always only in and through the concrete particular, the "fragment" or "example," the "image of perception" (*ibid.*). The knowledge of philosophy is always *explicit*, that of art *implicit*, so that philosophy, he says, is related to art somewhat as wine to grapes (*WR* ii, p. 407).

Schopenhauer's account of poetry (he includes under this term poetic drama – *theater*, that is, as he knew it) has, at its heart, this interplay of cognitive universality and perceptual particularity.

The poet's concern, he says, is with both "distinctness and vividness" (*WR* i, p. 242). On the one hand, he seeks vividness of communication with the imagination of the reader. To this end his skill lies in the fact that although he employs the same words as are used in the "driest prose" to communicate conceptual thought, he is yet able to combine them so as to stimulate the appearance of perceptual images before the imagination. In this connection, the use of, for example, adjectives and adverbs is particularly important, for through them the "sphere of a concept" is restricted more and more until perceptuality is reached. This is how the lines from Goethe's *Mignon*

> Where gentle breezes from the blue heavens sigh
> There stands the myrtle still, the laurel high

precipitate from a few concepts the delight (as we will see, a particularly Nietzschean delight) of the southern climate (*WR* i, p. 243).

On the other hand, however, poetry is concerned to present with clarity and distinctness the Idea of, above all, humanity. It is concerned with the communication of universal truth about human life. To this end (unlike history, which, according to Schopenhauer, presents huge, boring chunks of factual detail in which, since chronology provides the only principle of ordering, the trivial and the significant are lumped together in an undifferentiated mass) poetry selects for our attention only "significant characters in significant situations." By "holding up before us a clarifying mirror [*verdeutlichenden Spiegel*]" in which everything "essential and significant" is retained but everything idiosyncratic or trivial eliminated (*WR* I, p. 248), the poet tells us about *man* (*WR* I, p. 244) (unlike the historian who speaks only of *men* [*ibid.*]).

12 Schopenhauer experiences some difficulty in applying his general theory of art to lyric poetry. For since the lyric is, he suggests, distinguished from other forms of poetry by the fact that the depictor is also the depicted, "a certain subjectivity is essential to poetry of this kind" (*WR* I, p. 248). Since will-less objectivity is, according to his general theory of art, a condition of genuinely aesthetic perception, this leads to a devaluation of lyric poetry as not requiring genius for its production: "even the man who is not very eminent can produce a beautiful song," for all that is required is a "vivid perception" of his own state in a moment of emotional excitement (*WR* I, p. 249).

But this is a bad misunderstanding of his own general theory, for, as we saw in discussing the sublime (sec. 8 above), it is possible for the artist to be detached from, "objective" about, his own feelings as well as about the outer world. He can do this by ascending to the perspective of the "pure subject of knowing" a state in which, as Schopenhauer *correctly* put it in the case of the composer, "the man is entirely separate from and distinct from the artist" (*WR* I, p. 260). Presumably, it is the predominance of the personal pronoun in lyric poetry that misleads Schopenhauer into failing to give a unitary account of poet and musician.

Nietzsche saw that Schopenhauer had misapplied his own theory, and saw that in his "profound metaphysics of music" he "held in his hands the means" for a properly Schopenhauerian account of lyric poetry. Accordingly, in *The Birth of Tragedy*, he sets out to correct what Schopenhauer actually says, "in his spirit and to his honour" (*BT* 5). That he here understands the implications of Schopenhauer's general theory of art better than Schopenhauer himself is striking evidence of the depth of his Schopenhauerianism in this early phase of his career.

Art, the Schopenhauerian Nietzsche says, is *always* "objective": the "willing individual furthering his own egoistic ends" is *always* its antagonist. But this by no means requires that the lyric poet, say Archilochus, "should see nothing of the phenomenon of the man Archilochus." For Archilochus *qua* lyric "genius" is distinct from Archilocus *qua* "non-genius," *qua* "passionately inflamed, loving and hating man." This is so because, through a "mystical self-abnegation," he has become "the only truly existent and eternal self resting at the basis of things." From that perspective he may retain objectivity but still express his "primordial [i.e. universal] pain symbolically in the symbol of the man Archilochus" (*ibid.*). (Notice that Nietzsche offers here precisely the reconciliation of objectivity and expressiveness which, in section 8, I argued to be implicit in Schopenhauer's general theory of art.)

13 Schopenhauer says (as he must given both pessimism and the identification between aesthetic and cognitive value) that the highest expression of the poetical art is tragedy. His interest, as with both Aristotle and Nietzsche, lies in the nature of the "tragic effect," in the question of why we willingly submit to, even derive pleasure from, depictions of the misery and injustice of life. Schopenhauer's answer to this question is that pleasure in tragedy is the highest degree of the "feeling of the sublime." The "tragic catastrophe," he says, makes us feel

urged to turn our will away from life, to give up willing and loving life. But precisely in this way we become aware that there is still left in us something different that we cannot know positively but only negatively, as that which does *not* will life. Just as ... a red colour demands green, and even produces it in the eye, so every tragedy demands an existence of an entirely different kind, a different world, the knowledge of which can only be given to us indirectly as here by such a demand. At the moment of the tragic catastrophe we become convinced more clearly than ever that life is a bad dream from which we have to awake. (*WR* II, p. 433)[7]

Schopenhauer holds, then, that tragedy simultaneously produces "resignation" (*WR* I, p. 253) towards this life and makes us alive to the "supersensible side to our being." With the greatest tragedies – Schopenhauer thinks that on the whole ancient tragedies are inferior to Christian ones since they exhibit only stoic heroism in the face of misfortune – this serene, even cheerful, resignation is not merely the effect but is also depicted *in* the tragedy, a depiction which produces a further intensification of the effect. The drama, that is, portrays not merely a tragic development in the action but also the effect of this development upon the mind of the hero, an effect which culminates in a moment of metaphysical, world-transcending insight. Schopenhauer cites Bellini's *Norma* in this connection (*WR* I, p. 436), but one might think also of the film of Marcel Pagnol's, so it seems to me, deeply Schopenhauerian *Manon des Sources*: of the harvest of catastrophe reaped by Papet from his narrow, greedy willing and of his sudden transformation into a metaphysical figure of resignation and dignity as he learns that the man his rapaciousness has destroyed is, in fact, his own yearned-for son.

14 Schopenhauer regards music as an exception to his general theory of art, for it does not represent any individual or event of the type that belongs to everyday reality. There is, of course, the phenomenon of program music. But the representation of battles and bird-song (Schopenhauer reports here the conviction shared by all musical purists) is at best light-hearted and at worst an objectionable perversion of the true function of music (*WR* I, pp. 362–4). Properly employed, music never represents empirical objects. Hence neither does it represent any such object as Idea. The general theory which posits the Platonic Ideas as the topic of art does not apply to music. Schopenhauer thus propounds a radical dichotomy between music and the other arts which, as we will see, reappears in Nietzsche.

How are we to account for this exceptional, apparently "abstract" character of music? Leibniz held that music really *is* abstract, that it is "unconscious arithmetic," a mere play with numerical ratios, an uninterpreted syntax. But this, says Schopenhauer, must be rejected as incapable of accounting for the profound and powerful effect that music has on us. Music seems to *tell* us something, seems, that is, to be a "language" that represents, is about, something. Only by validating this intuition can we accommodate its depth and seriousness (*WR* I, p. 256).

What then is music about? Since it does not represent empirical reality, only one answer, within the dualism between appearance and thing in itself, is possible: it represents the thing itself, the will. The other arts, of course, are by no means precluded from intimating knowledge of the metaphysical: as bodily and facial movement and gesture can express an inner will, so representations of the "physiognomy" of nature can be representations of its inner will.

(Though Schopenhauer, of course, does not, it is perhaps helpful here to think of Van Gogh.) But only music has *direct* access to the metaphysical, only it provides us with an "immediate...copy" of the will. This is why, cognitively, it is the profoundest, the highest of all the arts: while the others speak always of the "shadow," it takes us directly to the "essence" of things (*WR* I, p. 257).

15 Notice that Schopenhauer's account of the aboutness of music has two aspects to it: on the one hand music is said to be about *metaphysical* reality, the "thing in itself"; on the other hand it is said to be about *psychological* reality, about "will." This double-aspectedness is responsible for an ambivalence in Schopenhauer's theory that comes to a head in the case of opera.

If we focus upon the first aspect, then the status of opera becomes highly problematic. For if music gives us direct access to the thing in itself and if, as Schopenhauer holds, the highest form of art is that with the greatest cognitive value – that which communicates knowledge of ultimate reality in the clearest and most vivid way – then it would seem to follow that the highest form of music is purely instrumental, as Wagner referred to it (derogatorily), "absolute" music. And if we further assume, as Schopenhauer tends to, that music has only one proper function, opera comes to appear (another aspect of the purist conviction) as a debased form of the art. For if music, by itself, gives us immediate knowledge of ultimate reality, then the addition to it of words (and action) would seem to be at best an irrelevance and at worst a positive distraction. If, to develop Schopenhauer's Platonic metaphor, music takes us directly to the Real World of sunlight what possible interest could one have in trying to guess at the character of that world by deciphering the shadows in the cave?

Insofar as Schopenhauer attends to *this* aspect of his theory we find him, as one would expect, in a frame of mind hostile to opera. Opera, he says, is "strictly speaking...an unmusical invention for the benefit of unmusical minds"; the truly musical mind desires only the "pure language of tones" (*PP* II, p. 437). The best that can be said by way of justifying libretto is to view it as a kind of doodling to occupy the intellects of lesser minds so that their musical faculties may be better able to attend to the music (*PP* II, p. 432). Again, we find Schopenhauer suggesting that the mass is superior to opera since the words, through constant repetition, come to function as a mere *solfeggio*, mere sounds (*PP* II, pp. 434–5). And of Rossini's operatic music he remarks that its greatness consists in the fact that "it requires no words at all, and therefore produces its full effect even when rendered by instrumental means alone" (*WR* I, p. 262).

16 To be set against these kinds of remarks, however, is the fact that Schopenhauer actually loved opera. And his writings, moreover, are full of glowing references to the individual operas of Mozart, Rossini, and, as we have already remarked, Bellini: *Norma* is described as "quite apart from its excellent music…and considered only according to its motives and interior economy…a tragedy of extreme perfection" (*WR* II, p. 436). These references are entirely innocent of any hint of the inferiority of opera to absolute music. The explanation of this, it seems to me, is that much of the time Schopenhauer ignores his official view that music is a representation of the *metaphysical* "will," treating it instead as a depiction of an entirely *human*, merely *psychological* reality.

Developed in this way, Schopenhauer's theory of musical representation posits, as its object, human emotions. Not, however, "particular and definite" emotions but, rather, their "inner nature" divorced from all "accessories and so also without any motives for them" (*WR* I, p. 261).

What is the "inner nature" of an emotion? Let us say that an emotion can be analyzed into on the one hand an intentional object and on the other an inner phenomenology that runs along dimensions such as intensity, waxing or waning, brevity or lingeringness, and innumerable others difficult or impossible to articulate in words. This latter, this inner "feel" of an emotion seems to be what Schopenhauer has in mind when he describes music, in particular melody, as representing the "secret history" of the "intellectually enlightened," that is human, will (*WR* I, p. 259) (a remark which seems, almost, to constitute the "program" for Strauss' *Ein Heldenleben*).

Understood in this way, Schopenhauer's theory of musical representation, treated psychologically, anticipates some aspects of that proposed in more recent years by Susanne K. Langer (see, for example, *Feeling and Form*).[8] For, like her, he treats the way in which music depicts, as we might call it, the feeling of feeling as a matter of isomorphic correspondence between, on the one hand, elements of the represented emotion and, on the other, elements (mainly rhythmic and melodic) in the music. The constant deviation of melody from the keynote, for example, corresponds to the perpetual striving of the human will, and the return to its satisfaction (*WR* I, p. 259). And the short phrases of rapid dance music correspond to the feeling of "ordinary happiness which is easy of attainment" while the longer phrases and wide deviations of the *allegro maestoso* seem to represent "a greater, nobler effort towards a distant goal and its final attainment" (*WR* I, pp. 260–1).

Understood in the above, nonmetaphysical way as a precursor of the theory of Langer, Schopenhauer's theory of musical representation becomes highly "opera-friendly," for on it, opera becomes not only legitimate but might even be regarded as (speaking from Schopenhauer's cognitivist point of view) the highest art-form. For if music depicts the inner reality of human life and words the outer, then music and words appear to be ideally suited to combine in the presentation of a stereoscopic vision of the world.[9]

17 I have labored the ambivalence in Schopenhauer's theory of music that manifests itself in his conflicting attitude towards opera because, as we will see in the next chapter, it is an ambivalence inherited by his two disciples, Wagner and Nietzsche. Let me, therefore, conclude this chapter by summarizing the exact character of the ambivalence.

Schopenhauer says that will, which is what music represents, constitutes the "inner" reality of the world. He also says that it is the "thing in itself" which lies beneath the surface of appearances. These two metaphors, the inner–outer and the surface–depth metaphors, run through all Schopenhauer's discussions of the will. Sometimes one assumes prominence, sometimes the other. Sometimes, in talking of music, Schopenhauer emphasizes the depth metaphor, for this captures his (romantic) intuition of its cognitive ultimacy. (As Nietzsche points out, this elevation of the composer into "a priest, a kind of mouthpiece of the 'in itself' of things, a telephone from the beyond" [*GM* III, 5] is undoubtedly connected with the attraction that Schopenhauer's philosophy of art held for Wagner – never one, as Nietzsche remarks, to ignore anything *in majorem musicae gloriam* (*ibid.*).) But to the extent that he speaks in this vein Schopenhauer's theory of music demands *absolute* music and is hostile to opera.

At other times, however, Schopenhauer emphasizes the inner–

outer metaphor. From this perspective the difference between music and the other arts lies not in its representing a different and deeper *level* of reality but rather in the object of its (direct) representation being a different *aspect* of reality. To the extent that Schopenhauer thinks in this way, music loses its cognitive superiority to the other arts; on the other hand the theory becomes entirely friendly to opera.

The difficulty with Schopenhauer's theory of music is that he tries to square the circle by combining the view of music as cognitively superior to the other arts with, at least at times, friendship towards opera. Nietzsche and Wagner, as we will see, follow him into a similar incoherence.

CHAPTER 2

The Birth of Tragedy

1 Nietzsche's first book, *The Birth of Tragedy*, was published in 1872, the same year as that in which the foundation stone was laid for the Festival Theater in Bayreuth. Politically and emotionally it is, like his next substantial discussion of art, *Richard Wagner at Bayreuth* (1876), dominated by the figure of Richard Wagner. The work is not only dedicated to Wagner (to whom, at this period, Nietzsche was accustomed to refer as *Meister*) but is conceived as, above all, a work of propaganda on behalf of the Wagnerian cause. (If one attempted to summarize the essence of its complex argument the following might be offered: we stand in need of a "solution" to the suffering and absurdity of life. The Greeks found such a solution in the art of their great tragedians. Our only hope for a solution – given the untenability of Christianity in the modern age – lies in the rebirth of such art in the music-dramas of Richard Wagner.) Nietzsche was dedicated to Wagner's cause and made proposals, both before and after the publication of *The Birth*, to abandon his professorship at Basle in order to work exclusively for the realization of the theater at Bayreuth.

Philosophically, however, the figure of greatest importance for the work is Arthur Schopenhauer. This is in no way inconsistent with its Wagnerianism, for the Wagner Nietzsche came to know (they first met at the end of 1868), the Wagner who had completed his whole musico-dramatic *œuvre* save for *Götterdämmerung* (1874) and *Parsifal* (1882), had been, since his discovery of Schopenhauer in 1854, himself dominated by the philosophy of the great pessimist.

Nietzsche himself discovered Schopenhauer in 1865 and became an immediate disciple. In letters of the following year he spoke of "my Schopenhauer" and described himself and Schopenhauer as "often the same thing." This passion, it is clear, is what first attracted him to Wagner: "I have found a man," he wrote of

Wagner to Karl von Gersdorff in 1869, "who reveals to me what Schopenhauer calls 'the genius' and is quite possessed by that [i.e. Schopenhauer's] wonderfully intense philosophy." Earlier in the same year he described his friendship with Wagner to Erwin Rohde as "like taking a practical course in Schopenhauerian philosophy," and at about the same time wrote to Wagner himself: "The highest and most inspiring moments of my life are closely associated with your name, and I know of only one other man, and that man your twin brother of intellect, Arthur Schopenhauer, whom I regard with the same veneration – yea even more, as *religione quadam.*"

In the light of these biographical observations concerning the years of its inception, it is natural to expect *The Birth* to be a work deeply Schopenhauerian in character. It comes, therefore, as something of a surprise to discover that the question of the nature and scope of the Schopenhauerian influence is a matter of deep controversy, and that many, particularly English-speaking, commentators are bent on minimizing its significance.

2 In *some* ways, that there is a Schopenhauerian influence is undenied and undeniable. There is, that is, fairly wide agreement that (as we will see) *The Birth* incorporates without modification Schopenhauer's metaphysics, that it incorporates substantial elements of his theory of art, especially his theory of music, and that Nietzsche found Schopenhauer's bleak portrait of the world and human life at least the authentic statement of a *problem*. What is highly controversial, however, is whether he also endorsed Schopenhauer's pessimism; whether, that is, he endorsed Schopenhauer's inference from the pain and purposelessness of human existence to its worthlessness. This question, which it is the main purpose of this chapter to answer, is the most crucial of all the questions which can be asked about *The Birth*, both with regard to understanding the meaning of the work itself and with regard to determining its relation to Nietzsche's later works.

3 After his break with Wagner in 1876 Nietzsche began to describe not just Wagner but Schopenhauer too (this is not surprising given the near-identity of the two in his mind) as "sick," "decadent," and – invariably a term of high abuse for Nietzsche – "romantic." And he started to represent his own philosophy as antipodal to Schopenhauer's in a way that centrally involves the issue of

pessimism: in opposition to Schopenhauer's "denial" of life, the later Nietzsche represents "life-affirmation" as the pervasive character and fundamental point of his own philosophy.

Aware of, and in agreement with, this self-characterization, many commentators have sought to incorporate *The Birth* into the body of Nietzsche's works by driving a wedge between Schopenhauer's "sick" philosophy and the healthier turn taken, even at the beginning, by Nietzsche's. In *The Birth*, they suggest, Nietzsche is already emancipated from his youthful infatuation with Schopenhauerian pessimism. In spite of its Schopenhauerian garb, its use of Schopenhauer's philosophy as a kind of "language," its fundamental message is anti-Schopenhauerian: the message is *opposed to* the medium. Hence *The Birth* is fundamentally continuous with Nietzsche's later works and may be incorported into the authentically Nietzschean canon.

Apart from Nietzsche himself (of whom more in a moment) the most important of these commentators is Walter Kaufmann.[1] Kaufmann is important on account of the tremendous influence he has, in the English-speaking world (witness the numerous references to "Apollinian," which as far as I know is not a word of English), an influence which stems partly from his mana as a pioneering (and generally very fine – the finest) translator of Nietzsche into English, but more dubiously from the many overintrusive, dogmatic footnotes which accompany those translations and which mean that many English readers imbibe text and Kaufmannic interpretations and opinions in the same gulp. Kaufmann denies that the work is pessimistic:

Instead of proving himself in his first book as an unswerving follower of Schopenhauer Nietzsche discovered in Greek art a bulwark against Schopenhauer's pessimism. One can oppose the shallow optimism of so many Western thinkers and yet refuse to negate life. Schopenhauer's negative pessimism is rejected along with the superficial optimism of the popular Hegelians and Darwinists: One can face the terrors of history and nature with unbroken courage and say Yes to life.[2]

This view is, I believe, quite mistaken (as mistaken as Kaufmann's attempt to deny Nietzsche's, on balance, thoroughly hostile attitude to Socrates). Nietzsche does, to be sure, offer a "solution" to pessimism, a way of, in a sense, "overcoming" (*BT* 3) it. In fact he offers two solutions. But these solutions, so I shall argue, represent, like Schopenhauer's, a flight from, a "denial" of human life. If we can establish this overridingly central point then we will be justified in regarding *The Birth* as a fundamentally Schopenhauerian work. And given that, as I shall suggest, in the so-called "positivistic" works produced after 1876 Nietzsche abandoned pessimism, we will be justified in regarding 1876 as marking a sharp break in his thought, in viewing *The Birth* as sharply discontinuous with those (though not the final) works.

4 Nietzsche's own retrospective comments on *The Birth* are, on the question of its pessimism, self-contradictory. On the one hand he writes, in *Ecce Homo* (1888), that "the Greeks were not pessimists: Schopenhauer went wrong at this point as he went wrong everywhere"; the Greeks "got over their pessimism,...they overcame it" (*EH* IV, 1). Since he almost always identifies (pre-Alexandrian) Greek attitudes with his own, this strongly suggests that by 1872 Nietzsche himself had abandoned pessimism. It is not surprising, therefore, that a few lines later in the same book, he writes that "the cadaverous perfume of Schopenhauer sticks only to a few formulas" in *The Birth*.

Kaufmann makes much of this self-assessment as he does of the remark in the 1886 preface to *The Birth* that its treatment of tragic art is utterly different from the life-denying "resignationism" which Schopenhauer takes to be its meaning (*BT*, "Attempt at a Self-Criticism," 6). But he fails to discuss the far greater number of passages which point in the opposite direction. In section 853 of *The Will to Power*, for example, Nietzsche says that pessimism counts in *The Birth* as a truth, and in section 1005 of the same work identifies 1876 as the year in which "I grasped that my instinct went in the opposite direction from Schopenhauer's: towards a *justification of life*," which seems to imply that at the time of *The Birth* he saw life as *un*justifiable. Even in *Ecce Homo* itself he identifies "the years of my lowest vitality" as the time when he "ceased to be a pessimist" (*EH* I, 2). Since it is always the period of the "free-spirited" works bounded by *Human, All-too-human* (1878) at the beginning and *The Gay Science* (1882) at the end that Nietzsche refers to in this way, this again implies that the author of *The Birth* was a pessimist. Another turn of discussion pointing in the same direction is constituted by the later Nietzsche's identification of life-denying pessimism with "romanticism" (e.g. in *GS* 370) together with a theme that runs through the prefaces to all the works of the "free-spirited" years, the assertion that the period of their authorship is one of recovery through "anti-romantic self-treatment" from a "dangerous" case of "romanticism" (*HH* II, Preface, 2). And in the 1886 preface to *The Birth* itself Nietzsche characterizes the work as "romantic," marked by a "deep hatred against "the Now," against "reality" and "modern ideas," and calls its author a "pessimist and art-deifier." Referring to the *metaphysical* "comfort" for the suffering of life which *The Birth* offers (as we will see), the mature Nietzsche advises "you young romantics" to seek rather a "*this-worldly* comfort" (*BT*, "Attempt at a Self-Criticism," 7). If we were to decide the issue by reference to Nietzsche's retrospective comments alone the balance would come down fairly decisively against Kaufmann. This, however, we should not do.

As we have already seen, Nietzsche's retrospective self-descriptions, considered from the point of view of scholarly accuracy, are deeply unreliable. To look at them from this point of view is, however, a mistake, a misunderstanding of their intended function. The mature Nietzsche holds, that is (as we will see in chapter 4), that a flourishing life demands the "redemption" of one's own past, a redemption which requires one to achieve a view of it as constituting, together with one's present and one's goals for the future, an aesthetic unit: one needs to "create" oneself as a literary hero, to view one's life as if it were a work of literature. Nietzsche was thus required to achieve such a view of his *own* past life, of, that is (since nearly all of it happened in books), his earlier writings. This not objective, scholarly assessment or introductory remarks intended to be helpful to the reader is the function of the array of prefaces, second prefaces, "self-criticisms," and philosophical autobiography (*Ecce Homo*) that the later Nietzsche interposes between the reader and the works. The aim, that is, is not to provide an accurate mirroring of the textual facts but rather to create (by the discovery of hints, undertones, "real" intentions, almost-utterances lurking between the lines, and by obscuring, where necessary, what is said on the lines) a work of art, an *aesthetically* convincing account of the intellectual and spiritual life of the man behind the works. In the case of *The Birth* Nietzsche was, I believe, divided between two aesthetic strategies, two scripts for his life. The dominant one is to view his life on the model of Saul–Paul with his sudden departure in the middle of the first Bayreuth Festival (1876) marking the satisfyingly dramatic moment of conversion (see *EH* VI, 2). But there is also a disposition to view his intellectual history as the story of the emergence of a butterfly from a chrysalis: to view the authentic Nietzsche as already present in the early works albeit wearing borrowed and unbecoming garb. ("I tried [in *The Birth*] to express by means of Schopenhauerian and Kantian formulas strange and new valuations which were basically at odds with Kant's and Schopenhauer's spirit and taste...obscured and spoiled Dionysian premonitions with Schopenhauerian formulations" (*BT*, "Attempt at a Self-Criticism," 6).

As Nietzsche-commentator, then, Nietzsche is to be viewed with greater distrust than most. We should, therefore, not try to decide the question of pessimism by appealing to his retrospective claims but rather by trying to achieve a clear-eyed perception of the work itself, a perception that avoids the distorting lenses through which Nietzsche the artist would persuade us to look.

5 What is *The Birth* about? Nietzsche gave the book two alternative titles: *The Birth of Tragedy* (in the first edition, *The Birth of Tragedy out of the Spirit of Music*) and *Hellenism and Pessimism*. These indicate its two central theses in the statement of each of which the celebrated (but elusive) distinction between the "Apollonian" and the "Dionysian" plays a crucial role. As a first approximation, these theses may be stated as follows. The first, "the birth-of-tragedy thesis" I shall call it, asserts that Greek tragedy came into being through the union of Apollonian and Dionysian elements. It "died" through the elimination of the Dionysian from Greek drama at the hands of Euripides acting under the baleful influence of Socrates. The second thesis, which I shall call "the Hellenism-and-pessimism thesis," asserts that although vividly sensitive (*BT* 3, 6) to the "terror and horror of existence" (*BT* 3) the Greeks were nevertheless able to survive and even thrive, psychologically speaking, through the effect of their art – through, more specifically, the effects of their two types of art, Apollonian and Dionysian art.

Stated in this way, the argument of *The Birth* has the air of thin-blooded scholarly detachment that one would expect from an author who was still Professor of Greek at Basle. Actually, however, the book is far removed from any such spirit for, in reality, it is engaged, evaluative, prescriptive, short on footnotes (Kaufmann's generous supply rather spoils this effect), long on fancy, fanciful to the point of falsification. The reason for this is that its primary concern is not to provide an historically accurate account of the Greeks and their culture at all. Its concern lies, rather, with *us* and *our* culture, Nietzsche's speculative account of the rise and fall of Greek art and culture having importance only as a "polished mirror" (*HH* IIa, 218) in which we can see aspects of our own culture reflected and clarified: The task of the classicist, he wrote in section 7 of the unpublished "We Philologists," is that of "understanding *his own* age better by means of the classical world." This demotion of classical scholarship, by a supposed professional in the field, from an end in itself into a means for understanding modern life and culture – his demand that it be "relevant" – goes a considerable distance towards explaining the scholarly fury with which the work was first received.[3]

In reality, it seems to me, Nietzsche's first thesis is not, in its most fundamental intention, a genetic thesis about Greek tragedy at all but rather an analytic and evaluative thesis about great art in general. The highest form of art, that is art which, seen in the "perspective of life" (*BT* 2, 5), is of the greatest service (as with classical scholarship and all forms of theoretical activity, Nietzsche always insists that art has value only to the degree that helps us in the practical task of living life), is a "fraternal union" in which, though "the Dionysian predominates," "Dionysus speaks the language of Apollo and Apollo speaks the language of Dionysus." When this happens "the highest goal of tragedy *and of all art* is attained" (*BT* 21, 24; my emphasis). Greek tragedy, Nietzsche holds, provides a paradigm example of such art and for this reason it merits close study. The fundamental purpose of *The Birth*, however, is to argue not the greatness of Greek tragedy but rather that we have, finally, another instance of the pattern of greatness first exemplified in the works of Sophocles and Aeschylus – the music-drama of Richard Wagner. Hence, Nietzsche holds, though our culture is "Socratic," devoid of the Dionysian, we can yet hope for its regeneration through the music which is to sound from Bayreuth.

With regard to the Hellenism-and-pessimism thesis the important point is that it is not just the Greeks but we,[4] too, who confront the pain and absurdity (*BT* 7) of existence. Hence the Greek art-solutions to pessimism were not only of interest to them but are of vital concern to us. Fundamentally, that is, the Hellenism-and-pessimism thesis is a recommendation as to how *we* should overcome pessimism.

The remainder of this chapter falls into five main parts: in the first (secs. 6–7) I attempt to understand the Apollonian–Dionysian dichotomy; in the second (secs. 8–9) the birth-of-tragedy thesis; in the third (secs. 10–13) the Hellenism-and-pessimism thesis; in the fourth (secs. 14–18) I attempt to establish my thesis concerning the Schopenhauerian, that is pessimistic, character of the work; I conclude (secs. 19–21) with some remarks concerning *Richard Wagner at Bayreuth*, a work that can be seen as something of a postscript to *The Birth*.

6 Nietzsche's talk of the Apollonian is hard to understand until one realizes that, as he admits (*BT* 1), he uses the term in different, though related, senses. (Alternatively put, since Nietzsche often says what he has to say by using Apollo as a symbol rather than "Apollonian" as a predicate, Apollo is, for Nietzsche, an ambiguous symbol.) Specifically, he uses the term in two senses: one when talking about art; the other, in its primary occurrence, when talking about metaphysics. In the metaphysical sense, Apollonian consciousness is consciousness of the world that is (Nietzsche repeatedly uses Schopenhauer's terminology) subject to the *principium individuationis* (*BT* 1, 2). It is, that is to say, that mundane consciousness which is the product of the limiting, delimiting, "boundary drawing" (*BT* 9) – as we sometimes say – "rational" faculty of mind which divides the world up into a plurality of discrete, spatio-temporal individuals. Nietzsche uses "Apollonian" in this sense in, for example, all those contexts in which he wishes to speak of the ethical and social consequences of various modes of consciousness and in which the Apollonian is opposed to the barbaric as the fundamental civilization-forming force. Apollo, he says, for instance, "wants to grant repose to individual beings...by drawing boundaries between them and by again and again calling these to mind as the most sacred laws of the world with his demand for self-knowledge and measure" (*ibid.*). This "majestically rejecting attitude of Apollo" (*BT* 2) created Greek civilization and preserved it from the "horrible mixture of sensuality and cruelty" (*ibid.*) of the surrounding barbarians.

Used in the metaphysical sense there is no necessary connection between the Apollonian and the beautiful: the object of consciousness is simply the world of the *principium individuationis* which may or may not be experienced as beautiful. Used in the aesthetic sense, however, the object of Apollonian consciousness *is* essentially beautiful: it is, not the mundane world, but rather that world raised to a state of glory; it is the "perfection" (*BT* 1), the "transfiguration" (*BT* 16), the "apotheosis of the *principium individuationis*" (*BT* 4). The aesthetically Apollonian is the metaphysically Apollonian perceived as beautiful.[5]

Nietzsche's first introduction of the objects of (aesthetically) Apollonian consciousness (*BT* 1) makes it clear that they are modeled upon Schopenhauer's "Platonic Ideas": in the Apollonian state, he says, we take delight in "beautiful appearances,"[6] appearances in which "all forms speak to us [and] there is nothing unimportant or superfluous," a description that closely follows Schopenhauer's conception of what it is to perceive an object as beautiful. Nietzsche even follows Schopenhauer in calling the objects of Apollonian art "archetypes" (*BT* 2), and the reference to them as "the eternity of the phenomenon" (*BT* 16) alludes similarly to the Platonic Ideas. It seems clear, therefore, that while that which is Apollonian in the metaphysical sense is Schopenhauer's world "as representation," that which is Apollonian in the aesthetic sense is Schopenhauer's world as "Idea."

Nietzsche connects the Apollonian with the metaphor of a dream image. In line with the ambiguity of the term, this metaphor, too, has a double function. On the one hand, it has the function of capturing the merely phenomenal status of everyday reality (Nietzsche gives a Schopenhauerian provenance for this use of the metaphor [*BT* 1]).[7] But on the other, since in dreams we simplify images, eliminate details not relevant to the dream's "narrative" or point[8] (Nietzsche is quite correct, it seems to me, to observe that "in our dreams we delight in the immediate understanding of figures; all forms speak to us; there is nothing unimportant or superfluous" [*ibid.*]), he is also able to use the metaphor to capture the idea of the pleasurable[9] contemplation of the beautiful, of the world perceived as Idea.

7 If dreams stand for the Apollonian, *Rausch* – "intoxication," "rapture," "ecstasy," "frenzy" – stands for the Dionysian. Dionysian consciousness is a "high," a state of literal or metaphorical drunkenness in which we overcome the "sobriety" of ordinary (metaphysically Apollonian) consciousness which presents the *principium individuationis* as absolute reality. In Dionysian rapture

one realizes that, on the contrary, reality is non-individual, a "primordial unity" (*BT* 1). This unity is nothing other than Schopenhauer's "universal will" (*BT* 17). The object of Dionysian consciousness is, therefore, Schopenhauer's "world as will."

It is important to observe a divergence between Schopenhauer and Nietzsche over the possible manifestations of Dionysian consciousness. For Schopenhauer, as we saw (ch. 1, sec. 15), the overcoming of plurality, the realization that all individual identities merge in that of the metaphysical will, constitutes the consciousness of the altruist. Hence the consequences of entering such consciousness are entirely benign. Nietzsche acknowledges this as an aspect of Dionysian consciousness: "under the charm of the Dionysian," he writes, all the "rigid hostile barriers" that the metaphysically Apollonian mind places between man and man and man and nature are broken down. In the Dionysian rapture of the participants in, for example, the Bacchic festivals of the ancient world or the carnivals of southern Germany, the barriers of "necessity" and "convention" are replaced by a "gospel of universal harmony" in which everyone "feels himself not only united, reconciled, and fused with his neighbour, but as one with him, as if the veil of *maya* [a term much used by Schopenhauer] had been torn aside and were now merely fluttering in tatters before the mysterious primordial being" (*BT* 1). This clearly is the *Gemeinschaft* of the Schopenhauerian altruist.

But Nietzsche also recognizes another side to Dionysian consciousness, a "horrible witches brew" of "sensuality and cruelty" (*BT* 2). (That "intoxication" contains the idea of both a benign and disgusting expression captures this double-edgedness of the Dionysian, its "dual nature" [*BT* 10].) And he is right to do so; Schopenhauer is mistaken in assuming that the benevolent actions of the moral altruist constitute the only possible expression of, as we called it (ch. 1, sec. 5), metaphysical solipsism. For if one identifies with a transindividual self then while one *may* be moved to act with sympathetic concern for others, one may also act barbarically, regarding particular individuals as insignificant, valueless, as dispensable as toe-nails. One may even affirm and celebrate one's  transcendence of individuality by the desecration or destruction of an individual. For this reason, Nietzsche holds, social life depends upon the confinement of Dionysian ecstasy to symbolic, artistic expression. (The manner of this containment will be examined in section 13 below.) This is what distinguished Greek civilization from the surrounding barbarism:[10] in the Dionysian festivals of the Greeks "nature for the first time obtains her artistic jubilee ... the destruction of the *principium individuationis* for the first time becomes an artistic phenomenon" (*ibid.*).

8 I want to turn now to the birth-of-tragedy thesis. To understand this we need to understand how "Apollonian" and "Dionysian," so far considered as attributes of consciousness, are applied to art. The important point to observe here is that Nietzsche accepts Schopenhauer's radical dichotomy between music and the nonmusical arts. The latter, being concerned with the beautiful representation of phenomenal reality are, in Nietzsche's terms, Apollonian: they embody and communicate (aesthetically) Apollonian consciousness. Music, however, at least when it performs its highest and proper function (program music is, for Nietzsche as for Schopenhauer, a perversion of the medium), has "a character and an origin quite different from all the other arts, because, unlike them, it is not a copy of the phenomenon but an immediate copy of the will itself, and therefore complements *everything physical in the world* and every phenomenon by representing what is *metaphysical*, the thing in itself" (*BT* 16). Music then is "the Dionysian art" (*ibid.*), for it is music that arises out of and communicates Dionysian consciousness.

From this initial understanding of the dichotomy between Apollonian and Dionysian art it seems to follow that according to the birth-of-tragedy thesis great art must consist in some kind of synthesis (a synthesis, remember, in which the Dionysian "predominates") between the beautiful representation of phenomenal reality – primarily, one assumes Nietzsche to hold, by means of speech and action – and music.

One objection one might wish to raise at this point is that, however the precise nature of the synthesis in question is to be spelled out, the thesis can be seen immediately to be vitiated by an arbitrary connecting of the value of a work of art to its medium, an unwarranted discrimination against nonmusical media. Why for instance, assuming Verdi's *Otello* to be a fine opera as operas go and Shakespeare's *Othello* a fine play as plays go, should Verdi's be a greater work of art merely because Shakespeare was not a composer? Viewed in relation to this objection *The Birth* exhibits, I believe, a tension between Nietzsche *qua* Wagner propagandist and Nietzsche *qua* philosopher of art.

Qua Wagner propagandist, Nietzsche was constrained to accommodate himself to Wagner's immodest portrait of himself (in, for
example, *Opera and Drama*) as the reborn, the German Aeschylus. In
view of the fact that its choral parts were sung, that is, Wagner was
able to represent Attic tragedy as the complete form of art, the
original *Gesamtkunstwerke* the spirit of which found its rebirth for the
first time in his own *Gesamtkunstwerke*. Hence, *qua* propagandist,
Nietzsche is more than happy to relegate all nonmusical artists to the
long trough that separates the Aeschylean and Wagnerian apexes of
artistic greatness. It is in line with this motivation that Nietzsche
formulates the birth-of-tragedy thesis in the manner we have seen
X and accords music a monopoly over the Dionysian, calling it "*the*
Dionysian art" (*BT* 16; my emphasis).

On the other hand, as a serious philosopher and as an aesthetic
man sensitive to the unsurpassed claims to greatness of Shakespeare
or Goethe, Nietzsche had to recognize that it cannot be demanded
of great art that it take the form of opera. In line with this, we find
that his more considered discussions moderate the demand that
great art should be literally musical to the requirement that it should
contain, should be generated out of, "musical mood" (*BT* 5); that
is, in the words of the original title of the book, "the spirit of music."

What Nietzsche means by "musical mood" is simply Dionysian
consciousness. (Though the force of the shift from talk of literal to
metaphorical music is to allow Dionysian content to artworks which
lack musical form, Nietzsche's continued association between music
and the Dionysian is readily understandable in Schopenhauerian
terms: music represents the metaphysical world *directly*, the nonmusical arts represent it, at best, only indirectly. Music, though no
longer "the [only] Dionysian art," remains "the Dionysian art *par
excellence*.") This consciousness, according to our new understanding
of the birth-of-tragedy thesis, is the generative force behind the
greatest works of art and is their fundamental meaning or content.
Great art, such as Greek or Shakespearean tragedy, that is, is the
attempt to give expression to Dionysian intuition in "symbolic
dream-images" (*BT* 5), beautiful images of the Apollonian world.
This means that there is something deceptive (see *BT* 21 and sec. 13
below) about such art. Though the surface of, for example,
Aeschylean tragedy is (aesthetically) Apollonian – simple, beautiful,
precise, and lucid (*BT* 9) – beneath it one senses an infinite,
"enigmatic depth" (*BT* 12): in spite of the lucidity of plot, action,

and speech, its figures carry with them a mysterious penumbra, a "comet's tail" (*ibid.*) of significance. Hence their actions are fuller of meaning than their words: they "speak, as it were, more superficially than they act," and this is because great art contains "a deeper wisdom than the poet himself can put into words and concepts" (*BT* 17).

Notice that this account of the greatness of great art as consisting in its being a vehicle for the communication of Dionysian insight – Nietzsche's portrait, that is, of the artistic "genius" as, through "mystical self-abnegation and oneness" with the "primal unity," becoming the "medium through which the one truly existent subject" speaks to us (*BT* 5) – is essentially continuous with the Kant–Schopenhauer conception of the artist as "genius." For, as with Schopenhauer, the artist is portrayed as essentially a bringer of metaphysical and hence (since, for Nietzsche as for Schopenhauer, the domain of the conceptual is confined to the phenomenal world) conceptually unparaphrasable news. This means that the later Nietzsche's satirical attack upon the romantic concept of genius, the deification of the artist into "an oracle, a priest, indeed more than a priest a kind of mouthpiece of the 'in itself' of things, a telephone from the beyond ... [a] ventriloquist of God" (*GM* iii, 5) is an attack not merely upon Schopenhauer and Wagner but also upon his own youthful self – as he later, sometimes, concedes (e.g. *Z* i, 3).

9 Must art have a hidden metaphysical curriculum? Is the possession of metaphysical, "afterworldly" (*ibid.*) meaning a condition of greatness in art? There seems to be absolutely no reason to suppose this, no reason to suppose the art of the immanent to be, *a fortiori*, inferior to the art of the transcendent. Nietzsche's insistence that it is is, in my view, a product of the distortion of aesthetics by pessimism. Given, that is, that art has value only to the degree that it serves life, and given also my claim that, in the end, *The Birth of Tragedy* holds this life not to be worth living, it follows that art can ultimately only be of service to us by bringing, like religion, hope of another kind of life. Just how it is supposed to do this will be discussed shortly.

What of the other side to the birth-of-tragedy thesis, the claim that the Apollonian is a necessary component in great art? Is this really so? Is it really necessary that great art should represent phenomenal reality, should be, in the everyday sense, representational or figurative art? The central problem here (though it could be raised, too, by reference to abstractness in the visual arts) is created by the phenomenon of purely instrumental, as Wagner called it, "absolute," music.

Regarding absolute music, we find again a tension in _The Birth_ between the demands of propaganda and those of philosophy, a tension that exists, too, between Wagner's earlier and later aesthetic writings, and, as we have already seen (ch. 1, secs. 14–17), in Schopenhauer. On the one hand, we find Nietzsche claiming, as the birth-of-tragedy thesis demands he should, that "music at its highest stages _must_ seek to obtain its highest objectification in images" (_BT_ 17; my emphasis). This remark reflects the view taken by Wagner prior to his discovery of Schopenhauer's philosophy of music that absolute music is a functionless absurdity (Beethoven's introduction of Schiller's words into the finale of the Ninth made it the "last symphony"), that music demands words in order to achieve its function which is "realise the poetic intention for the feelings"[11] to bring home to feeling, what words and action present to the intellect and senses. On the other hand, however, we find Nietzsche writing that "music in its absolute sovereignty does not need the image and concepts, but merely endures them as accompaniments. [Words]... can express nothing that does not already lie hidden in the vast universality and absoluteness of the music...Language can never adequately render the cosmic symbolism of music" (_BT_ 6). This, which is inconsistent with the birth-of-tragedy thesis, reflects of course the Schopenhauerian view that since music takes us to a domain deeper and more significant than words can go, words, to the truly musical listener at least, are a distracting irrelevance.

The fact is that _The Birth_ has no consistent position with respect to absolute music but constitutes, rather, a necessarily confused attempt to combine a defense of Wagnerian opera as the highest form of art with Schopenhauer's metaphysical interpretation of music. The insistence upon the necessity of the Apollonian element in great art reflects the former constraint. But the phenomenon of absolute music shows that it is a mistaken insistence:[12] the task of the aesthetician is to accommodate the fact that Beethoven's last string quartets belong to the highest level of art, not to legislate, absurdly, that they do not.

10 I turn now to the Hellenism-and-pessimism thesis. The Greeks, Nietzsche asserts, though deeply sensitive to the "terror and horror"

of existence, were able, psychologically, to survive on account of their art. And we too can surmount the horror of life through art. More strongly, it seems – given the famous assertion that "it is *only* as *aesthetic phenomenon* that existence and the world are eternally *justified*" (*BT* 6, 24; first emphasis mine) – Nietzsche asserts that *only* through art can we overcome life's terror.

Before examining the thesis itself I want to raise the question of just what it is that constitutes the terror and horror of life. Commentators typically deal rather briefly with this question, taking it to be rather obvious that disease, natural disasters, the loss of close friends, and such like are the kinds of things Nietzsche has in mind. But this is an inadequate answer. For what the terror and horror does, Nietzsche holds, is to bring one to the brink of an affirmation of pessimism: an affirmation of the "wisdom of Silenus" ("best of all is not to be born, not to *be*, to be nothing. But the second best for you is – to die soon" [*BT* 3]) which leads to action-paralyzing "nausea" (*BT* 7) and a "longing for a Buddhistic negation of the will" (*ibid*.). The ultimate practical expression of this state of mind is suicide (*BT* 15). But a mere *Candide*-like catalogue of life's ills cannot adequately motivate such a response. It cannot, that is, reveal it as anything other than pathological. But Nietzsche does not take the response to be pathological: it is something that (but for the life-saving power of art) *all* intellectual and spiritually sensitive people stand in danger of.

In section 7 of *The Birth* Nietzsche says that that which threatens "Buddhistic negation of the will" is "the terrible destructiveness of so-called world history" and the "cruelty of nature." Both of these phrases have a strongly Schopenhauerian ring to them. The latter, particularly if taken in conjunction with Nietzsche's reference to the "curse of individuation" (*BT* 9) and to individuality as the "primal cause of evil" (*BT* 10), evokes Schopenhauer's picture of nature as *bellum omnium contra omnes*, his portrait of pain and anxiety as the "keynote" of one's life as an individual (*WR* 1, p. 373). And it evokes his horror at nature's (the will's) callous indifference to the suffering of the individuals to which it gives rise. The former phrase evokes the Schopenhauerian, anti-Hegelian sense that history conceived as a story of evolution or progress is merely "so-called," that in a sense history does not exist at all, since all there is is the endless repetition of the same meaningless patterns (see e.g. *WR* 1, p. 315). To the Schopenhauerian and of course Nietzschean eye the world lacks teleology: its course resembles that of not an arrow but a circle.[13] Even as superb and apparently progressive a construction as the Roman Empire seems doomed to last only a brief moment before being reduced to the rubble from which it arose. In *The Antichrist* it becomes clear that much of Nietzsche's bitterness against Christianity stems from the fact that, like Gibbon, he holds it responsible for the collapse of that Empire, an empire "fit to last a thousand years."

Nature, then, is not merely cruel, it is also purposeless. Individuals do not merely suffer; they suffer senselessly, "absurdly" (*BT* 7), for there is no goal in which their suffering might find justification as its necessary means. These thoughts are connected in Nietzsche's mind, with the threat of world-disgust. But they are still not sufficient to constitute it. For someone might acknowledge *nature* to be both cruel and purposeless yet hold that this is merely its *de facto*, not its *de jure* character, something contingent and in principle alterable. From this standpoint, while one might deny parts or phases of the world, that *cosmic* world-disgust which embraces not merely the past and present but also all possible futures is impossible.

To adopt the standpoint in question is to adopt what Nietzsche calls "Socratism"; the view that human and more particularly scientific thought is "capable not only of knowing being but even of *correcting*" it (*BT* 15). Nietzsche makes three observations about the Socratic outlook (sometimes called the outlook of "theoretical" or "scientific man"). First, that up to a point it has value as an antidote to pessimism. Since he believes, that is, in the merely contingent character of life's ills, in our, in principle, "limitless power" (*BT* 18) to control both nature and human nature, life presents the Socratic type with only solvable problems. And though nature, unaided by man, may lack teleology, it is nonetheless possible for us to remedy this by ourselves imparting progressive movement to world history. Theoretical man is even likely to *welcome* the terror and aimlessness of nature as a challenge, a spur to scientific research and action, a source of excitement: "theoretical man finds infinite delight in whatever exists, and this satisfaction protects him against... pessimism" (*BT* 15). He experiences a "blissful affirmation of existence that seeks to discharge itself in actions" (*ibid.*). (Presumably, the lay inhabitant of a scientific culture can to some degree share vicariously in the scientist's delight.)

Nietzsche's second point (to which we will return in section 14 below) is that our culture, with its faith in "democracy," scientific "optimism," "rationality," and "utilitarianism" (*BT*, "Attempts at a Self-Criticism," 4), faith that is, in the ultimate triumph of "earthly happiness for all" (*BT* 18), is Socratic. The third point is that the Socratic belief in the unbounded power of science is a terrible error. The reason for this is revealed by, in a broad sense, *science itself*, *Wissenschaft*. Science itself, that is, reveals that ultimate reality is *not* accessible to scientific rationality. (A rather similar theme has reappeared in recent years in the works of W. V. Quine.) For, as "the extraordinary courage of Kant and Schopenhauer" has shown, all we can understand "with the aid of causality" is the phenomenon, never the world in itself (*ibid.*).

The truth of Kant and Schopenhauer's idealism might show Socratism to be an error, but why a *terrible* error? One might, after all, though admitting the unknowability and hence uncorrectibility of ultimate reality by human agency, have faith, with Kant, in the existence of a nonhuman agent that imparts progressive direction to the course of world history.

Nietzsche, however, rejects the possibility of such faith for he *knows*, or at least has a picture of, the character of ultimate reality. According to this Schopenhauerian–Heraclitean picture, the ultimate nature of the world is ceaseless flux, a boiling sea of eternal "becoming" in which everything is fluid and nothing stable or permanent, no "being," is to be found (see *EH* iv, 3). This provides a metaphysical *guarantee* that world history cannot possess teleology. The structures we build in order to impress our wills upon the world are mere "frail bark[s]" (*BT* 1) poised, as it were, on the crest of a wave that is bound to break. It is, therefore, a metaphysical certainty that history is a cycle of creation and destruction. It is guaranteed that whatever happiness and security a society or individual achieves will, in the end, be smashed. For this inevitable catastrophe the Socratic type is entirely unprepared.

The "Dionysian" type, on the other hand, knows the Heraclitean truth of things. The (pre-Socratic) Greeks knew it: they were possessed of "Dionysian truth," "tragic vision." That they were susceptible to "overwhelming dismay in the face of the titanic powers of nature, the Moira [fate] enthroned inexorably over all knowledge" (*BT* 1) is recorded in their myths; in particular, in the tragic myths of the humanitarian Prometheus and the wise Oedipus (*ibid.*). (Notice the resemblance between "Dionysian wisdom" and Schopenhauer's "feeling of the [dynamically] sublime" [see ch. 1,

sec. 8]. This provides a hint as to the kind of solution to the terror
of life Nietzsche will ultimately propose.) It is this that threatens life-
denying nausea, Buddhistic negation of the will: "Dionysian man
resembles Hamlet: both have once looked truly into the essence of
things, they have *gained knowledge*, and nausea inhibits action; for
their action could not change anything in the eternal nature of
things;...knowledge kills action; action requires the veil of illusion"
(*BT* 7). But the Greeks did act, for through their art they were saved
from nausea. How did it do this? I turn first to Nietzsche's discussion
of Apollonian art.

11 The Apollonian "prophylactic" (*BT* 11) against pessimism is
pictured, by Nietzsche, as belonging to the earlier, Homeric period
of Greek culture. The Greeks of this period "overcame...or at any
rate veiled" (*BT* 3) the terror of life by producing, in their art, a
"radiant glorification" of the phenomenal world (*BT* 16), by
interposing between themselves and the realities of life, in particular,
the "radiant dream-birth of the Olympians" (*BT* 3). In their stories
of the gods, that is, the Greeks erected no non- or antihuman ideal
(here Nietzsche anticipates his later critique of Christianity) but
rather a "transfigured" *self*-portrait, a glorification of *human* life
(*ibid.*). In this way the Homeric Greeks "seduced" (*BT* 18)
themselves into continued existence – "existence under the bright
sunshine of such gods is regarded as desirable in itself" (*BT* 3) –
and into action.

What exactly is transfiguration? Nietzsche's most common
explanatory notion is that of "illusion" or "lie" (*BT* 3, 7, 16, 18; cf.
WP 853) which, together with the ancient link between dreaming
and wish-fulfillment – the world-picture engendered by Apollonian
art stands to reality, he says, as does the "rapturous vision of the
tortured martyr to his suffering" (*BT* 3) – suggests that the Greeks
overcame pessimism by dwelling in a realm of sentimental fantasy in
which really nasty things are no more allowed to exist than they are
in the world of Enid Blyton or the television commercial. In fact,
however, this cannot be a correct understanding: first, because
Homer is nothing like Enid Blyton; and second, because Nietzsche
says that in Apollonian art "all things, whether good *or evil* [*böse*] are
deified" (*BT* 3; my emphasis), and speaks of it as "transform[ing]
the most terrible things by the joy in mere appearance and in
redemption through mere appearance" (*BT* 12). Apollonian art,

therefore, in some way and to some degree, *acknowledges* and does not eliminate from consciousness the terrible in life. Illusion it may offer us; but in some sense it is a *truthful* illusion.

The clue to understanding how life can be rendered beautiful without censorship of the ugly can be discovered, I believe, by returning to the fact that it is Schopenhauer's "Platonic Ideas" that provide the basis for Nietzsche's conception of Apollonian art. Schopenhauer holds, it will be remembered, that since anything expresses an Idea to some degree, *anything* can be beautiful provided it possesses "significant form." Extrapolating from this to perception of art, we may say that beauty lies not in *what* is represented but in the *way* it is represented. Nietzsche repeats this: to enjoy the beautiful is, he says, to "delight in beautiful forms" (*BT* 16).

If beauty is, in this way, divorced from content then it is possible for the beautiful and terrible to coexist, and for the terrible to be "redeemed" by its beauty. Nietzsche says that in Apollonian art "beauty triumphs over the suffering inherent in life" (*BT* 16). This would be possible if, in such art, one's attention is focused upon the beauty of the portrayal and away from the terribleness of the portrayed. And this seems to be Nietzsche's conception of what happens. Unlike theoretical man, whose interest is only in "uncovering" truth, the artist, he says, whenever truth is uncovered (we may assume that it is nausea-threatening, Dionysian truth Nietzsche has here in view) will always "cling with rapt gaze to what still remains covering after such uncovering" (*BT* 15).

How, to turn from art to life, does this suggest a style of living capable of overcoming pessimism? What it suggests, I think, is an outlook in which one is disposed to describe life as "terrible but magnificent." (One of Nietzsche's images of human existence, an image to which we shall return, compares us to soldiers in a grand and beautiful oil-painting of a battle [*BT* 5] – one thinks, perhaps of Uccello's *Battle of San Romano* [see jacket].) Such an outlook, while not flinching from acknowledging that Hector suffered a terrible fate at the hands of Achilles, nonetheless focuses upon the beauty of its heroes, their powerfulness, courage, the sheen of their armor, their "style." In this respect Homer does for his heroes what that modern (but regrettably dying) epic, the Western, does for its.

Part of such an outlook, it seems to me, must be (as in the Western) a strong insensitivity to the inner reality of human suffering: for the horror of Homeric warfare not to swamp one's

enjoyment of the magnificence of its sweep and style one must avoid
empathy, avoid identification with the suffering of its victims. This,
Nietzsche holds, is what happens in the Apollonian outlook: the
"mirror of appearance" (*Schein*), he says, prevents the Apollonian
artist from "becoming one and fused with his figures" (*ibid.*). We
are, as it were, so dazzled by the beauty of the Homeric figures that
we cannot see the inner reality of their suffering. The Apollonian
outlook is characterized by an externality, a *profound* superficiality.[14]
(Schopenhauer makes a similar observation about the Homeric
world: objects and events are portrayed, he says, with a unique
"objectivity," are untouched, that is, by human feelings and moods
[*PP* II, p. 444].)

12 Why, given that Apollonian art does acknowledge the terrible,
does Nietzsche connect with it the notion of "lying"? For, I think,
two reasons. First, because, though acknowledging the existence of
life's horrors, it fails to present them from the inner perspective, fails,
that is, to bring home to us their inner reality, their feeling. Hence, in
that it implicitly claims to offer a comprehensive vision, the whole
truth about the world, what it offers is, "in a sense [*in einem gewissen
Sinne* – Kaufmann's translation omits this important qualification],
lies" (*BT* 16). The second reason is that, in Nietzsche's account, the
Greeks of course *knew* that Apollonianism does not offer the whole
truth about the world: they lied to themselves. Self-deception is at
the heart of the Apollonian solution to pessimism. (Nietzsche offers
a slightly different perspective upon the Apollonian lie in *Human, All-
too-human*, in a brilliant passage that seems to say as much about the
Irish as about the Greeks:

Playing with Life – The facility and frivolity of the Homeric fantasy was
necessary for soothing the immoderately passionate disposition and over-
subtle intellect of the Greeks and temporarily banishing them. When their
intellect speaks, how cruel and bitter life appears! They do not deceive
themselves, but they deliberately and playfully embellish life with lies.
Simonides advised his compatriots to take life as a game, they were only too
familiar with its painful seriousness (for the misery of mankind is among the
favourite themes for song among the gods), and they knew that even misery
could become a source of enjoyment solely through art. As a punishment for
this insight, however, they were so plagued by a delight in telling stories
that it was hard for them to desist from lies and deception in the course of
everyday life – just as all poetical people take a delight in lying, a delight
that is moreover quite innocent. The neighbouring nations were no doubt
sometimes reduced to despair by it. [*HH* I, 154].)

13 The Apollonian "veiling" of the horrors of life strikes one as a somewhat fragile prophylactic against pessimism. Though it may seduce one into a general valuing of life, its "superficiality" appears to leaves one unprotected against suffering that thrusts itself upon one in a personal and unavoidable way. But Nietzsche does not represent it as an ideal. The solution he favors is the Dionysian solution, the solution offered by Greek tragedy. This, he says, belongs to a higher stage of Greek culture and offers a "more profound" world-view than that offered by Apollonian art (*BT* 10).

What then is the Dionysian solution? Nietzsche says that whereas Apollonian art tries to convince us of the joy of existence by a glorification of phenomenal reality, Dionysian art "teaches us that we are to seek this joy not in phenomena but behind them" (*BT* 17). It brings us, that is to say, a certain "metaphysical comfort" for the "terrors of individual existence" (*ibid.*). How does it do this? This question is the question of Nietzsche's account of the "tragic effect," the question of why, paradoxically, we derive pleasure from, voluntarily subject ourselves to, confrontations with, indeed in a certain sense, experiences of, the painful and catastrophic in life.

The *general* character of Nietzsche's answer to this question is clear. In Dionysian art, in Greek tragedy in particular, the destruction of the tragic hero is presented in a way that is exulting: though forced to witness the tragic catastrophe "we are not to become rigid with fear: a metaphysical comfort tears us momentarily from the bustle of changing figures. We really are, for a brief moment, the primodial being itself" (*ibid.*).

It seems to me clear, in spite of attempts by the later Nietzsche and others to suggest that his account of the tragic effect is entirely original (*BT*, "Attempt at a Self-Criticism," 6), that this is a version of Schopenhauer's account of the tragic effect as our highest experience of the "feeling of the sublime" – as indeed, in *The Birth*, Nietzsche *admits*: the "artistic taming of the horrible" is, he says, "the sublime" (*BT* 7). Our tragic joy consists in an at least momentary escape from the terror of individual human existence, in an intimation of our "higher," suprahuman destiny: tragedy "in the person of the tragic hero... knows how to redeem us from the greedy thirst for this existence, and with an admonishing gesture... reminds us of another existence and a higher pleasure for which the tragic hero prepares himself by means of his destruction not by means of his triumphs" (*BT* 21).

Unlike Schopenhauer, however, who reports the sublime effect but never really attempts an explanation of how it occurs (see ch. 1, sec. 13 above), Nietzsche attempts such an explanation, at least with respect to Greek tragedy. Some of its details are obscure, but it is clear that the crucial idea is that the Greek audience, though (as in Schopenhauer's account of the experience of the sublime) partially identifying with the individual threatened by tragic destruction – it "shudders at the sufferings which will befall the hero" (*BT* 22) – has, as its primary identification, the chorus.

Nietzsche suggests that the singing of the chorus (the original prototype of tragedy, the drama being, as it were, born out of it at a later date [*BT* 7]) "nullifies" the *principium individuationis* (*ibid.*), draws the hitherto soberly Apollonian spectator into the Dionysian world. From this perspective he experiences with *joy* the annihilation of the tragic hero. As, that is, the barbarians celebrated their ecstatic absorption into the primal oneness in acts of real violence performed on real individuals, so the Greek audience performed the same act symbolically (the first "artistic jubilee" of the Dionysian impulse [see sec. 7 above]). Tragedy offers, as it were, a symbolic sacrifice to Dionysus. A joy which appears to rest on cruelty, appears to be *Schadenfreude*, is in reality, an exuberant affirmation of one's supra-individual identity that resembles the burning of banknotes as an expression of sudden accession to great wealth.

Nietzsche says that tragedy offers us "a profound and [note this word] pessimistic view of the world." It offers "the conception of individuation as the primal cause of evil" but also "the joyous hope that the spell of individuation may be broken in augury of a restored oneness" (*BT* 10). And he speaks in apocalyptic terms of the yearning of the Dionysian initiates for a "rebirth of Dionysus, which we must now dimly conceive as the end of individuation" (*ibid.*). But if this is the character of the tragic effects, why did the Greeks not lapse into Schopenhauerian "resignationism" (*BT*, "Attempt at a Self-Criticism," 6), a pessimistic nausea, and "Buddhistic negation of the will"? Social organization, action, in particular political action, that is, demands the world of Apollonian individuation: a distinction between actor and that which is acted upon, a distinction, in the case of the defense of the state, between *us* and *them*. But Dionysian man knows both the futility of action – that it can change nothing "in the eternal nature of things" – and the joy of a higher, non-Apollonian state. It surely follows, then, that "from [Dionysian] orgies a people can take one path only, the path to Indian

Buddhism" (*BT* 21). And yet the Greeks acted: among things, they ✗
defeated the Persians. How was this possible?

Nietzsche answers by saying that situated between the Indian
culture of actionless contemplation on the one side and the Roman
culture of action and assertion on the other, the Greeks "exhausted
themselves neither in ecstatic brooding nor in a consuming chase
after worldly power and worldly honour" but succeeded, at least
during the short period of their high tragedies, in producing a
synthesis of Indian passivity and Roman assertiveness, a third form
of culture both "fiery and contemplative" (*BT* 21). Through
tragedy, that is, we are brought tidings of a "higher existence," a
"metaphysical comfort" which "stimulates, purifies and discharges" our feelings of nausea at our habitation of the world of
individuals (*ibid.*). Now, however, the Apollonian part of tragedy
must be brought into play. Through it we are subject to the "noble
deception" (*ibid.*) that the meaning of the play concerns only the fate
of an individual in a world of individuality: the tragic hero as it were
"relieves us of the burden" of Dionysian insight (*ibid.*). Even the
author, as we have seen, cannot properly understand the meaning of
his work (*BT* 17).

The same is true of Wagner's *Tristan*. No completely musical soul
would be able to experience the third act as absolute music with
"expiring in a spasmodic unharnessing of all the wings of the soul"
(*BT* 21).[15] Fortunately, however, the Apollonian drama exists to
restore "the almost shattered individual with the healing balm of
illusion" (*BT* 17). Tristan wakes up from metaphysico-sexual
reverie and so do we, unable to understand the metaphysical
meaning of our musical experience. The effectiveness of Dionysian
art, therefore, is that while on the one hand affirming to us our
ultimate deliverance from the pain and anxiety of individuality, on
the other – as if recognizing that "action requires the veil of
illusion" (*BT* 7) – it acts like a fairy godmother and draws a veil of
forgetfulness over what we have experienced. In this way we are
returned to the world strangely comforted but yet able to act.

14 We are now in a position to return to the question of whether or
not *The Birth* is a pessimistic work, whether or not it affirms or rebuts
Silenus' evaluation of life, his view that the best response to human
existence is "to die soon."

It is, it seems to me, completely clear that the Apollonian solution

to suffering implies a pessimistic assessment of the value of human life:
that *were* Nietzsche to endorse it as *his* solution there would be no
question as to his pessimism. For what the solution offers as a way of
overcoming pessimism, of avoiding the pessimist's judgment on life,
is self-deception, telling oneself "lies." But this implies that in the
fullness of knowledge one would *not* affirm life as worth living. It
implies, more briefly, that life is not worth living.[16]

But it is also clear that the Apollonian solution is not and cannot
be Nietzsche's solution. It cannot be the solution he endorses since,
given the birth-of-tragedy thesis's account of the highest form of art,
and given also the thesis that the greatest art is that which performs
the greatest service for life, Nietzsche *has* to endorse Dionysian, tragic
art as offering the best solution to the suffering of life. The question
of *Nietzsche's* pessimism turns, therefore, on the question of whether
Dionysianism implies a pessimistic assessment of human life.

It seems to me clear, even obvious, that it does. One intimation of
this is to be found in the language used to describe the effect of
Dionysian art. Dionysian art, he says, "seduces" us into continued
life, provides a "metaphysical comfort" for life (in later works
Nietzsche sometimes speaks of art as *enhancing* life), turns the horror
and absurdity of life into "notions with which one can live" (*BT* 7).
None of these turns of phrase suggests human existence to be a
particularly attractive state of being. And it should be borne in
mind, too, that "intoxication," the central metaphor for Dionysianism, though not perhaps necessarily, nonetheless most naturally,
carries with it pessimistic associations. The need for intoxication,
that is, is to be discovered typically where the realities of life are
found to be unacceptable. (Nietzsche makes the connection between
intoxication and pessimism explicit in later works, describing those
who "seek rest, stillness, calm seas, redemption from themselves
through art...intoxication, convulsions, anaesthesia and madness"
as "romantic pessimists" [*GS* 370].)

The best way, however, to see that *The Birth* is a life-denying work
is to note its fundamentally religious character and to conjoin this
observation with the well-known view of the later Nietzsche that
religion, in particular Christianity, is the product of those who,
damaged and demeaned by life, are fundamentally hostile to it.
(Although claiming, in *Ecce Homo*, that *The Birth* already shares in his
later abhorrence of Christianity – it exhibits, he claims, a "profound
and hostile silence about Christianity" [*EH* IV, 1; cf. *BT*, "Attempt

at a Self-Criticism," 5] – the truth is that it in fact interprets at least German Christianity, Lutheranism, as a rebirth of the Dionysian [*BT* 23].)

That *The Birth* has religion as its fundamental concern, that it seeks to find through art – through "art-deification" – something to fill the void left by the demise of the Christian God is manifested in its account of the role of the tragic theater in Greek life – an account which, remember, is supposed to provide a model for the regeneration of modern culture. The Greek theater, he says, had the function of "stimulat[ing], purify[ing], and discharg[ing] the whole life of the people" (*BT* 21) (a fanciful claim, given the probability that during the period of the great tragedies the Greek audience was mainly, if not exclusively, male). In so describing it, he transforms Greek theater (and demands the same status for Wagnerian theater) into, in all but name, a church, a church which possesses the centrality to social life possessed by the church of medieval Christendom, and which fulfills the same function of providing metaphysical consolation for the horrors of human life.

That it is a religious role Nietzsche assigns to theater becomes ever more clear when we attend to his (impressive) critique of the positivistic spirit of contemporary industrial culture and to his remedy for its ills. As Greek tragedy was killed by the insistence of Socrates, that "despotic logician" (*BT* 14), that the beautiful, and hence the admissible, in art should imitate reality (as conceived by Socrates) in being fully intelligible to the Apollonian mind (*BT* 12), so the scientistic refusal of the modern age to countenance anything inaccessible to the rational mind has produced a "decisive secularization" (*BT* 23) of our culture and has thereby created a climate in which myth – tragic, Dionysian myth in particular – cannot flourish. Several consequences follow from this. First, a lack of both artistic and political unity, for only the sharing of an "unconscious metaphysics" can prevent "the powers of the imagination and of the Apollonian dream from their aimless wandering" (*BT* 23), and only a state in possession of the "unwritten laws" of a "mythical foundation that guarantees its connection with religion and growth from mythical notions" (*ibid.*) can achieve genuine cohesion. Second, modern, mythless man, denied any culturally endorsed solution to the suffering and absurdity of life, is led to a feverish plundering of other and earlier cultures in a restless quest for satisfaction of the "metaphysical drive" (*ibid.*). Hence

western culture contains a "pandemonium of myths and superstitions" (*ibid.*), a "revolting" smorgasbord of religious and quasi-
religious remedies for life. And hence, too, the vulgar materialism of
western culture, its dominance by the "burden and greed of the
moment,"[17] a worthless and desperate hedonism of the moment, a
feverish consumerism. Lacking the perspective of eternity, we find
our only locus of satisfaction to be the sensuality of the *now* (*ibid.*; cf.
WB, pp. 219–20).

The closing pages of *The Birth* are (like some of his later works)
dominated by Nietzsche's presentiment of the imminent collapse of
western culture. Only a rebirth of Dionysian myth, which will occur,
if anywhere, in the "pure and vigorous core of the German
character" (*BT* 23), can transmute it into a culture of dignity and
value, for "any people – just as, incidentally, any individual – is
worth only as much as it is able to press upon its experience the
stamp of the eternal; for thus it is, as it were, desecularised and shows
its unconscious inward convictions of the relativity of time and of the
true, that is metaphysical significance of life" (*ibid.*).

It is clear from all this that the task for Bayreuth is to achieve not
merely a rebirth of tragedy but the recreation, too, of a religious
culture. This is why art, in the words in which *The Birth* is dedicated
to Wagner, is the highest task and truly metaphysical (Nietzsche
could equally have said religious) activity of this life (*BT* Preface).

15 Exception might be taken to the implicit assumption in the above
discussion that to identify *The Birth* as a religious work is *a fortiori* to
identify it as a pessimistic work. For a religion need not, it may be
said, and in Nietzsche's case *is* not, a denigration or denial of this
world in favor of another. For Nietzsche's religion is a religion, a
celebration of *life*, a joyous "Saying Yes to life even in its strangest
and hardest problems, the will to life rejoicing over its own
inexhaustibility even in the very sacrifice of its highest types" (*EH*
IV, 3), rather than, as in the case of Christianity, the promotion of an
antihuman ideal by means of which to condemn, "say No to," life.
Coupled with this objection may be the further one that in my
account of the tragic effect I failed to mention that, according to
Nietzsche, one not only identifies with the primal unity but also
experiences in "creative joy" its eternal "satisfaction in [the]...
change of phenomena," its "raging desire for and joy in existence"
(*BT* 17). Surely, it may be said, when the tragic effect is fully

described in this way we see that, as he claims, Nietzsche's account of that effect is indeed far removed from Schopenhauer's pessimistic "resignation" from life. Finally, it may be protested, in representing Nietzsche as a pessimist I have ignored the famous assertion that, considered as an aesthetic phenomenon, the world is "eternally justified."

16 Let me begin to answer these charges by attending to the last point first; but considering the import of the assertion that "only as an *aesthetic phenomenon* is existence and the world eternally justified" (*BT* 5, 24).

The first point to investigate is the question of the force of the "only." What other kind of justification is being rejected? The answer is that it is *moral* justification he rejects: "confronted with morality," he writes in the 1886 Preface, "life must continually and inevitably be in the wrong...crushed by the weight of contempt and the eternal No" (*BT*, "Attempt at a Self-Criticism," 5; cf. *KG* IV 3, p. 388, Fragment 30 [51]). The point here, a point taken over from Schopenhauer, is the impossibility of reconciling the character of the world with a morally perfect, omnipotent creator – the ludicrous impossibility of Christian theodicy: Schopenhauer holds, as we saw (ch. 1, sec. 4), that if we insist in anthropomorphizing the creative source of existence then not benevolence but sadism is the character we must attribute to it.

There is, however, Nietzsche suggests, a third possibility: we may conceive of the source of existence as neither saint nor sadist but as, rather, "an entirely reckless and amoral artist–god" (*BT*, "Attempt at a Self-Criticism," 5), a "world-building force" which "the dark Heraclitus compares to a playing child that places stones here and there and builds sand hills only to overthrow them again" (*BT* 24).[18] In Dionysian ecstasy, then, it is with this child–artist–god that we identify: sharing in his "creative joy" we take delight in the "artwork" "we" have created and finding it beautiful[19] see it as "justified." The world we see contains, of course, terrible catastrophe, arbitrary, unmerited suffering, tragic "dissonances" (*BT* 24) – the "ugly and disharmonic," in the language of the later Nietzsche. But, as in music, these artistically employed dissonances can be seen to increase the aesthetic pleasurability of the whole. And if, as sober, Apollonian individuals, we feel inclined to protest that we do not enjoy being part of those dissonances, let us not forget that we individuals are not the creator of the world but "merely images and artistic projections for the true author, and that we have our highest dignity in our significance as [his] works of art" (*BT* 5). We resemble soldiers painted on a canvas of a battle scene (*ibid.*). Our protest that the world should have been kinder to us is as laughable as their protest would be.

As aesthetic phenomenon, then, the world is an object of pleasure; beautiful, "justified," affirmable. But *to whom* is it justified? Not, clearly, to individual human beings, but rather to the world creator. There is no suggestion here at all that humans find or can find *their* life to be pleasurable or justified. To suggest otherwise would be to suggest that because a concentration camp "justifies" itself to its sadistic (or perhaps merely playfully mad) commandant as a pleasurable "entertainment" (*BT* 6), so too must the inmates find it justified. If Nietzsche's account of the tragic effect is right, human beings can, with luck, be transported briefly out of the role of protagonist in the tragedy of life and into that of its "sole author and spectator" (*ibid.*). But this does nothing to justify the life of an inmate to an inmate. And such a justification indeed – Nietzsche is quite explicit – is not offered. The world, he says, evincing an artist's megalomania of truly Wagnerian proportions, was not created "for our betterment or education" (*BT* 5). Consequently, justification from *our* perspective is something we have no right to demand.

It is possible that we have misunderstood Nietzsche's Dionysianism by taking the discussion too literally, too metaphysically? Should we not perhaps[20] take metaphysics as metaphor and understand *The Birth* to take the Dionysian to be not really a metaphysical, but rather a *psychological*, state? On this interpretation, the "end of individuation" is not a matter of absorption into a higher metaphysical domain but rather the achievement of a state of love for and security with one's fellow human beings – Schopenhauerian *Gemeinschaft* (see ch. 1, sec. 5), in other words. On this view Nietzsche's Dionysianism would not be an escape from, denial of, the human self and life, but rather an affirmation of the higher potentialities of that life and self.

The answer is that while it is possible to *reconstruct* Nietzsche in this way, to derive from *The Birth* inspiration for a Nietzsch*ean* (or, more correctly, Schopenhauerian) ethics of altruism, it is not possible *correctly to interpret The Birth* in this way. For two reasons. First, because, as we will see in the next chapter, the later Nietzsche's critique of the postulation, intimation of, or yearning for, a "metaphysical world," whether it be in religion, art, or philosophy, a critique begun in his "positivistic" years, is very clearly a *self*-critique: he describes the metaphysical interpretation of life with an authenticity and intimacy that only a former inhabitant of that interpretation could achieve. Indeed, he *tells* us this in the already-quoted (n. 19 above) passage in *Zarathustra*, a passage that can refer only to *The Birth*: "At one time Zarathustra too cast his delusion beyond man, like all the afterworldly. The work of a suffering and tortured god. The world then seemed to me..." (*Z* 1, 3). To view *The Birth*'s metaphysics as mere metaphor deprives Nietzsche of an object for this self-critique. The second reason is that, as Schopenhauer realized – and as Nietzsche, given his close acquaintance with Schopenhauer cannot have failed to realize too – altruistic identification with the totality of *human* lives does not solve the problem of pessimism. If I identify – empathize, that is – with humanity in general then, though the quality of my suffering may change, given that the wisdom of Silenus was a problem to start with, it *remains* a problem: if human life is in general a confrontation with horror and absurdity, then it remains so notwithstanding my solidarity with the numerous other individuals who find themselves in the same predicament. (One is not the less likely to drown just because there are others in the lifeboat.) Indeed, if Schopenhauer is right, identification with others *increases* one's awareness of the horror of life (see ch. 1, sec. 5). Since, therefore, overcoming pessimism is *the* problem for *The Birth*, it is important to resist the temptation to read Nietzsche's Dionysian solution as a matter of identifying with other *human* beings. Rather, one identifies with a *non*human being, the primal unity, or "will-to-live" which celebrates, says yes to, not the inexhaustibility of human life but rather "*its own* inexhaustibility" (see sec. 16 above; my emphasis), the wanton pleasure of its own eternally boyish existence as the creator–spectator of the fate of the human flies (see *A* 48).

17 Let me bring the discussion of *The Birth* to a close. The question of the stance taken in it towards pessimism is, I suggested, the question of whether or not the Dionysian solution to suffering is pessimistic. But it is pessimistic, I have argued, since the only being to whom the life lived by human beings is said to have any kind of value is a nonhuman, external spectator. Human beings are offered,

as a solution to their suffering, a transcendence of their humanity, an escape from individuality into a feeling of absorption into the Primal One. Clearly though, it seems to me, this does nothing to rebut the wisdom of Silenus: the best things for human individuals is indeed not to be born and the second best is to die soon; or at least to "kill" the consciousness of what it is like to be human with heady draughts of Dionysian intoxication.

Like Schopenhauer, therefore, Nietzsche offers flight from human individuality as his solution to its pain and absurdity. Like him therefore, he denies (human) life. Later on, in *Assorted Opinions and Maxims*, he distinguishes between one who "wants to enjoy his own nature by means of art" (clearly a descendant of the Apollonian glorifier of the phenomenon) and one who "wants with its aid to get above and away from his nature" (*HH* IIa, 371). The latter is clearly the "romantic pessimist" (see sec. 14 above). And it is also, in his Dionysian vein, the author of *The Birth of Tragedy*.

18 Is there then no difference between the Schopenhauerian and Nietzschean solutions to suffering? There is a difference, for whereas the Nietzschean hero, Dionysian man, identifies with the world-will, the primal source of the world as phenomenon, the Schopenhauerian stance is unable to stomach such an identification. Moral repugnance against the creative source of that hell which the world is leads him, as we have seen, to a horrified rejection of the will. Thus, though Schopenhauer and Nietzsche are at one in denying human existence they differ in that in Schopenhauer there is a *double* denial, a denial, in Nietzschean terminology, of not just Apollonian but of Dionysian reality in favor of identification with a *we* know not what, a something "beyond" the will (see *WR* II, p. 198).

This occurs because Schopenhauer fails to adopt the Nietzschean stance "beyond good and evil." Nietzsche, that is, suggests that only aesthetic criteria are to be employed in judging the world and its creator. Schopenhauer, on the other hand, judges according to moral criteria and condemns the creator for failing to be constrained by moral ideals (see *WP* 1005). It has to be said, I think, that, given Schopenhauer's and Nietzsche's identical assessment of the character of the human world, Schopenhauer's response is the more attractive, the more *human*. There is, it seems to me, something ugly, inhuman even, one is tempted to add, Wagnerian about a willingness not only to condone but even to inhabit a state of mind willing to deploy human individuals as mere means to the production of the artist–god's spectacular, bloody, cosmic epic.

19 After *The Birth*, Nietzsche's only other sustained discussion of art prior to the radical change of stance represented by *Human, All-too-human* is the last of his four *Untimely Meditations, Richard Wagner at Bayreuth*. This work, a portrait of Wagner at a time at which only *Parsifal* (1882) remained to be written, was published in 1876, the year of Nietzsche's dramatic flight in the middle of the first Bayreuth Festival, his final break with the Wagner phenomenon. It is one of Nietzsche's weakest works (he himself has serious doubts about its publishability), weak in structure, short on argument and analysis, long on rhapsodic yet (in contrast to *The Birth*) somehow inauthentic attempts to evoke the power of Wagner's music. It also, I shall suggest, has nothing of substance to add to *The Birth*: in print, at any rate, Nietzsche's thought about art remained static from 1872 until 1876.

Nietzsche wrote the work with difficulty. The reason is that by the time of its writing his attitude towards Wagner had changed from adulation to ambivalence. Though outwardly still devoted to both Wagner and his cause, privately he was full of reservations: his notebooks for the two years preceding the work's publication raise many of the accusations – that Wagner was insincere, a populist, an "actor," a German nationalist – which were to constitute the foundation of his later case against Wagner.

The device Nietzsche adopted to enable him to write out of this divided state of mind was to compose an idealized biography in which Wagner's "higher" self eventually triumphs over the errors and weaknesses of his "lower" self (see especially *WB* 8). This enables him to combine hagiography with a warning to Wagner to remain true to his highest ideal. Thus Wagner is pictured, in the first stage of his career, as a composer of grand opera, a power-hungry striver after cheap and empty "effects" and "artifices" with which to "wrest a success from the public" (a description that may call to mind certain composers of the contemporary "musical"). Never, comments Nietzsche, can so great an artist have started out so deeply involved in error, nor engaged in a more "revolting" form of his art (*ibid.*). Of the next stage, that of the social revolutionary, it can at least be said that it is distinguished from the first by a certain nobility of feeling. The mature Wagner, however, transcends this stage too, realizing that the transformation needed by art and by humanity concerns not social institutions but rather the individual heart (*ibid.*). This mature Wagner now becomes Nietzsche's *mouthpiece*.[21] Under the rubric "Wagner holds that" we are in fact told what he, Nietzsche, believes about art and about life.

What does this Wagner–Nietzsche figure tell us? As in *The Birth*, the underlying premise is pessimism; that life is something to be endured rather than embraced. The individual, we are told, has a desperate need to be delivered from "terrible anxiety which death and time evoke" (*WB* 4), a metaphysical yearning for deliverance from this life which is experienced, as in *Tristan*, as "evil, deception and separation" (*WB* 8).

The solution (here Nietzsche reiterates the illusory character of "Socratic," scientific optimism) is not to be found in action: "suffering pertains to the essence of things" (*WB* 8) and cannot be eliminated. And power, *all* power, is, as Wotan shows us in the *Ring* cycle, evil; Wotan's renunciation of power is a model for us all to follow (*WB* 11). At the beginning of *Wagner at Bayreuth* Nietzsche says that the most vital question for philosophy is the extent to which the world is alterable; vital, he says, making an active-*sounding* remark, so that once it is answered we may "set about *improving that part of it recognised as alterable*" (*WB* 3). But at the end of the work it turns out to be not the world but only our attitudes to it that are capable of alteration. One can believe in the future, he says, only because the Socratic attitudes of our modern culture towards art and the metaphysical are, at least possibly, capable of being changed, not because any changes in the fundamental character of human existence are possible (*WB* 11).

Art, that is to say in particular Wagner's music, is capable of endowing life with a metaphysical dimension. It is capable of bringing the individual to an identification with "something higher than himself" (*WB* 4), of transporting him (a Kantian phrase this) to a "realm of freedom" (*WB* 7). When, "strangely consoled," we return from this realm we possess a "new feeling of security." Towards our fellows, since we have realized the merely phenomenal status of the *principium individuationis*, the illusoriness of individuality and separateness, we feel "abundantly benevolent." And we have difficulty taking our previously so-distressing life seriously since, because we have taken *art* so seriously, ordinary life now appears to us as an unimportant fragment of the total experience we have traversed in our ecstatic, musical absorption (*ibid.*).

20 This, then, is what art does for life: it returns us to life able to face it with grace and benevolent serenity, our knowledge of the inevitability of suffering and death alleviated by a sense of life's vanity, rendered trivial by being viewed in the perspective of eternity. Or rather, this is what art *can* do for life. Modern music-less, mythless theoretical man, however, has cut himself off from such redemption. Convention has alienated him from other human beings and from himself. In its adaptation to cognitive ends, language has ceased to perform its original function of communicating strong feelings, so that human beings can only communicate about the "objective." Culture, instead of being the outer manifestations of inner "content," has become mere artifice so that we are, even to ourselves, mere "appearance," "out of touch" with our feelings so that we are unable to admit to ourselves how wretched we are; how full our lives are of "hoary impotence, nagging discontent, industrious boredom, dishonourable wretchedness" (*WB* 5). "Modern art" has become a form of "quiet dipsomania" (*Stille Trunksucht*) (*ibid.*) in which we seek to drown our disquiet. But this must be replaced by the "dithyrambic" art first exemplified by Aeschylus and now reborn in the art of Wagner (*WB* 7) so that men can once more become "naive," "candid," authentic. For only the natural, "free" man is capable of "genuine satisfactions and redemptions," capable, as it were, of receiving the "sacrament" offered by redemptive art (*WB* 11).

21 It is clear from the foregoing précis that *Wagner at Bayreuth* both shares in the pessimism of *The Birth* and offers us the same metaphysical comfort for it; as we called it, the Dionysian solution. The last of the *Untimely Meditations* is an uneasy repetition of *The Birth of Tragedy* – with the difference, since its focus is upon music, that there is no mention of Apollonian art nor of an Apollonian solution to pessimism.

CHAPTER 3

Human, All-too-human

1 At about the time *Richard Wagner at Bayreuth* appeared Nietzsche began work on *Human, All-too-human,* which he published in the spring of 1878. In 1886 it was republished as volume I of a work with that same title, volume II comprising *Assorted Opinions and Maxims,* first published in 1879, and *The Wanderer and his Shadow* of 1880. This body of material, together with *Dawn* (1881), is the topic of this chapter. Accordingly, the chapter falls into four parts: in the first (secs. 2–13) I discuss *Human, All-too-human* (to avoid confusion I shall refer only to the work of 1878 under that title); in the second (secs. 14–22) *Assorted Opinions and Maxims;* in the third (secs. 23–5) *The Wanderer and his Shadow;* and in the fourth (secs. 26–9) *Dawn.*

2 *Human, All-too-human* is subtitled *A Book for Free Spirits.* The foremost spirit thus referred to is, he explains in *Ecce Homo,* himself: the book, he says, is a work of liberation, the work in which "I liberated myself from that in my nature which did not belong to me" (*EH* VI, 1). Emotionally, the book marks his "liberation" from Wagner, his first "coming out" as a non- indeed anti- Wagnerite. Though the last meeting between the two had occurred eighteen months prior to its publication, the devastatingly deflationary portrait of the artist posing as romantic, prophetic, quasi-priestly "genius" (Wagner, that is, in all but name) which, as we will see, the work contains, placed the rupture between the two beyond repair. (A sign, however, of Nietzsche's all-too-human emotional confusion, a sign that the liberation from Wagner was less than total is the fact that he sent both Richard and Cosima copies of the book hoping, of course in vain, for some kind of approval.) Philosophically, the book marks a liberation from certain aspects of Nietzsche's Schopenhauerism. Gone is the Schopenhauerian reverence for the transcendence of rationality, for "the saint" and "the genius" (see *EH* VI,

1) and gone too, as we will see, is Schopenhauer's pessimism. Stylistically, the book marks a liberation from the nineteenth century. Gone are the long, heavy, humorless passages of overripe prose that marked *The Birth of Tragedy*. In the short, dry, witty aphorisms that replace them we escape and breathe, in fact, for the first time, the air of the modern world.

3 *Human, All-too-human* marks, it is clear, a tremendous departure from the world of *The Birth of Tragedy*. The most startling departure is that it adopts and inhabits that stance identified in *The Birth* as the antithesis of Nietzsche's own Dionysianism, the stance of "theoretical," "Socratic," or "scientific" man.

This adoption reveals itself in the disappearance of the quality of "untimeliness" that characterizes *The Birth* and indeed, in one way or another, all of Nietzsche's other published works. *Human, All-too-human*, it seems to me, is unique in its abandonment of the "wanderer" pose (see *GS* 380), the stance of the outsider alienated from his time and culture. In the work he abandons the neoromantic critique of modern culture presented by its predecessors and comes, instead, to inhabit and affirm the science-based, "progress"-affirming *Weltanschauung* of his age. Though most of the characteristics of modern culture for which, in *The Birth*, it was condemned are again recorded, the *Gestalt* is now entirely different. Thus, for example, though again recording the collapse of the old national cultures and their replacement by a new, international, "motley" culture, rather than lamenting their demise he now says that we should feel proud to live in an "age of comparisons." And we should feel excited at the possibilities, in particular, for the achievement of peace (*HH* I, 23–6). "Progress" conceived, it seems, in terms of health, education, welfare, and peace is possible (the question of the meaning of such progress, of whether it constitutes an affirmable end-in-itself, prominent in Nietzsche's later work, is conspicuous by its absence). Pessimism is rejected: away with this "overused" word, says Nietzsche, "occasion for using [it] ... is growing less day by day" (*HH* I, 28). The increasing human ability to abolish suffering, even one day perhaps death (*HH* I, 128), is, he adds, a "bad lookout for the writers of tragedy – for there is less and less material for tragedy because the realm of inexorable, implacable destiny is growing narrower and narrower" (*HH* I, 108). But disappearing too is the need for the myths that, according to *The Birth*, were embodied for us in tragedy: "serious occupation" with symbolic thinking "has become [now] a mark of a lower culture." What we value now are not the grand "errors handed down by metaphysical and artistic ages of men" but the "small unpretentious truths" we discover by "rigorous thinking" of which earlier ages were incapable (*HH* I, 3).

4 The main target for criticism in *Human*, that from which Nietzsche would finally and totally liberate both himself and us, is "the metaphysical world" (*HH* I, 9), sometimes the "thing in itself" (*HH* I, 1). What do these phrases encompass?

In *one* sense, it is fairly clear, *Human* affirms a metaphysical world. In section 9 Nietzsche says that since we cannot but perceive the world through the human head there must be a gap between appearance and reality: the human picture of the world must, that is, be a mere interpretation, an interpretation guided by biological constraints (see ch. 1, sec. 1). In section 19 Nietzsche talks of the error of believing in temporally enduring "things" – science, he says, is "resolving everything thing-like (material) into motions" – and in section 29 he says that, through science, we are getting closer and closer to knowledge of the "true nature" of the world. Putting these remarks together we derive (1) a biologically based idealism with regard to the layman's world-view, (2) an affirmation of scientific realism – the world *is* the way a completed natural science claims it to be – and (3) the affirmation that science is moving towards a dynamic rather than mechanistic view of nature (see ch. 1, nn. 3, 4).

Now all this, surely, suggests that Nietzsche's view of nature in *Human* is little, if at all, removed from the Heracliteanism subscribed to in *The Birth* (see ch. 2, sec. 10), an impression strengthened by the affirmation in section 2 that "everything has become: there are no *eternal facts*." But this, surely, amounts to the affirmation of a particular metaphysical view of the world. What then is the metaphysical world that is to be rejected?

Part of the answer is that it is the literally metaphysical world, that is rejected, the supranatural world, the Kantian "thing in itself" that is beyond space and time, as we at least ordinarily conceive them. Naturalism[1] is a fundamental assertion in *Human, All-too-human*.

Another way of describing the world that is to be rejected is to say that it is the *excitingly* metaphysical world, the world pregnant with implications of practical (rather than theoretical) import. The *Kantian* "thing in itself," that is, was important as the focus of

everything "valuable, terrible, delightful" (*HH* I, 9). It was the
world affirmed by religion, demanded by morality, and intimated by
art. The thing in itself revealed by science, however – the metaphysical world retained by Nietzsche – is, from the point of view of
"happiness, salvation and life," utterly uninteresting; knowledge of
it is even more useless than is knowledge of the composition of water
to a sailor in danger of shipwreck (*ibid.*). The metaphysical world
revealed by science is a "root" not a "blossom," for it does nothing
to give life meaning, direction, or "color" (*HH* I, 29). (Actually, it
deprives the world of color since the dissolution of objects into
"motions" results, presumably, in the relegation of "secondary
qualities," sounds, odors, colors, and so on, to the realm of
appearance.)

5 A question which presents itself at this point is that of *why*
Nietzsche's own metaphysical world should be regarded as so prosaic
given that it is essentially the same Schopenhauerian–Heraclitean
world as that affirmed in *The Birth of Tragedy*. In *The Birth*, that is,
it was the fact that beneath or behind the flickering and painful
world of individuals there exists the "primal unity," the one force,
energy, or will whose manifestation or appearance all individuals
are, that was the presupposition and ground of the "Dionysian
solution" to the horror and terror of existence. For according to this
solution, it is by realizing that our real identity is constituted by the
One that we overcome the nausea and pessimism engendered by
knowledge of the essential character of the life of individuals. But if
now, the One still remains, why should this metaphysical fact be of
any less practical interest than it used to be?

Presumably what Nietzsche would now point out, in his new,
tough-minded, scientific mood, is that to anthropomorphize the
totality of the world's energy – to speak of it either as a
child–artist–god or as one's own real self – is nothing but romantic
"hype," poetic fiction, sentimental illusion. There are people, and
there is totality of the world's energy. The former are sentient
individuals, the latter is not. *Ergo*, no person is the "primal unity."
The "primal unity" is not a person. It is worth noticing that at one
strange point Nietzsche seems to take this stance in *The Birth* itself.
In section 18 he describes "the metaphysical comfort that beneath
the whirl of phenomena eternal life flows on indestructibly" as,
along with the Apollonian and Socratic remedies for life's suffering
one of "three stages of illusion." What he means here, presumably,

is not that the dichotomy between the primal One and the *principium individuationis* is illusion. What is romantic illusion, rather, is the notion that the being of the one constitutes the "eternal life" of any person.

6 In *Human, All-too-human*, therefore, the metaphysics of *The Birth* has undergone a process of de-anthropomorphization. The primal One belongs now to the physicist, no longer the tragedian. Nonetheless, since, apart from this de-anthropomorphization, the metaphysics of *The Birth* remains, the question presents itself as to how it is that the pessimism of the former, a *pessimism which, as we saw* (ch. 2, sec. 10), *was grounded in that metaphysics*, has been replaced now by scientific optimism. The answer can only have to do with an alteration in Nietzsche's conception of nature and power of natural science. In what way can it have changed?

In *The Birth*, it will be remembered, the terrible thing for Nietzsche (as for certain contemporary "chaos" theorists) about the "destructiveness of world history" was its *randomness*. The essence, that is, of metaphysical flux, of the "Dionysian child-god," was its capriciousness: as humans we can never anticipate when it will again be overcome by the creative urge, when its "sandcastles" will become boring, when it will smash them in order to build others. (In *Human* Nietzsche identifies "arbitrariness" as an essential feature of primitive, animistic world-views; when everything is the product of conscious, volitional agents, he suggests [in one of his brilliant excursions into speculative anthropology], nature is not predictable. Religion begins as the attempt to win the favor of the deity by means of the same kind of techniques as a tribe seeks to propitiate a stronger tribe. Its aim thereby is to *make* nature predictable [*HH* I, 111].)

It was this randomness, it will be remembered, that rendered the optimistic assumption that the world is capable of scientific "correction" a disastrous illusion. Science, that is, was perceived as inhabiting, along with common sense, the "frail bark" of the *principium individuationis*. The Schopenhauerian–Heraclitean world of the fluctuating will was, therefore, something it could not know and so not tame.

I want now to propose the hypothesis that somewhere between 1872 and 1878 Nietzsche reevaluated his assessment of science as unable to conceive of the world in terms appropriate to its Heraclitean reality. What adds support to this hypothesis is that we know that though, through F. A. Lange's *History of Materialism*,

Nietzsche had some acquaintance with the history and contemporary state of natural science as early as the 1860s, it was not until 1872[2] that he began his serious study of Roger Boscovich's *Philosophia Naturalis*, the work which convinced him (for a time – see ch 4, sec. 5) that *from a strictly scientific and not merely philosophical viewpoint* there are no "things." Boscovich, that is, proposed that there are no atoms, no matter, but only force organized round various extensionless points, or "*puncta*": "Boscovich taught us to abjure belief in…'substance,' in 'matter,' in the earth-residuum and particle atom: it was the greatest triumph over the senses hitherto achieved on earth" (*BGE* 12; cf. ch. 1, n. 3). But if this is how the world looks *to science* then, it seems, science is *not* inexorably locked into the conceptual scheme of "things," does *not*, after all, inhabit the *principium individuationis*. What I want to suggest, then, is that in between *The Birth* and *Human* Nietzsche came to the view that far from there being, as he had originally supposed, an opposition between his metaphysical Heracliteanism and the scientific world-picture, there is, in fact, a perfect congruence.

Boscovich's physics, of course, since he took himself to be developing Newton's was entirely deterministic: the total state of the universe at a later time is a function of its state at any earlier time. Hence Nietzsche must have come to see that the world can *both* be flux, in the sense of there being no material objects that persist through time and change, and be predictable. In Boscovich, flux does not, as it does in *The Birth*, place reality beyond the reach of scientific understanding and "correction."

This account of Nietzsche's reevaluation of science is, as I say, hypothetical. What is not hypothetical, however, is that in *Human* nature, for whatever reason, has become (in principle) wholly predictable. In section 107 (cf. *GS* 109) he speaks of "the new knowledge" (the context implies it is new to *him*, thereby tending to confirm the hypothesis that *Human* was written under the *recent* impact of Boscovich) according to which everything is "necessary," and in section 106 he applies this knowledge to that ostensibly least predictable part of nature, human action:

At the sight of a waterfall we think we see in the countless curvings, twistings and breakings of the waves capriciousness and freedom of the will; but everything here is necessary, every motion mathematically calculable. So it is in the case of human actions; if one were all-knowing, one would be able to calculate every individual action, likewise every advance in knowledge, every error, every piece of wickedness.

(The conclusion Nietzsche draws from this is "the complete unaccountability of man for his actions" [*HH* I, 107], an exhilarating, liberating conclusion since what follows is the "innocence" [*ibid.*] of man, our freedom from guilt and the dread that accompanies it.)

7 The main aim of *Human*, to resume the main thread of the discussion, is, as we observed in section 4 above, to do away with the metaphysical world, to abolish all "idealism," every setting of human nature and destiny in a suprabiological, suprahuman context: the title of the work means, says Nietzsche, "where *you* see ideal things, *I* see what is human, alas, all-too-human! – I know man better" (*EH* VI, 1). Thereby, we are to create a "free spirit," a spirit free of the myths and superstitions of more primitive ages.

Why does this ambition appear to be so important to the author of the work? Because although, as we saw in *The Birth*, the comforts and delights of metaphysical perspectives "sooth and heal" they do so "only provisionally, only for a moment" (a specific rejection, this, of the Dionysianism of *The Birth*). What is worse is that "they… hinder men from working for a real improvement in their conditions by suspending and discharging in a palliative way the very passion which impels the discontented to action" (*HH* I, 148). The more a man inclines towards a metaphysical interpretation of life, says Nietzsche, continuing in his Marxian vein,

the less attention will he give to the cause of the ill and to doing away with it; the momentary amelioration and narcoticizing, such as is normally employed for example in the case of a toothache, suffices him in the case of more serious sufferings too. The more the domination of religion and all the arts of narcosis declines, the stricter attention men pay to the actual abolition of the ill. (*HH* I, 108)

But how *can* life be supportable without a metaphysical crutch of one sort or another? Is not (in the words of Schopenhauer's famous chapter title) "Man's need for metaphysics" (*WR* II, ch. XVII) an inalienable part of human nature such that life cannot be borne without its satisfaction? People assume, replies Nietzsche, that the "metaphysical need" is immutable because they assume that human nature is. But both assumptions are false (*HH* I, 2, 110). The metaphysical need has come into existence ("Christianity has first to burden the heart so as afterwards to be able to lighten it" [*HH* I, 119]) and can therefore go out of existence (*HH* I, 131). Though a too violent withdrawal is not to be recommended – to this extent metaphysical art and philosophy (for example, *The Birth of Tragedy*) in which we enjoy at least the mood of religion (*ibid.*) are useful as "substitutes" to ease the withdrawal from the "hard" stuff supplied by religion proper (*HH* 1, 27) – the proper response to the metaphysical need is to work towards its weakening and ultimate extermination (*ibid.*). For only when we escape finally and completely from the clutches of the metaphysical, only when we cease to abase ourselves before the nonhuman, will we fully escape "guilt" and "depression" (*HH* 1, 133), only then will we achieve as humans genuine "self-love," "self-valuation" (*HH* 1, 134).

8 How does art fall within the scope of this spiritual spring-cleaning that is to produce the self-love of the "free spirit"? Why, that is, does art invite and perpetuate the metaphysical interpretation of existence?

As has already been intimated,

Art raises its head when the religions relax their hold. It takes over a host of moods and feelings engendered by religion, lays them to its heart and itself grows more profound and soulful, so that it is now capable of communicating exultation and enthusiasm as it formerly could not. The wealth of religious feelings, swollen to a torrent, breaks forth again and again and seeks to conquer new regions; but the growth of the Enlightenment, undermined the dogmas of religion, and inspired a fundamental distrust of them; so that the feelings expelled from the sphere of religion by the Enlightenment throw themselves into art... Wherever we perceive... higher, gloomier colouring, we can assume that dread of spirits, the odour of incense and shadows of churches are still adhering to them. (*HH* 1, 150)

(Note the stark contrast between this and the demand in *The Birth* for the "desecularization" of society [*BT* 23; cf. ch. 2, sec. 14].) Art, in other words, enables us to enjoy religious sentiment without the need to subscribe to any conceptual content (see *HH* 1, 131) – a point not only admitted but emphasized as constituting its central value by, in particular, Kant. Art in a secular age provides, as it were, a catacomb in which the religious habit of mind can continue to exist. For what it offers is religious feeling without cognitive responsibility. We have, says Nietzsche, in a penetrating and surely self-analytical remark about the romantic imagination, a tendency to ontologize the intentional objects of "deep" and serious feelings, to assume, as does astrology, that what we have "essentially at heart" *must* constitute also "the essence and heart of things" (*HH* I, 4). But the objects of the quasi-religious feelings engendered by art are so intangible and vague that they constitute no challenge to the accepted verities of a secular age.

Above all, *music* provides a home for the continued existence of the religious feeling. (It comes as no surprise, given that in *The Birth* it was viewed as *the* metaphysical art, that it is now viewed with particular distrust.) "Art," says Nietzsche,

> *makes the thinker's heart heavy.* – How strong the metaphysical need is, and how hard nature makes it to bid it in a final farewell, can be seen from the fact that even when the free spirit has divested himself of everything metaphysical the highest effects of art can easily set the metaphysical strings, which have long been silent or indeed snapped apart, vibrating in sympathy; so it can happen, for example, that a passage in Beethoven's Ninth Symphony will make him feel he is hovering above the earth in a dome of stars with the dream of *immortality* in the heart: all the stars seem to glitter around him and the earth seems to sink further and further away. – If he becomes aware of being in this condition he feels a profound stab in the heart and sighs for the man who will lead him back to his lost love whether she be called religion or metaphysics. It is in such moments that his intellectual probity is put to the test. (*HH* I, 153)

If art functions for us as a substitute for religion then the artist must occupy a role similar to that of the priest or prophet. And so, says Nietzsche, in the romantic "cult of genius" (a cult that reaches something like its ultimate expression in the claim that art represents "the highest task and truly metaphysical activity of this life" [*BT* Preface]) he does. One ascribes to artists, as Nietzsche's newly satirical phrasing puts it, "a direct view of the nature of the world, as it were a hole in the cloak of appearance, and believes that, by virtue of this miraculous seer's vision, they are able to communicate something conclusive and decisive about man and the world without the toil and rigorousness required by science" (*HH* I, 164; cf. *GM* III, 5).

9 How does Nietzsche propose to liberate us from faith in the "ideal," metaphysical, more-than-human world? How, in particular, from such faith as is presented in art?

He would like to convince us that (like Descartes) he has discovered a new *method*, a method for exposing the errors of metaphysics; a purported branch of "natural science" which investigates the origin of ideas, feelings, and practices which he calls "historical" (later he prefers the term "genealogical") philosophizing (*HH* I, I). The old "metaphysical philosophy," he announces to us at the very beginning of *Human*, found various phenomena, moral (the altruist), religious (the saint), and aesthetic (the genius), to be inexplicable save for the postulation of "a miraculous source in the very kernel and being of the 'thing in itself.'" Historical philosophy, however, demonstrates the redundancy of such a postulation by providing a "chemistry of the moral, religious and aesthetic conceptions and sensations," a demonstration of how even "the most glorious colors" are derived from "base," that is "human" – from the point of view of the old metaphysical yearning "All-too-human" – materials (*ibid.*).

But in fact Nietzsche has no single method for disposing of the metaphysical. For in his demolition of the aesthetic home of the metaphysical (as in his demolition of its other homes), "historical" considerations function as only one ingredient in an opportunistic mixture that also includes (1) the surgical application of the tools of, as we now call it, "analytic" philosophy, and (2) more and less subtle uses of rhetoric.

Examples of Nietzsche's deployment of rhetoric against the metaphysical in art we have already seen. Recall, for example, how the language of section 164 (quoted at the end of sec. 8 above) draws us into a conspiracy in which we both ridicule the romantic artist and feel angry that he should try to achieve the kudos of the scientist with none of the effort. And notice the brilliance with which in section 153 (quoted in the penultimate paragraph of section 8 above) Nietzsche first demonstrates in the rhapsodic yet accurate beauty of his evocation of the finale of Beethoven's Ninth that he, too, the unbeliever, can generate the illusion of immortality but then punctures it with the brisk coldness of the final sentence. The conjurer's art is, as it were, given a magnificent performance and then we are made to feel that it is nothing more than a cheap trick.

Nietzsche's rhetoric (like all rhetoric) is to be viewed with suspicion since it gives us the *experience* of having overcome the metaphysical interpretation of life without providing *reasons* for rejecting it. He *himself* offers us "something conclusive and decisive about man and the world without the toil and rigorousness required by science" (*HH* I, 164). Less problematic are his excursions into analytic philosophy. With respect to metaphysical art, the analytic mode of philosophizing is one he inhabits mainly in discussing the spectator's response. The main thrust of his argument here can be summarized as "presentiments are not arguments." Thus, he points out, certain moods bring with them the "sympathetic resonance" of many related moods, sensations, and thoughts so that they come to be experienced as unities. Referring to these we speak of religious or moral feeling (*HH* I, 14). We call such feelings "profound" believing them to be pregnant with metaphysical import. But in fact,

such feelings are profound only insofar as when they occur certain complex groups of thoughts which we call profound are, scarcely perceptibly, regularly aroused with them; a feeling is profound because we regard the thoughts that accompany it as profound. But a profound thought can nonetheless be very distant from the truth as, for example, every metaphysical thought is; if one deducts from the profound feeling the element of thought mixed in with it, what remains is the *strong* feeling, and this has nothing to do with knowledge as such, just as strong belief demonstrates only its strength, not the truth of that which is believed. (*HH* I, 15; cf. 220, 222)

To someone trained in analytic philosophy, these observations – thoughts not feelings are the bearers of cognitive content, strength of conviction is quite distinct from strength of evidence – may appear to be of a fairly elementary order. But in relation to their specific target, romantic wistfulness, they are pertinent and necessary observations. Thus, for example, it is quite true, as Nietzsche suggests, that in romantic philosophy one finds "the justifications of metaphysical hopes and the profound peace to be attained through them" based on "presentiments" such as that to be derived from "the whole sure evangel in the glance of Raphael's Madonna" (*HH* I, 131). (Without naming him, Nietzsche is here remembering Schopenhauer. What Schopenhauer actually says is that to banish the idea that there exists an absolute "nothingness" beyond this world of suffering we have only to contemplate the saint's "ocean-like calmness of the spirit, that deep tranquility, that unshakable confidence and serenity, whose mere reflection in the countenance as depicted by Raphael or Correggio, is a complete and certain gospel" [*WR* I, p. 411].)

10 Nietzsche's deployment of specifically "historical" observations is directed against the deification of the artist. In the romantic cult of genius in, for example, Schopenhauer's characterization of the

composer (or Nietzsche's own characterization of the lyric poet as one who, through "mystical self-abnegation," becomes identical with "the only truly existent and eternal self resting at the basis of things" [*BT* 5; cf. ch. 1, sec. 12]) the artist is perceived as a quasi-priestly figure in special and mysterious communion with another world. This perception Nietzsche portrays as grounded in no way in the reality of artistic creation, but in, rather, a (largely unconscious) conspiracy between artist and audience for the purpose of mutual gratification. On the artist's side, Nietzsche suggests, he *of course* encourages the idea of himself as someone with direct access to a "beyond," for this is a potent means of increasing his power and influence (*HH* 1, 146). To this end he employs various, as it were, conjuring tricks. He carefully hides, for example, all signs of effort and temporal development in the production of the artwork so that it may "tyrannise" us by its perfection: the finished work "repulses all thinking as to how it became" so that (one thinks here, perhaps, of the importance of the illusion of omnipotence in the instru-mentalist's achievement of the virtuoso effect) we feel the work to be the "casual improvisation of a god" (*HH* 1, 145).[3]

The reality, however, beneath this deceptive veneer is utterly different. Beethoven's notebooks, for example, reveal the huge industry of sorting, sifting, rejecting, and transforming by means of which a glorious and apparently effortless melody is distilled out of a mass of material in which good, bad, and indifferent are mixed together (*HH* 1, 155). Inspiration is, in reality, perspiration. The requirements for art are "inexhaustible" energy, industry, courage, education, taste, and judgment (*ibid.*) and also, in certain respects, an arrested development. The artist's imagination, that is, is stuck in childhood (notice the rhetorical suggestion that, as adults, we should be slightly ashamed of our devotion to art), that primitive stage of the individual which, like dreams, recapitulates the world of primitive man. In a way, that is to say, art really *does* transport us to another world. It is, however, not a *supra*scientific but a *pre*scientific world, an animistic world "imbued with soul," full of "gods and demons" (*HH* 1, 12, 13, 147, 159; cf. sec. 6 above).

Artistic creation is, then, a mundane, human (all-too-human) phenomenon that is passed off by the artist–magician as something pregnant with supernatural overtones. But as with the conjuring-trick proper, we, the audience, connive at our own deception. One motive for this is provided, as we saw, by our need for a surrogate outlet for all those feelings denied religious expression by the dominance of scientific rationalism (*HH* 1, 150), our need for, as Nietzsche later puts it, the art of "spiritual pleasure" (*GS* Preface, 4). (We, as it were, do not want to be without our "drug" even though we cannot take it in the "hard" form anymore.) Another is provided by our vanity: by regarding the artist as a different *order* of being we avoid having to think less well of ourselves on account of our own inability to produce art: "to call something 'divine' means: 'here there is no need for us to compete'": the stars, in Goethe's words, one does not covet (*HH* 1, 162).

It is easy to pick holes in these brilliant but exaggerated observations. Does not Beethoven's *Grosse Fuge display* his life-long battle with the art of fugal writing? Are we not impressed by Cézanne's integrity precisely because the painful consideredness of each brush stroke is often so visible? On the other hand, is not Schubertian or Mozartian perfection sometimes a *genuinely* effortless phenomenon? And while the observations concerning the vanity of the audience may correctly analyze the gushing worship of the "maestro" or "diva" of many a bourgeois opera *aficionado*, is there not such a thing, too, as genuinely humble gratitude for art? But these objections are, I think, beside the point. For the point of Nietzsche's "historical" observations is to give us the *idea* of the technique of demythologizing art. His argument, that is, seems to me implicitly inductive: though art is a highly complex activity, Nietzsche suggests, with devastating effectiveness, there will always be some non-"miraculous" (*HH* 1, 162) interpretation of those phenomena which prompt the romantic's flights of fancy, some account that will show aesthetic activity to be of the same order as human activities of an uncontroversially mundane kind.

11 In sections 7 and 8 we saw Nietzsche's objecting to the metaphysical interpretation of life in general and to metaphysical art in particular that by intimating to us promises of other-worldly comfort for our ills it diverts us from remedial action in this world. Though, that is, we have in our hands the means, science, for undertaking a *cure* for life's ills, art seduces us away from this into merely symptomatic treatment of short-lived efficacy. The consequence of this is that art is (1) redundant and (2) pernicious. Having performed its function of easing the passage from an explicitly religious to a fully secular outlook it should, therefore, be allowed to fade away. Indeed it *is* so fading. We live, says Nietzsche – exhibiting

as nowhere else the "timeliness" of his current mood – in the "evening twilight" of art; the artist will soon be regarded as a "glorious relic" (*HH* I, 223) of a more primitive culture, someone whom we honor for past services, but (like Plato and for Plato's reasons – art distracts us from "reality and truth") show firmly to the door. For the future belongs to science: "the scientific man is the further evolution of the artistic" (*HH* I, 222).

But surely, one wishes to object, this argument presupposes what is clearly false: that all art is other-worldly art. This, moreover, is something that the author of *The Birth of Tragedy* – with its fundamental distinction between art that glorifies the world of human actuality and art which takes us behind "the phenomenon" – ought to be particularly conscious of. There is the art of *this* world as well as the art of "the beyond."

Nietzsche does acknowledge, in *Human*, in effect Apollonian as well as metaphysical (as it used to be called, "Dionysian") art; a type of art which "lays a veil over reality" in such a manner that it "now conceals, now brings into prominence." To one seeking comfort, it "makes the sight of life bearable by laying over it a veil of unclear thinking" (*HH* I, 151; cf. 154). But as the rhetoric indicates, Nietzsche for the moment has little more taste for Apollonian than he does for metaphysical art. The explanation for this, I think, is that Nietzsche is now clearly aware that Apollonian art is, in a sense, as other-worldly as is Dionysian. In terms, that is, of the contrast between disposing of an ill by getting rid of its cause and by bringing about a "change of sensibility" (*HH* I, 108) with regard to that ill, Apollonian as much as Dionysian art does the latter. As much as the art of metaphysical flight, the fuzzy glorification of the phenomena by Apollonian art is a "narcoticizing of human ills" (*ibid.*) and hence an impediment to action. Pain, in short, is good. We do not want reality to be made "bearable" by any kind of art because it is pain that prompts us to action.

12 What, then, to raise Nietzsche's own question (*HH* I, 222), remains of art? Above all, he says, art

has taught us for thousands of years to look upon life in any of its forms with interest and pleasure, and to educate our sensibilities so far that we at last cry: "life, however it may be, is good!"[4] This teaching imparted by art to take pleasure in life and to regard human life as a piece of nature... without being too violently involved in it has been absorbed into us, and now reemerges as an almighty requirement of knowledge. One could give up art but would not thereby relinquish the capacity one has learnt from it...If art disappeared the intensity and multifariousness of the joy in life it has implanted would still continue to demand satisfaction. The scientific man is the further evolution of the artistic. (*HH* I, 222)

This passage seems to postulate the preservation of the Apollonian attitude to life – the stance of detached, "objective" delight – in the activity of science, though presumably, since clarity of thought belongs to the essence of science (*HH* I, 3), it is an Apollonianism from which "unclear thinking" is expunged, an *honest* Apollonianism. (Why there should be any *necessary* connection between delight in life and science is mysterious; the scientist must, of course, be *interested in* at least parts of the world, but it is not at all clear that this entails that she must be *delighted by* it. And Nietzsche soon changed his mind, coming to see science as, at least often, serving the "ascetic ideal" [*GM* III, 25].)

13 What are we to make of the dismissal of art in *Human, All-too-human*? The important thing to notice, it seems to me, is the length of the shadow cast by *The Birth*. *The Birth*, that is, was dominated by a pessimistic account of life and by the thought of our impotence to improve its character through action. Against this background the function of art was either to conceal or to comfort us for life's horrors. Now, however, pessimism has evaporated. Art, therefore, is left without a function. Against this line of argument at least two important objections need to be raised. The first consists in pointing out the excessively hasty nature of Nietzsche's abandonment of pessimism, of his newly discovered faith in action. Nature, as we saw, becomes in *Human* knowable, predictable. From this Nietzsche infers the possibility of a fundamental kind of "progress"; he infers, in the language of *The Birth*, that nature is capable of "correction." But this inference is mistaken, for all that *follows* from the predictability of Nature is that future sufferings, if and when they occur, are, like death and taxes, *predictable* sufferings. It by no means follows that they are *eliminable*.

The second objection is that even if science were able to eliminate human suffering it would not follow that art was functionless. For it is not true – to state the obvious but nonetheless necessary – that the sole function of art is to ameliorate the problem of human suffering. It is not true, to put the point in an equivalent way, that all art is the art either of Apollonian glorification or of metaphysical escape. The Apollonian–Dionysian distinction is not, as Nietzsche explicitly supposes in *The Birth* and implicitly supposes in *Human*, an exhaustive one. Art, rather, has a variety of actual and potential functions – cognitive,[5] expressive, decorative, hortative, and so on – so large that it is probably impossible to specify all of them. When attacking the Kant–Schopenhauer view that disinterestedness constitutes the essence of the aesthetic attitude (see ch. 5, secs. 3–6 below) Nietzsche himself emphasizes the *variety* of our responses to art. Art may, for example, he says, serve as an occasion for communication: our pleasure in understanding an art work may be the pleasure of decoding a kind of riddle; or it may give us pleasure by commemorating a past pleasure, a victory, a hunt, or a wedding; or again art may have the function of moving and rousing the audience to action through, for example, the glorification of revenge or danger (*HH* IIa, 119). Strangely, however, when offering his own assessment of the value of art Nietzsche always ignores this awareness of its plurality of functions. There is always some *one* function the fulfillment of which confers – or, in *Human*, *fails* to confer – value on art. Nietzsche's idea as to what this unique value-conferring function is undergoes, as we will see, kaleidoscopic transformations. But the unwarranted predilection for identifying some one thing as *the* (deep, serious, important, value-conferring) function of art is never questioned.

14 Nietzsche described *Assorted Opinions and Maxims*, together with its successor, *The Wanderer and his Shadow*, as "continuations and appendices" (*HH* II, Preface, 2) of *Human, All-too-human*. Insofar as both works continue to debunk the metaphysical in all its guises, and continue to inhabit the stance of the scientific optimist, the description is justified. With respect to art, however, it is seriously misleading. For whereas art, in *Human*, is consigned to the realm of glorious memory, in *Opinions*, Nietzsche recovers his sense of its indispensability. Art, we will see, is assigned the vital role of "signposting" the future, an assignment that brings with it a revival, in transmuted form, of *The Birth*'s conception of the artist as agent of cultural regeneration. It follows that though there are sound reasons for regarding Nietzsche's works between 1876 and 1882 as a unity, as together constituting a "positivistic" or "middle" period, there are, nonetheless, important transitions within this period.

Why the change? Why does the future no longer belong to "scientific man" alone? The answer, I believe, is that Nietzsche has come to confront a problem neglected in *Human* – value. Scientific man, the "free spirit" (at least at this stage in Nietzsche's conception of the latter), has abandoned all the old metaphysical presuppositions which gave value to the world – distinguished, that is between "good" and "bad" actions – but has, as Nietzsche says, nothing to communicate (even to himself) except his joy in this liberated condition (*HH* I, 34). Such joy, however, must evaporate as soon as the problem of action presents itself. For above the level of biological need and lust, scientific man, so Nietzsche seems to believe, cannot act but is rather a mere uninvolved spectator of life's pageant (see sec. 12 above). The reason for this is that, as he later puts it, science "never creates values" but rather requires something external to itself to be "an ideal of value, a value creating power in the service of which it could believe in itself" (*GM* III, 25). The scientist is thus perceived as a mere purveyor of hypothetical imperatives, instructions as to effective means of achieving given ends. Categorical imperatives, those ends or values themselves, must be created and disseminated by some other agency.[6] That agency, as we will see, is art.

15 What kind of art can perform this vital, art-redeeming function? *Not*, first of all, the art of metaphysical flight. Nietzsche distinguished two types of art and artist: the one "wants to enjoy his own nature by means of art"; the other "with its aid to get above and away from his nature for a while" (*HH* IIa, 371). This looks like a reappearance of the old duality between Apollonian and Dionysian art. But the lighting conditions are now very different. Dionysian art, any art which takes us away from the actuality of human existence, is now completely out of favor. Away, demands Nietzsche, with "all those fantastic, superstitious, half-mendacious, faded subjects upon which certain poets demonstrated their powers." The "good poet of the future" (notice that there are now to *be* poets in the future) is to confine his attention to the world of human actuality: "only reality" (*nur Wirkliches*) (*HH* IIa, 114; cf. 135, 169) is his legitimate topic.

He is *not*, however, to indulge in slavish naturalism: "only reality but by no means every reality! – he will depict only a selected reality" (*ibid*.). Why is this? Because artists are to become again, like the Greek artists of old, "transformers of animals, creators of men," "sculptors and re-modelers of life," "teacher[s] of adults" (*HH* IIa, 172). They are, that is, to dedicate their powers

not so much to the representation of the contemporary world or to the reanimation and imaginative reconstruction of the past, but to signposting the future – not, though, as if the poet could, like a fabulous economist, figuratively [*im Bilde*] anticipate the kind of conditions nations and societies would prosper better under and how they could then be brought about. What he will do, rather, is to emulate the artists of earlier times who imaginatively developed the existing images of the gods and *imaginatively develop* a beautiful [*schön*] image of man: he will scent out those cases in which, in the *midst* of our modern world and reality and without any artificial withdrawal from or warding off of this world, the great and beautiful soul is still possible. (*HH* IIa, 99)

This selected reality he is to raise to "the status of a model and in so doing, through the excitation of envy and emulation, help to create the future" (*ibid.*) (precisely Nietzsche's own ambition, it may be added, in constructing the glowing portrait of the *Übermensch* in *Zarathustra*).

16 Writing, as I do, in the former colony of New Zealand, one is particularly aware of the significance of art in its "signposting" role. For the contribution made by art to the creation of an authentically local identity (and the intensity of the demand made of it that it *should* thus contribute) is in this part of the world quite obvious. It is not, I think, to be doubted that, for example, the apotheosis of the vocabulary and speech-rhythms of the rural New Zealand male in the novels of Frank Sargesson or of the peculiarly harsh, "hard-edged" quality of the New Zealand light in the paintings of Rita Angus and, later, Colin McCahon have made significant contributions in this respect. New Zealand art has had as its particular preoccupation, the task of liberating New Zealanders from the need to inhabit pale and ill-fitting identities imported from the mother-country. Nietzsche's observation that art helps, or can help, to create the future is particularly true of an ex-colony. But of course it is true, also, elsewhere. Art, in general, has the capacity to create (as the unlovely jargon has it) "role models." In unheralded ways it *legislates* (here we find an echo of the *Birth*'s concept of artist as prophet) values for the future.

Notice that in the idea of "signposting" we find a rehabilitation of Apollonian art. For it is clear that in discussing the creation of ideals out of the mass of material presented by past and present life we are discussing the "transfiguration" of reality – the activity which defines Apollonian art. Notice, however, that though signposting art employs the familiar Apollonian techniques of selecting, "concealing and reinterpreting" (*HH* IIa, 174) and so on, its old associations of "lie" and "illusion" have been discarded. Apollonian art has become "honest" because it has ceased to make truth-claims. In *The Birth*, that is, the Apollonian artist, as it were, held up a distorting mirror to nature and said (mendaciously): "the world is thus." Now, however, she holds up the same mirror but says: "make yourself thus!" (In terms of a Wittgensteinian distinction: the "sentence-radical" is the same but the mood-indicator has changed.)

17 What kind of art signposts the future? Not, we have seen, the art of other-worlds. Only this-worldly art can construct the future of this world. (Not musical art either, so, at least some of the time, it seems. Since according to section 171 music is always backward-looking – "all truly meaningful music is a swan-song" – it seems to be excluded from future-oriented activity.) And not the art (about which more will be said shortly) which consists in "the barbaric if enthralling spluttering out of hot and motley things from a chaotic, unruly soul." For the image of the "great and beautiful soul" can be embodied *only* in forms that are "harmonious and well-proportioned." The poems, therefore, of artists who signpost the future

will be distinguished by the fact that they appear to be secluded and secured against the fire and breath of the *passions*: the incorrigible error, the shattering of the entire human instrument, mocking laughter and gnashing of teeth, and everything tragic and comic in the old customary sense will be experienced as a tedious, anachronizing coarsening of the human image when confronted with his new art. Strength, goodness, mildness, purity and an involuntary inborn moderation in the characters and their actions: a level ground which it is repose and joy to the feet to walk upon: countenances and events mirroring a luminous sky: knowledge and art blended to a new unity: the spirit dwelling together with its sister the soul without presumptuousness or jealousy.[7] (*HH* IIa, 99)

They will be characterized by that at least apparent "coldness and sobriety" (*HH* IIa, 142), "unconscious astringency and morning chilliness, an avoidance of passion" (*HH* IIa, 126), "moderation, symmetry" (*ibid.*), "proportion and limit" (*HH* IIa, 131) which characterized both the souls and the art of the great artists of the past (*HH* IIa, 126).

18 The above remarks amount to an equation between good, that is (to Nietzsche's current way of thinking), signposting art and *classical* art. (In section 144 he explicitly identifies "great" with "classical" art.) For the features he says that signposting art "will" (i.e. *must*) have are just the attributes which, in eighteenth-century Germany, had been identified as constituting the essence of Greek art. Here, for example, is the enormously influential Johann Joachim Winckelmann (1717–68) assimilating to his account of the spirit of Greek art the seemingly most intractable case, the famous Laocoon group, a sculpture depicting the Trojan priest and his sons in the grip of the sea-god's serpents:

The universal, dominant characteristic of Greek masterpieces … is noble simplicity and serene greatness in the pose as well as the expression. The depths of the sea are always calm however wild and stormy the surface: and in the same way the expression in Greek figures reveals greatness and composure of soul in the throes of whatever passions. This spirit is depicted in Laocoon's face, and not in the face alone, in spite of the most violent sufferings. The pain which is manifest in all the muscles and sinews of the body … does not express itself with any violence either in the face or in the position as a whole. This Laocoon, unlike the hero of Virgil's poem, is raising no dreadful cry … The pain of the body and the greatness of the soul are equally balanced throughout the composition of the figure and seem to cancel each other out. Laocoon suffers; but he suffers like Sophocles' Philoctetes; his misery pierces us to the soul; but we should like to be able to bear anguish in the manner of this great man.[8]

Notice that Winckelmann, too, was interested in deriving from art models that will "excite envy and emulation." Nietzsche's equation between signposting and classical art is, in fact, *doubly* backward-looking, for it is an attempt to return to the outlook of eighteenth-century German Hellenism that culminated in the Weimar classicism of Goethe and Schiller:[9] in section 99 he explicitly says that "many a path to this poetry of the future starts out from Goethe." Why, however, should we accept the equation?

19 Let me try to recapitulate, in a somewhat organized fashion, the structure of Nietzsche's route to the validation of his neo-Hellenistic demands upon art.

Good art, we have seen, is required to be *didactic*; the artist is to become a "teacher of adults." She is to do this by "transfiguring" the mundane, by constructing beautiful images of the "great and beautiful soul," images which, by exciting "envy and emulation," help to create the future. Now art, of course, may influence the future in various ways: it may point it in directions both desirable and undesirable. It may do either because the archetypes it constructs may be models of either desirable or undesirable personality types. Nietzsche's demand is, of course, that it should do the former. Good art, then, so begins Nietzsche's route to neo-Hellenism, is art which offers vivid and seductive models of desirable personality types. Call this premise *one*. Premise *two* offers an account of the "great and beautiful soul": it is a soul "secured against" (but not unacquainted with) the "fire and breath" of passion, a soul in which "spirit" is not "jealous" of her rational "sister" (see n. 7 above) and hence a soul in which strength, purity, mildness, goodness, moderation, and self-mastery reign. Since we have here a pretty exact description of Plato's ideally just soul (mildness looks like Plato's "temperance," "goodness" like his "justice" [see n. 7 above]), we may refer to Nietzsche's ideal personality type as "Platonic man." Nietzsche's *third* premise makes the claim that only those forms which are (for us) limited, balanced, symmetrical, and harmonious are capable of expressing the collection of character traits which make up the beautiful soul. Models of Platonic man can only be expressed by classical forms. From these three premises the conclusion follows that good art can only be (neo-)classical art.

20 What are we to make of this peculiar argument? The third premise, first of all, is, I am inclined to accept, true. Its basis is in human physiognomy. Extreme and violent passion distorts facial (and bodily) features, displaces them from their normal – harmonious, reposeful – state. Hence we naturally associate disharmonious forms with violent passion: the expression of the calm passions demands harmony, symmetry, proportion. Or it is, at least, very hard to imagine how mildness, serenity, security from passion – particularly security *in the face of* the passions (*vide* the quotation from Winckelmann in sec. 18 above) – could be depicted by anything but forms which conform to the classical ideal. (The difficulty of imagining otherwise resembles the difficulty of imagining, *in detail*, the exchange of brains and personalities between the refined prince

and the coarse pauper.) Violent passions, it is true, appear on occasion in, for example, Mozart. But when they do – in, for example the wailing, tonality-threatening D-minor scales of the Commendatore's music at the end of *Don Giovanni* (scc *HH* 11b, 165) – they seem to be accompanied by a corresponding distortion of classical form.

Nietzsche's first premise, however, is much more questionable. Why should it be that the *only* legitimate function of art is the creation of desirable role models? Even if we accept, as I for one do, that good art (or good anything else) must in *some* way be of service to life, why should we for a moment suppose that only by the creation of "improving" role models can it do that? Even if we were to accept the more specific claim that art must be of service to life by helping to construct the future there are ways of doing that other than the presentation of beautiful images. One might, for example, after the manner of Dickens or Zola (see further, ch. 5, sec. 13), construct images of ugliness and depravity that excite not "envy and emulation" but rather horror, outrage, and the demand for reform. I have had occasion before to draw attention to Nietzsche's tendency to monomania – his disposition to deny the *variety* of the (useful) functions of art. It is this monomania that helps here to give Nietzsche's neo-Hellenism the face of aesthetic Stalinism. More exactly described, Nietzsche's position smacks of aesthetic *Platonism*: having, in *Human, All-too-human*, dismissed art from his brave new world for exactly the reasons given in book x of the *Republic* – that art distracts the mind from that "truth and reality" which is accessible to (but only to) the scientific mind – he now seems to mimic book III of the *Republic*, which, while banning Homer, admits to the classrooms of the ideal state stories in which justice is always rewarded, wickedness punished, and the gods never act in anything but the *nicest* of ways.

An objection one wishes to bring against Nietzsche's second premise is that there is *no* single personality type to which it is desirable that everyone should conform. (The suggestion that there is is the other aspect of his argument that gives it the face of Stalinism.) Ants are not what we want.[10] Nietzsche tries to accommodate this objection by talking about "tender distinctions" within the "all-embracing golden ground" constituted by Platonic man (*HH* 11a, 99), but it is not easy to imagine a multiplicity of unique and contrasting individuals all of whom share the "golden ground" of strength, purity, goodness, mildness, self-control, moderation, and so on.

Even if one can, the question still needs to be raised as to whether it is *always* the case that a desirable future is best promoted by the general predominance of the Platonic type of soul. In section 119 Nietzsche says that "it is everything orderly and regular in life which alone we have ... to thank for our well-being." Since this strongly recalls the thesis of *The Birth* of the essentially Apollonian character of social life – its dependence upon the rejection of barbarism by the impulse to "measure" and "moderation" – we may hypothesize (1) that the future Nietzsche is concerned with is a *social*, not an individual one – his concern is to promote the well-being of society as a whole – and that (2) his assumption is that the well-being of the social organism demands the constant and vigilant promotion of the Platonic virtues of order and regularity against the forces which threaten to demolish them.

But is this latter assumption correct? In the 1960s artists (and others) promoted images of "letting go," "getting in touch with" our feelings, abandoning reverence for "reason" and science. Was all this (*pace* Allan Bloom) *necessarily* bad? Is it always respect for law and order that needs to be reinforced? Surely not. Surely when, for example, a political order becomes unresponsive, exhausted and sterile, subversion, the promotion of precisely *anti*-classical ideals of being and action may be just what is required. Romantic images of extremities of freedom and immoderate heroism may, at a time, promote social regeneration while classical images of mildness and measure may serve only to entrench a repressive order.

True to his habit of not being able to maintain an evident falsehood very long or very consistently, Nietzsche, in a quiet way, admits this, even in *Opinions* itself. "Baroque" (soon to be called "romantic") art is, he says, the art of "so-called inorganic composition bedecked with the most marvellous means of expression" (*HH* IIa, 131). It is art that is "rhetorical and dramatic," that deals in "the eloquence of strong emotions and gestures, of the sublime[11] and ugly, of great masses, of quantity as such ... the glow of twilight, transfiguration or conflagration [of] ... strongly constructed forms" (*HH* IIa, 144). It is the art of Wagner, art which replaces "limit and proportion" by a kind of "swimming" movement in which one "surrenders unconditionally" to a "watery element" (*HH* IIa, 134). Baroque art is, he says, inevitable:

If we follow the history of an art, that of Greek rhetoric for instance, as we proceed from master to master and behold the ever increasing care spent on obedience to all the ancient rules and self-limitations and to those added subsequently, we are aware of a painful tension in ourselves: we grasp that the bow *has* to break and that... the baroque style of Asia[12]... was sooner or later a necessity and *almost* an *act of* charity. (*HH* IIa, 131)

It is also, in some circumstances, to be welcomed: anticlassical "unchainers of the will"; artists dedicated to "unharnessing, unfettering, destroying" may sometimes be "liberators of life" (*HH* IIa, 172).

There is then – Nietzsche at times agrees – *no* man for all seasons, no image of humanity which, from the point of view of the social organism, we timelessly want to be promoted. And if the predominance of different types of soul is needed at different times then, though one of the ways in which art can be of benefit to society is, it seems impossible to deny, by constructing role models, this service is one it can and will perform by constructing different models at different times. In the *Gay Science*, it is worth noting, Nietzsche clearly recognizes this. Images of destruction and change, of "becoming," he suggests, require a dual interpretation: on the one hand, they may express (and also promote) mere anarchic resentment: the hatred of the existing order by the "ill-constituted, disinherited and underprivileged." But on the other, they may express (and encourage) "an overflowing energy that is pregnant with future (my term for this, as is known, is 'Dionysian')" (*GS* 370).

A final and, I think, the most damning objection against Nietzsche's second premise is that its enunciation is fundamentally inconsistent with the role and conception of the artist mapped out in the first. The fundamental thought behind the first, that is, is that artists are uniquely *creative* – creative of *value*; they are "tamers of the will, transformers of animals, creators of men... sculptors and remodellers of life" (*HH* IIa, 172). They are *not*, let it be noticed, conceived as mere technicians skilled in the seductive packaging and propagation of ideals designated and chosen by some external agency. Rather, they are the choosers, discoverers of value themselves. What Nietzsche wants is an as it were poet–king (an ambition realized literally, as I write, for the first time in modern European history in Czechoslovakia), a *legislator* of value, no mere propagandist on behalf of values chosen by the party. Why the artist should be thought especially suited to this role is not made clear in

Opinions. But presumably the idea (an idea which will become clearer in ch. 5) is that the artist not only produces transfigurations but *sees* the world in a transfigured and simplified way which makes her particularly able to "scent out those cases in which, in the *midst* of our modern world and reality... the great and beautiful soul is... possible" before going on to "imaginatively develop a beautiful image of man" (*HH* IIa, 99). (In *The Gay Science*, a quotation we will return to in the next chapter, Nietzsche says that "only artists have given men the eyes and ears to see [themselves]... simplified and transfigured, to discover the hero that is concealed in everyday characters" rather than losing it in a mass of "foreground" detail [*GS* 78].)

Nietzsche's second premise, however, undercuts this special valuing of the artist. For here the petty party bureaucrat (Nietzsche is, of course, a great artist, but on occasions such as the present one speaks as a bureaucrat) *tells* the artist what she must see, announces, in the manner of Stalin, the program to which the artist must adhere. And this produces a contradiction: in the first premise the artist is someone we, the ordinary, need on account of her unique powers of mediocrity-transcending vision; but in the second the mediocre tells the artist what she is to see, thereby ensuring precisely that mediocrity of vision one sought to avoid.

21 In *Opinions* Nietzsche discovers a vital occupation for the artist that rescues her from the oblivion to which she was consigned in *Human, All-too-human* (though he also, I have argued, partially spoils the discovery by attempting to shackle her with the chains of Hellenism). Coexisting with this discovery, however, is a skepticism about art – "the art of works of art" (*HH* IIa, 174) – which seems to apply quite generally and not merely the forms of art of which we have seen Nietzsche explicitly disapprove. In section 102, for example, he describes art as

An excuse for many a fault – The ceaseless desire to create on the part of the artist, together with his ceaseless observaton of the world outside him prevents him becoming better and more beautiful as a person, that is to say, from creating *himself*... he possesses only a fixed quantity of strength: that of it which he expends upon *himself* – how could he at the same time expend it on his *work*? – and the reverse.

And in section 174 he emphasizes that "art is above and before all supposed to *beautify* life, thus making *us* ourselves endurable, if possible pleasing to others."

Is it possible to reconcile these two themes? Section 174 attempts to do so by making it clear that Nietzsche stands not for the abolition of art, but is concerned, rather, to oppose the deification of "the art of works of art," to set it in its proper place as an "appendage" to the art of living. A man or society, he says, who possesses an "excess" of beautifying power, will, in the end, "discharge" it in works of art as well as in life. The mistake, however, is to believe that "the art of works of art is the true art out of which life is to be improved and transformed." Life, rather, is to be transformed by applying artistic powers to it directly. Art is the "dessert," not the main course.

Nietzsche's position here seems to rest on the Schopenhauerian perception of the artistic genius as someone endowed with exceptional energy (see *WR* ii, p. 377). It seems that, in spite of the suggestion in section 102 that everyone has only a limited quantity of energy, the exceptional person has in fact energy enough to create herself as a work of art (this is a notion we shall explore in detail in the next chapter) and also to create artworks in the literal sense. So the overall position seems to be that the true artist legitimately engages in the production of artworks and these will have value as "signposts" to the future. Ordinary people, on the other hand, are required to devote their limited creative energies to their lives and are not to delude themselves that either by producing minor artworks or by having elevated experiences in art galleries are they doing anything of life-transforming significance.

But this attempt to present a consistent position is a failure. For if the providing of "signposts" to the future is really an important, artwork-justifying function, then *regardless* of the question of whether or not their production involves the diversion of energy from the beautification of life, the artist, surely, is legitimately employed in their production. Many people have taken the view that, often at least, the price of great art is a deficient or diseased personality. If that is so then the price of art is *lack* of "beauty" in the artist's life. But that, surely, if art has the function of creating ideals or values for the future, is a price that may be worth paying. The run of humanity, that is, in the endeavor to beautify, to give shape and coherence to their lives stand in need of archetypes that only the exceptional person, the artist, can provide. This, in a fine passage in *The Gay Science*, Nietzsche came later to understand. The "con-

templative" type, the "poet," he says, sadly fancies that he is a mere
"spectator and listener who has been placed before the great visual
and acoustic spectacle that is life." But this is a "delusion." For it is

really the poet who keeps creating this life. Of course, he is different from the
actor of this drama, the so-called active type; but he is even less like a mere
spectator and festive guest in front of the stage. As a poet he certainly has
vis contemplativa and the ability to look back upon his work but at the same
time also and above all *vis creativa* which the active human being *lacks*,
whatever visual appearances and the faith of all the world may say. We
who think and feel at the same time are those who really continually fashion
something that had not been there before: the whole eternally growing
world of valuations, colours, accents, perspectives, scales, affirmations and
negations. This poem that we have invented is continually studied by so-
called practical human beings (our actors) who translate everything into
flesh and actuality, into the everyday. (*GS* 301)

22 The conclusion to be drawn from the reflections of the previous
section is that in *Opinions* contrary impulses are at work. On the one
hand, continuous in this respect with the debunking of the romantic
vision of art and the artist in *Human*, there is disposition to debunk
everything connected with "high" art, with concert halls, art
galleries, and the like. (The examples he gives in section 174 of the
beautification of life through the direct application of the aesthetic
impulse – the creation of "social forms," "rules of decency,
cleanliness, politeness, of speaking and staying silent at the proper
time" – have a humble, almost William Morris flavor to them.) On
the other hand, the theme of the artist as prophetic regenerator of
culture reappears in the work in a way that restores to the artist a
pedestal not that much lower than the one so recently removed.
Opinions is, with respect to art, an unresolved work.

23 Like its predecessor, *The Wanderer and his Shadow* is concerned
with the elevation of the classical ideal over the "art of today." A
new synonym for "classical" is introduced: "the grand style." This
Nietzsche defines (echoing yet again the metaphysics of *The Birth*) as
occurring when "the beautiful carries off victory over the monstrous" (*HH* IIb, 96).
   What is "the monstrous"? Nietzsche says the following:

A Chief reason for corruption of style – To desire to *demonstrate* more feeling for
a thing than one actually *has* corrupts one's style, in both language and all
the arts. All great art, rather, has the opposite tendency: like every man of

moral consequence, it likes to arrest the feelings on their course and not allow them to run *quite* to their conclusion. This modesty which keeps the feelings only half visible can be observed at its fairest in, for example, Sophocles; and it seems to transfigure the features of the feelings when they present themselves as being more sober than they are. (*HH* ɪɪb, 136)

Style or form, according to this aphorism, is corrupted by histrionics, the display of fake or falsely exaggerated feeling. Nietzsche develops the idea of such corruption into yet another attack on Wagner. Coupling the massively enhanced resources of the romantic orchestra with, as he sees it, Wagner's neurotic exaggeration of feeling, he castigates the "music of today" as the music of "strong lungs and weak nerves" (*HH* ɪɪb, 166). And referring to the relegation of art in our "industrious age" to a mere "recreational activity," he laments its corruption into a bombastic display of "narcotics, intoxicants, convulsives, paroxysms of tears" designed to "overpower the tired and weary, arouse them to a fatigued over-liveliness and make them beside themselves with rapture and terror" (*HH* ɪɪb, 170). Art, particularly music, "in the age of work," in other words, has become the art of "[melo]dramatic" "high relief," the art of the empty "effect" (*HH* ɪɪb, 165).[13]

Notice the rhetorical trickery contained in this discussion of aesthetic corruption. Section 136 (the long quotation in the previous paragraph), though if read closely can be seen to acknowledge *three* ways in which feeling can be related to artistic form, seeks to present the appearance that we are compelled to choose between, on the one hand, the "modesty" of classical restraint and proportion and, on the other, the fake or falsely exaggerated feeling of "modern" art. The discussion of Wagner collaborates in presenting us with such a choice: "modern" art, the art of dramatic contrasts and unreposeful forms – "baroque" art, as *Opinions* called it – is corrupt, inauthentic. Thus Nietzsche seeks to force on us the equations: authentic = classical, modern ("baroque") = corrupt. If we accept them then we are forced, of course, to agree to a further equation: good art = classical art.

But, of course, there are really *two* ways in which the constraints of classical "modesty" can be disrupted in art: they can be disrupted in the endeavor to display unfelt feelings; but they can be disrupted, too, in the expression of entirely *genuine* feeling. In the expressionist tradition, in, for example, the paintings of Edvard Munch (a painter, paradoxically, who greatly admired and indeed produced a celebrated portrait of Nietzsche), one finds art which, while as far removed as possible from the constraints of classicism, is equally far removed from the production of empty "effects." Far from inauthenticity, Munch gives us almost an excess of painful, self-revealing honesty.

24　Good art, we have seen, is supposed to be restrained, "modest." Though not devoid of spirit or feeling, it is a "dancing in chains" (*HH* IIb, 140). What constitutes these chains? Nietzsche explains:

> With every Greek artist, poet and writer one has to ask: what is the *new constraint* he has imposed upon himself and through which he charms his contemporaries (so that he finds imitators)? For that which we call "invention" (in metrics, for example) is always such a self-imposed fetter. "Dancing in chains," making things difficult for oneself and then spreading over it the illusion of ease and facility – that is the artifice they want to demonstrate to us. Already in Homer we can perceive an abundance of inherited formulae and epic narrative rules *within* which he had to dance: and he himself created additional new conventions for those who came after him. This was the school in which the Greek poets were raised: firstly to allow a multiplicity of constraints to be imposed upon one; then to devise an additional new constraint, impose it upon oneself and conquer it with charm and grace: so that both the constraint and its conquest are noticed and admired. (*ibid.*)

Chains, then, are "conventions" governing aesthetic form. What, however, apart from the demand, of the *tour de force*[14] is so good about the observing of conventions? Nietzsche explains:

> Three-quarters of Homer is convention; and the same is true of all Greek artists who had no reason to fall prey to the modern rage for originality. They lacked all fear of convention; it was through this indeed that they were united with their public for conventions are the *achieved* artistic means, the toilsomely acquired common language, through which the artist can truly communicate himself to the understanding of his audience. Especially when, like the Greek poets and musicians, he wants to conquer *immediately* with each of his works – since he is accustomed to contend publicly with one or two rivals – the first condition is that he should also be *understood immediately*: which is possible, however, only through convention...As a rule what is original is admired, sometimes idolized, but rarely understood; obstinately to avoid convention means wanting not to be understood. To what, then, does our modern rage for originality point? (*HH* IIb, 122)

It points, Nietzsche would presumably have one think, to the unfittedness of the "modern" artist to the signposting of the future.

For if one's models are to excite envy and emulation, if like the Greek poets one is to be a "teacher of adults" (*HH* IIa, 172), then of course one's art must be readily understood. But the modern artist, the "romantic" ("Both those spirits of a classical and those of a romantic bent – the two species exist at all times – entertain a vision of the future; but the former does so out of a *strength* of their age, the latter out of its *weakness*" [*HH* IIb, 217; cf. 184][15]), has no response to the future except *fear*, and so has no contribution to make towards its construction. Once again we are presented with an invidious comparison between "modern" and classical art; between the fearful and useless "romanticism" of the former and the world-building confidence of the latter.

But the argument is a trick which depends upon a pun on "chains." Classical art, we are told, is "modest." As with the reposeful, or at least controlled, physiognomy, passion is not allowed to destroy the balance or symmetry of form. Feeling is "chained" down by the will to preserve those formal and spiritual values; beauty is victorious over the monstrous. Art that seeks to communicate, however, is chained by a quite *different* set of constraints: the constraints of communication, those conventions which constitute the common aesthetic "language" of the artist's age. These *may* at least be quite different from the constraints of classical style. In a romantic or baroque age, for example, the forms that create ease of communication will be nonclassical. And the abrupt introduction of classical constraints (one thinks here of the reintroduction of "doric" order and severity by Schönberg or the Bauhaus) is likely to impede communication, to lead, initially at least, to shock and rejection. In section 140, as we saw, Nietzsche contrasts the conventional in art with "originality." This is the correct opposition: that which threatens aesthetic communication is the temporally and culturally fluctuating phenomenon of originality. It is not, at least not necessarily, departure from the unchanging ideals of classicism.

25 Like its predecessor, *Wanderer* is concerned to elevate classical art over the "art of today." The alternative to classicism, it is suggested, is the meretricious parade of empty, inauthentic "effects," or[16] again, an uncommunicative straining after originality. Both suggestions should, however, be resisted. Classical art has a monopoly over neither authenticity nor intelligibility.

26 *Morgenröte*, "Dawn" or "Daybreak," which appeared the year after *Wanderer*, preoccupied as it is with the critique of morality and of Christianity, touches only rather peripherally on art. Those of its remarks which do deal with art are concerned in the main to amplify first the critique of metaphysical art offered by its "positivistic" predecessors, and second their critique of Wagnerian or, as I shall now call it, "demagogic" (see *D* 255) art. Though the observations on art made in *Dawn* are uniformly hostile, it nonetheless shares, I shall suggest, that valuing of a certain kind of art which distinguished both *Opinions* and *Wanderer* from *Human*.

27 In *The Birth*, we saw, the value of art lay in its capacity to bring us "comfort" for (or else to disguise) the horror and terror of existence. In *Human* Nietzsche loses (temporarily) the Schopenhauerian sense of life as a tormenting "riddle"; the idea that there is a philosophical problem of pessimism is reduced to ashes by the heat of scientific optimism. Yet there remains, of course, the undeniable phenomenon of depression: "distress of the soul" (*D* 269) as an *individual* phenomenon has to be acknowledged. The difference is that it has lost its epistemological validation. It is no longer a deep, truth-perceiving, philosophically *justified* state of mind, but is, rather, a mere neurosis. With this Nietzsche is now brisk, militaristic, and (as in *Wanderer* [see *HH* iib, 1, 84]) physiological. He recommends "change of diet and hard physical labour" (*D* 269). (This crudely physical approach contrasts sharply with the, as it were, "talking cure" for depression that he discovers, as we will see, in *The Gay Science*.)

Unfortunately, however, he continues, people resort to "means of intoxication: to art, for example" as a cure for their distress (*ibid.*). This, though perhaps alleviating the problem for a short time, in the long term only exacerbates it. For as is the habit of drugs, it produces both serious side-effects and dependency. One begins to identify one's real life and self with one's intoxicated state and to view one's ordinary existence as a drab impediment to access to one's real self. In this way addicts (such as, for example, the "untimely" author of *The Birth of Tragedy* – the passage is unmistakably self-referential [see *BT*, "Attempt at a Self-Criticism," 7]) come to "harbour feelings of revengefulness towards their environment, their age, their entire world" (*D* 50).

In spite of the mark of deadly truth with which this passage, considered as phenomenology of a certain species of afflicted consciousness, is stamped, it is time to enter a protest against the *general* truth of the assertion which constitutes its heart; the assertion, in Schopenhauerian language, that affirmation of a metaphysical world *always and inevitably* entails denial of this one; in Nietzschean language, the assertion that such affirmation is always and inevitably "romantic."

28 In discussing *The Birth* we saw Nietzsche himself turning to an "intoxicated" kind of metaphysics for comfort on account of his "incurable pessimism" (*BGE* 59) about the possibility of ameliorating the awfulness of the human condition through action. In section 7 of the present chapter we saw it objected that metaphysics in general and metaphysical art in particular stifles the attempt to improve the world through action. And in *Dawn*, as we have just seen, metaphysical art is represented as a form of "intoxication" that is both effect and cause of alienation from human reality. (Notice that the favor with which Nietzsche regards *Rausch* varies inversely with his hopefulness with regards to human existence.) Throughout Nietzsche's writings runs the thesis that affirmation of the metaphysical entails – is both symptom and intensification of – denial of the physical. This, the heart of Nietzsche's critique of the metaphysical in art (and in general), it is now time to subject to critical scrutiny.

The *brilliance* of Nietzsche's analysis of the impulses to metaphysical art (a brilliance closely related to that of his account of the roles of resentment and revenge in the impulse to Christian affirmation) is his discovery of the roles of disability, defense, and compensation in the – in *Nietzsche's* sense[17] – romantic spirit. Considered, as I have suggested, as *pathology* of the metaphysical impulse, there can be no doubting this brilliance. Nietzsche's rhetorical trickery, however, lies in the presentation of pathology as if it were anatomy. Another part of his trickery is to present his pathology in a manner so dazzling as to inhibit, through fear of appearing boring, the making of the mundane points which expose it as *merely* pathology. The points, nonetheless, need to be made.

We need, that is, to remind ourselves of such obvious phenomena as the theology of salvation by *works* rather than grace, to remember that it is by no means a general truth that metaphysical affirmation stifles action – empirically, in any case, a fatuous assertion. Again, we need to remind ourselves that a Christian view of life, through increasing one's sense of ultimate worth and security, may have as its effect, fearlessness, effectiveness, and delight in this life; that the location of ultimate bliss in a future life does not preclude, and may facilitate the discovery of, relative bliss in the present. And that, in any case, the nature of "salvation" is conceived, in some theologies, not in terms of a future state at all, but in terms, rather, of a present "relatedness" to the Divinity.

In addition to all this we need to recall that not all metaphysical affirmations are of an even covertly theistic character, so that even were it true that theism generally involves a critique of the moral standing of human beings, it would not follow that metaphysical affirmation as such does. It is true that a sense of the metaphysical involves, in general, a blow to our *epistemological* self-esteem; an awareness of the puniness of the human intellect in relation to the vastness of what exists to be known. But the bitterness involved in this, as in all encounters with the sublime, is more than compensated for by the scale and richness that the cosmos possesses for one, by the avoidance of epistemological claustrophobia. Affirmation of the metaphysical does, it is true, reduce human self-esteem. But that such a reduction is invariably a matter for regret is far from clear.

The trouble with Nietzsche's thesis that other-worldly affirmation entails this-worldly denial is that it predicates of the whole that which is true only of the part. Metaphysical affirmation is identified with Christian affirmation and that, in turn, with something like Calvinism. (More accurately, it is identified with Schopenhauer-ianism. Schopenhauer, who claims that in denying the possibility of salvation by works, in affirming asceticism and world-denial, his philosophy captures the essence of Christianity [*WR* I, p. 386] seems the dubious source of most of Nietzsche's "theology.") For all the psychiatric brilliance of its deployment, the thesis is, therefore, false. Indeed it is *obviously* false – which makes this hard to say.

29 *Dawn*, as I mentioned, continues to prosecute the attack against Wagner. The characterization of his music as the art of empty "effects" is expanded. It is now characterized as the art which "seeks to exalt without being exalted" (*D* 223), as a "bombastic," "in-flated" art that seeks not to discharge but to *create* a feeling of "swollenness" (*D* 332), as an art in which every move is calculated to "assemble delighted looks," to stupefy, convulse, shatter, in general

to possess and manipulate the feelings of the audience (*D* 255). Wagner's art is the art of market forces, the art of a "demagogue" (*ibid.*).

The question presents itself as to just what is so wrong with the art of consumer demand. (It is easy, one reflects, to see Andrew Lloyd Webber as a shallow, but difficult to see him as a deeply pernicious, phenomenon.) The epithet "demagogic" is particularly significant here because it suggests an answer. It suggests, that is, that Nietzsche sees Wagner in the same light as Plato, particularly in the *Gorgias*, sees the rhetoricians.[18]

In section 165 of *Wanderer*, Nietzsche says that although the art of high, melodramatic relief ("the music of the [Don Giovanni's] stone guest" that Mozart produced on just this *one* occasion) may indeed produce the greatest effect on a contemporary audience, to produce an effect on "the people" is something the "noble" artist should never *want* to achieve (see *D* 269). This reproduces Plato's objection that an attitude of slavish groveling towards the *demos* is unworthy of a freeman (*Gorgias* 495). But Plato's fundamental objection to the rhetoricians is that whereas the true statesman ought to be improving and educating his people, *qua* rhetorician, all he possesses is the ability to *follow* them, to tailor and present his proposals in a way calculated to appeal to their lower instincts. This, I think, is Nietzsche's fundamental objection to Wagner. The business of art, we saw in *Opinions*, is to signpost the future. It is, as *Dawn* continues the theme, to "improve" its audience, for example, as Corneille did "with pictures of knightly virtue, stern duty, magnanimous self-sacrifice, heroic self-restraint" which demonstrate that "greatness [*Grösse*] and humanity are *possible* together" (*D* 191). With Wagner, however, we find the reverse of what we should find. Artist as legislator of high values for the future has been replaced by artist as panderer to low tastes of the present. Clearly, a presupposition of this critique is that Wagner had the *capacity* to fulfill the mission of art. It is a *noble* mind which, failing to heed the veiled warning of *Wagner at Bayreuth*, is now revealed as overthrown.

CHAPTER 4

The Gay Science

1 How gay, actually, is *The Gay Science*? The retrospective Nietzsche would have us believe that, as its title suggests, the book is "affirmative, profound but bright and benevolent," that "in practically every sentence profundity and exuberance go hand in hand" (*EH* VIII). And by and large he has been successful. Here, for example, is how Richard Schacht views the work:

In tone and content, the volume deserves its title. After having struggled through a period of some years of intellectual crisis, its author has attained a new philosophical and spiritual health, of the sort he describes at the fifth book's end (382). He has become profoundly and joyfully affirmative of life and the world and has discovered that "all the daring of the lover of knowledge is permitted again" (343). He is in love with knowledge and with life and the world, and with the humanity emerging out of them; for, having earlier become hard and disillusioned by them, he has now become newly appreciative of them. Thus he cheerfully and confidently sets out to explore them as they stand revealed in the "new dawn" that has broken in the aftermath of "the news that 'the old god is dead'." (343)[1]

Schacht, I want to suggest in this chapter, has been duped. In spite of its title, *The Gay Science*, it seems to me, is a work in which the only kind of gaiety its author achieves is a kind of manic frivolity which is really no more than a symptom of desperation and despair.

2 Before getting down to the substance of this chapter some preliminary, bibliographical observations. Although I have called the chapter "*The Gay Science*," I in fact intend to discuss in it not merely *The Gay Science* but also the related parts of all of Nietzsche's works published between 1882 and 1887: in addition to *The Gay Science*, that is, *Thus Spoke Zarathustra* and *Beyond Good and Evil*. There are good chronological reasons for treating this body of work as a unity. For of *The Gay Science* only books I–IV appeared in 1882, book V and the preface to the second edition not appearing until 1887.

These two parts of the work thus bracket *Zarathustra* (parts I–II appeared in 1883, part III in 1884, part IV in 1885) and *Beyond Good and Evil* (1886).

The reason I make *The Gay Science* the center of this unity is that all of the major ideas touching upon the topic of art which appear in the works of this period are found first in it: in fact, in its first four books. (The one exception to this, the critique of the Kant–Schopenhauer notion that aesthetic perception is "disinterested," I shall reserve for discussion in chapter 5.) All the other works may be regarded as commentaries on, elucidations of *The Gay Science*. It is true that Nietzsche himself suggested that the latter could be regarded as commentary on the yet-to-be-written *Zarathustra*[2] but the truth, so it seems at least to me, is if anything the reverse. Thoughts which first appear in *The Gay Science* and, because it stands so close to their creation, are expressed in difficult and unclear ways, not uncommonly appear with much greater clarity and simplicity in *Zarathustra*. *Wissenschaftliche* prose, strangely, finds its elucidation in poetic fiction.

3 Let us begin at the beginning; with the title of the work. Why should anyone entitle a book *The Gay Science*? Why should anyone subtitle it *la gaya scienza*, a phrase of Provençal that refers to the culture and poetry of the medieval troubadours; to their, as Nietzsche describes it, gay, free, exuberant, childish, mocking, dancing, light, floating spirit? Why insist – and insist, as Nietzsche does, so *repeatedly* – on how infused and permeated by that spirit is the book? Why preface and conclude the work with a set of poems – as if in fear that someone might fail to get the point that in it the spirit of the troubadours is reborn? A prudent reader, it seems to me (a "philologist" or "psychologist" in Nietzsche's sense), ought to suspect that someone who displays, parades their alleged gaiety so insistently – and in the end tediously – is closely acquainted with suffering and despair.

In the Preface (on which, since it was written last and therefore constitutes Nietzsche's last word in the work, I shall place considerable weight) Nietzsche admits to a *past* acquaintance with suffering. The book is, he says, "nothing but a bit of merry-making after a long privation," filled with the "intoxication of convalescence" (*GS*, Preface, 1) of one who has endured a "long slow pain" (*GS*, Preface, 3). What we have to decide is how correctly this pain is consigned to the past.

4 But let us first do away with metaphor. What is the "long slow
pain" to which Nietzsche refers? It is, in a word, the death of God,
an event which, though formally announced for the first time only
in section 125 of *The Gay Science*, was in fact acutely present to
Nietzsche from the very outset of his philosophical career. The pain
is the pain of confronting the "terror and horror," the "heartbreaking and cruel character" of existence – "what I desire most,"
he wrote to Heinrich von Stein in December 1882, "is a high point
from which I can see the tragic problem lying beneath me. I would
like to take away from human existence some of its heartbreaking
and cruel character" – without the "metaphysical comfort"
brought to us by theistic belief. The problem is suffering and our
vulnerability to it: not all suffering (not the pain of dentistry, for
example) but rather suffering for which we can discover no
redeeming purpose or justification, suffering that disposes us to view
life as "nauseating." Without God life appears to be "absurd" and
(save for extinction) there appears to be no deliverance from it.

In *The Birth of Tragedy*, as we saw, Nietzsche discovered a
substitute for God in art. In experiencing tragic art we receive the
"metaphysical comfort" of becoming aware of our supraindividual
identity, our oneness with the "primal unity" that is the
metaphysical reality beneath the illusory world of individuality. In
Human, All-too-human, however, the idea of art as a substitute for
religion, the idea of a "metaphysical world" in both its overt and
covert manifestations, is exposed to ridicule and is demolished. The
world, as Nietzsche confronts it at the beginning of *The Gay Science* is
completely "naturalized," fully "dedeified" (*GS* 109). There is no
metaphysical redemption from its horrors.

5 But, surely, one might reflect, the dedeification of existence was
already confronted by Nietzsche in *Human, All-too-human*. And there,
surely, there was nothing painful about the absence of the
metaphysical world. Its destruction seemed, on the contrary, a
necessary, even joyful, task. Why then, at the beginning of *The Gay
Science*, has its absence become painful?

In *Human, All-too-human*, as we saw, Nietzsche came to occupy the
hitherto despised stance of "Socratic," scientific optimism. "Progress" through science seemed possible, and this both provided a telos
to the world and gave meaning to the life of the *Wissenschaftler* able
to think of himself as participating in the process of its realization.

This is what provided the rationale for the destruction of the metaphysical world: the point was to liberate our energies so that we could turn to the elimination of the causes of suffering rather than merely "narcoticizing" their effects. Nietzsche, in short, was sustained in his rejection of the old faiths by the acquisition of a new one: faith in science. Not an other-worldly state but rather a future state of *this* world is seen as redeeming life from its present horrors and terrors.

But in *The Gay Science*, in Nietzsche's anguished demand for consolation over the death of God (*GS* 125), the old pain and the old yearning for "metaphysical comfort" has returned. Something, therefore, must have altered in his assessment of the nature and capacities of science.

What has altered has, it is fairly clear, *something* to do with "perspectivism"; that is, "phenomenalism," idealism: "the essence of phenomenalism and perspectivism as I understand them:... the world of which we can become conscious is only a surface and sign-world" (*GS* 354), a world of "appearances," in more traditional language. *The Gay Science* is full of remarks in a similar vein: "Delusion and error are conditions of human knowledge," he says in section 107, and in the *Preface* he announces the abandonment of his "youthful" quest to unveil the statue of reality since, "we no longer believe that truth remains truth when all the veils are withdrawn" (sec. 4).

Perspectivism, though the term is first introduced in *The Gay Science*, goes back in one form or another to the beginning of Nietzsche's thought. In *The Birth of Tragedy*, as we saw, its scope was conceived as embracing all that can be produced by the Socratic mind. It was this, as demonstrated by "the extraordinary courage and wisdom of Kant and Schopenhauer," that placed "being" beyond the knowledge and hence control of the Socratic mind. In *Human, All-too-human*, however, its scope diminished: only the lay, common-sense, thing-affirming image of the world was held to the ideal, the scientific image, in particular the thing-dissolving image of Boscovichian physics, being affirmed as real. Being appeared as knowable, as predictable, and hence as in principle capable of "correction."

What is it in this view of things that has altered by the time of *The Gay Science*? The issue is shrouded in mystery so that the following can be offered as no more than an hypothesis.

What I suggest is that in *The Gay Science* Nietzsche came to see that whatever reasons there are for applying perspectivism to the common-sense image of the world are reasons, equally, for applying it to the Boscovichian image. In *Beyond Good and Evil*, recalling, perhaps, his thoughts from the *Human, All-too-human* period, Nietzsche expresses his gratitude to Boscovich, who "taught us to abjure belief in... 'substance', in matter, in the earth-residuum and particle atom: it was the greatest triumph over the senses hitherto achieved on earth." "One must, however," he adds, "go still further and also declare war on the 'atomistic need'" (sec. 12). Why does Boscovich not go far enough? Because, I suggest, though abolishing the *extended* atom, his *puncta* (see ch. 3, sec. 6), though unextended, mimic the extended atom in being spatially mobile, temporally persistent entities. Boscovichian physics, therefore, still remains gripped by, still caters to, the "atomistic need." Boscovich's *puncta* are really just immaterial atoms.

In section 111 of *The Gay Science* Nietzsche suggests that "the concept of substance" is (1) "indispensable to logic," yet (2) such that "in the strictest sense nothing real corresponds to it." By "logic" he means here the grammatical structure of language, and by "substance," I think, any object of reference. It follows that Boscovich's *puncta* are as much human projections, grammatical fictions, as are the extended atoms of the theorists he opposed: "physics too [even the superior physics of Boscovich] is only an interpretation and arrangement of the world" (*BGE* 14). Reality as such is ineffable, in principle incongruent with *any* structure proposed by human thought or language. Existence outside of one perspective or another, "existence without interpretation" is, he says, "nonsense" (*GS* 374).

But *not*, notice, non-existent. Although some of his formulations of perspectivism *might* be interpreted as an affirmation of, in Kant's language, "absolute idealism" – the world contains nothing but interpretations (and perhaps interpreters)[3] – such, in fact, is not Nietzsche's position. The world outside the mind, beyond our interpretations, is still there in *The Gay Science*: "The total character of the world... is in all eternity chaos [or 'nonsense'] in the sense not of a lack of necessity[4] but of a lack of order, arrangement, form" (*GS* 109), everything there could make it congruent with, graspable by, conceptual thought or language. As Arthur Danto has put it,[5] because Nietzsche wants to say that all our beliefs about ultimate reality are (not truth-valueless but rather) false, "errors," he is constrained to introduce a world for them to be false to or about, a world which (like the Kantian noumenon) is to all eternity ineffable, chaotic relative to the distinctions drawn by conceptual thought, yet for all that indisputably *there*.

6 What does the impact of, as we may call it, *comprehensive* perspectivism mean with regard to Nietzsche's earlier optimism with respect to scientific progress? Had perspectivism been correctly interpreted as absolute idealism the answer would have been: nothing at all. For then there would have been nothing "out there," nothing to be incongruent with our scientific world-interpretations. But there *is* something; something which has its own "necessary" nature yet is ineffable to reason and hence unknowable by science. Something, moreover, which is permanently liable to "disorderly motion" (see n. 4 above), liable to disrupt the ordered structures created by human science and technology. In effect, therefore, we have returned to the position of *The Birth of Tragedy*. Being, perpetually threatening to human well-being, is unknowable and hence incapable of "correction." Scientific optimism is again (and again the agent of disillusionment is science, philosophy, itself) exposed as illusion. This time, however, the effect is devastating; devastating because Nietzsche *himself* had succumbed to its charms. This is why the realization in *The Gay Science* that "delusion and error are conditions of human knowledge" threatens such an extreme reaction: "nausea and suicide" (*GS* 107).

7 To summarize: at the beginning of *The Gay Science* what Nietzsche confronts is a *triple* loss of faith. We cannot justify, redeem, bring ourselves to affirm our existence by accepting the claims of religion that this life is a brief and necessary stage on a journey to an ultimate, transcendent salvation. And neither can we accept the intimations in art of a vaguer, less articulated version of the same world-interpretation. But neither, finally, do we possess the power to eliminate the "horror and terror" that afflicts us. There is only one world and its eternal character is, as it were, nasty, brutish, short, and meaningless (see *WP* 853). Humanity appears condemned, for some nameless crime, to a kind of Kafkaesque prison (see Z II, 20) that it can neither alter nor escape. Nausea and suicide threaten.

Nietzsche sums up his predicament at the end of section 3 of the

Preface. Life, he says, has become "problematic." This may seem a rather mild term for the kind of *Angst* we have been discussing. But in fact *problematisch* is a deeply pregnant expression which takes its resonances from Schopenhauer's greater chapter "On man's need for metaphysics" (*WR* II, ch. XVII; cf. p. 170). It is the word Schopenhauer uses to capture the sense of life as a tormenting "riddle," an anguish-ridden phenomenon which, according to Schopenhauer, creates the "metaphysical need," the demand for another world to provide us with its "solution" (*ibid.*).

What Nietzsche confronts, therefore, at the beginning of *The Gay Science* is the Schopenhauerian "riddle" (see Z II, 20; Z III, 12[3]). But in the work, he claims, he discovers a solution. What is that solution?

8 Nietzsche says that the pain of confronting the riddle is peculiar to, or felt in its acute form at least only by, "we philosophers" (*GS*, Preface, 3). Felt, that is, by Nietzsche together with his thoughtful and sensitive contemporaries. (As he suggests [*GS*, Preface, 2], the fluctuating states of "Herr Nietzsche's" spiritual well-being as such are of interest to no one except Herr Nietzsche. It is only *qua* epitomizer of the crisis of his times, the crisis of modernity, that Nietzsche's travails are of general and philosophical interest.) Distinguished from "the people" (*GS* 3) by the "will to truth" (*GS*, Preface, 4), by "honesty" (*GS* 335) or the "intellectual conscience" (*GS* 2), the philosopher is compelled to inhabit, to constitute, the "bad conscience" of his time (*BGE* 212). He is compelled, that is, to pick at the scab[6] constituted by the conventional comforts of the age, subject their foundations to the most rigorous examination. Ordinary people, people who, free of the philosopher's scruples about evidence and truth, are moved to belief by what is comfortable rather than by what is true, accept without difficulty the comfort brought by faith in religion, art, or science. The Faustian thinker, however, "that being in whom the impulse for truth and...life-preserving errors clash for their first fight" (*GS* 110), cannot do this. He is set apart.

In view of this, it is not surprising that a strong element of misology, hatred of reason, characterizes Nietzsche's solution to the riddle. "We philosophers," he says, gripped as we were by the will to truth, descended to our "ultimate depths," became "profound." But as a result we were "burned," betrayed by our love of truth. For the truth we discovered was "Baubo" – the Greek demon who personified the obscene. "We artists," however, he continues (reminding us again that the author of *The Gay Science* is a poet, a troubadour, one who has, as it were, encapsulated the philosophy of *The Gay Science* within the healing balm of poetry) have discovered a better wisdom. As artists "we now learn to forget well, and to be good at *not* knowing." We learn to love not depths but surfaces, "the fold, the skin,…forms, tones, words,…the whole Olympus of appearance" (*GS*, Preface, 3, 4). As a "counterforce" to the "over-severe demands" of our "irritable honesty" we have discovered the "cult of the untrue," the "*good* will to appearance" (*GS* 107). Like the Greek artists we have learnt to be "superficial – *out of profundity*" (*GS*, Preface, 4). "As an aesthetic phenomenon existence is still *bearable* [*erträglich*] for us" (*GS* 107).

Such a transformation of outlook, however, demands, is equivalent to, nothing less than the transformation of the self. We must turn not just the world but also the *self* into an "aesthetic phenomenon" (*ibid.*). We must, says Nietzsche, continuing a theme from *Assorted Opinions and Maxims* (see ch. 3, sec. 21 above) become artists who produce not (or not primarily) "the art of works of art" but rather their own lives. We must learn the art of "staging…ourselves" (*GS* 78), we must become "poets of our lives" (*GS* 299).

How are we to do this? By copying the work of artists in the literal sense (artists who produce "the art of works of art"), by emulating their techniques. Particularly crucial here is "distance" (*GS* 78), "artistic distance" (*GS* 107). By standing back from our lives we bring it about that there is "a good deal that one no longer sees and there is much that our eye has to add if we are still to see them at all" (*GS* 299). Distance, that is, gives us the creative freedom to script for ourselves a new character. We can write out all those memories, character traits, and ambitions which gave us the personality and the problems of the profound, weighty (*GS* 107), troubled, burnt thinker, and write in, in its place, a new kind of "superficial" personality, that of someone who experiences the world in a "light, fleeting, divinely untroubled, divinely artificial" way, someone whose world, "like a pure flame, licks into unclouded skies" (*GS*, Preface, 4). We write out, in particular, the demands of our honesty and thereby create for ourselves an "exuberant, floating, dancing, mocking, childish and blissful…*freedom above things*" (*GS*, Preface, 4): an incredible lightness of being, in short, *la gaya scienza*.

This, it seems, is Nietzsche's solution. We transform ourselves from weighty thinkers into intellectual and spiritual "lightweights": from the deep and gloomy Schopenhauer into the "gay," "staged," frivolous, "divinely artificial" Oscar Wilde. (It is not an accident, I think, that Wilde, who said he had put his genius into his life, only his talent into art, was an almost exact contemporary of Nietzsche.) We find relief from (to change the image) the "over-severe honesty" of modernism in the decadent superficiality, the whimsically allusive love of surfaces of postmodernism. We solve the problem of the riddle by simply "forgetting" about it. That was someone *else's* problem, a problem in which *we* are childishly uninterested. Like Albert Finney in his neglected *Charlie Bubbles*, as the heavy social realism of the marital drama reaches its torrid climax, we slip away to the end of the garden where, by divine artifice, a gaily colored balloon awaits us. The terror and horror we leave behind and below us as we float off, receding like a flame, into unclouded skies.[7]

9 But will the balloon fly for very long? The essence, after all, of Nietzsche's solution to the riddle is self-deception, acting, role-playing. Becoming an appearance to oneself, deplored in *Wagner at Bayreuth* (*WB* 5), is now, it seems, just what is proposed. Repression, the denial of desires and character traits, the pretense that traumatic events of the past never happened, is seen now as a vital, life-saving activity. But does this not lend a brittle, desperate, doomed quality to Nietzsche's *gaya scienza*? Truth, as poor, silly Wilde's tragedy exemplifies, cannot easily be kept at bay. And even if, for a time, it can, the price exacted by such repression in terms of neurotic symptoms is (if we believe Freud at all) a high one.

Another question to ask, however, is whether the advocacy of profound superficiality *really* constitutes Nietzsche's last word by way of a solution to the riddle. What gives force to this question – and makes *The Gay Science* a very puzzling text to decipher – is that although the Preface is dominated by the perceived need at all costs to fly from, eradicate, the will to truth, the body of the work is dominated by the attachment of tremendous *value* to "honesty," to the "intellectual conscience" (*GS* 2, 335), to the avoidance of that "suicide of reason" for which, in *Beyond Good and Evil* (229), he condemns Pascal. Moreover, and most importantly, *The Gay Science* is the place where the doctrine that being able to will the eternal recurrence is the mark of the ideal stance towards the world receives its first enunciation (*GS* 341). And the point of this doctrine, as we will shortly see, is that ideally one should be able to accept, love, will to recur *all of the truth about the world*, down to the very last detail.

10 The solution to this puzzle is to be found, I believe, in the fact that like *The Birth of Tragedy*, *The Gay Science* offers not one but rather *two* solutions to the problem of the riddle. As in *The Birth* one of these solutions is preferred to the other. And as in *The Birth*, too, one essentially involves illusion, the other ecstasy (*Rausch*). In fact the parallels with *The Birth* are so strong that, without wishing to imply that *The Gay Science* is by any means a simple rewriting of *The Birth*, I shall call the one solution, the one we have already looked at, "Apollonian," and the other, preferred solution, "Dionysian."

The key to seeing that there is this duality is to notice that profound superficiality, the Apollonian solution, is intended specifically for "we convalescents" (*GS*, Preface, 1, 4). (In *Zarathustra* it is said that the convalescent needs to sing a "different song" from the healthy man [*Z* II, 13].) It is intended, that is, for people who have made *some* kind of a recovery from a sickness (to the question of just what the sickness is I shall return later, but what Nietzsche has in mind, it may be helpful to state here, is closely connected with Christian belief) but are still far from completely healthy. This suggests that the Dionysian solution is intended for, will be achieved by (and only by), someone who is fully healthy.

11 What does the Dionysian solution look like? In *Beyond Good and Evil* Nietzsche couples the life of *la gaya scienza* with the Christian interpretation of existence, as *both* species of profound superficiality. Both the transcendentalization of existence by "*homines religiosi*" and the "impassioned and exaggerated worship of 'pure forms' among both philosophers and artists" illustrate, he says, "how much wisdom there lies in the superficiality of men. The instinct that preserves "these ["burnt children"] teaches them to be flighty, light and false." (Notice that this coupling provides, given Nietzsche's well-known antipathy to *homo religiosus*, a further reason for doubting that *la gaya scienza* constitutes Nietzsche's final response to the riddle.) Both, he continues, are products of artistry, artistry inspired by "fear of truth," fear of an "incurable pessimism" that would result were one to "get hold of a truth too soon." But he mentions, too, another, nonsuperficial, truth-*embracing* approach to existence that one could take were one "strong enough, hard enough, artist

enough" (*BGE* 59). This indicates, firstly, that the Dionysian solution will abandon the Apollonian "falsification" of the image of life (*ibid.*), that it will be in some way "honest," and, secondly, that it, too, will somehow involve artistry. As in *The Birth of Tragedy*, therefore, we are provided with two *art*-solutions to the riddle.

12 How is art involved in the Dionysian solution? As with the Apollonian, it requires one to view, to create oneself as an "aesthetic phenomenon." Imitating again the techniques of artists in the literal sense, especially the technique of aesthetic distance, one is required to view the self from a distance so that rather than regarding it "in the spell of that perspective which makes what is closest at hand and most vulgar appear as it were vast and reality itself," rather than its being "nothing but foreground," we learn to see the wood for the trees, to see ourselves "simplified and transfigured," "to see and...esteem the hero[8] that is concealed in everyday characters" (*GS* 78). Elsewhere Nietzsche says that what is "needful" is to "give style" to one's character, by fitting the various aspects of one's "nature" into a pleasing totality according to an "artistic plan" (*GS* 290).[9] One is, in other words, to come to view all the details of one's life as fitting together into the kind of coherent unity that we demand of a well-executed character in literature.

13 How, it might at this point be wondered, is the Dionysian any different from the Apollonian solution to the riddle? For that too seemed to involve giving oneself a certain style, viewing oneself very much as if one were a character in literature.

The answser has to do with Nietzsche's repeated injunction to "become who you are" (*GS* 270), an injunction that he clearly regards as being of central importance since his final, autobiographical work, *Ecce Homo*, is subtitled: *How One Becomes What One Is*. There are two aspects to the injunction, the epigrammatic conjunction of which helps to give it its paradoxical appearance. The first is the anti-Delphic idea that the self is something one "becomes," that is (*GS* 335 makes this clear), *makes* or *creates* rather than *discovers*. It is a fundamental position of the later Nietzsche that there is no real, *given* self waiting to be discovered, neither a self conceived as a persisting Cartesian object – "soul atomism...that belief which regards the soul as being something indestructible, eternal, indivisible, as a monad, as an atom...ought to be expelled from science" (*BGE* 12) – nor a self conceived in the related Schopen-hauerian or Freudian manner (see n. 9 above) as a set of "real," innate, and unalterable, but largely repressed desires. The self, Nietzsche holds, resembles the state; it may be conceived as a "social structure of drives and affects" (*ibid.*). As such, though its *elements* may be given, it, like the state, is the product of free creative activity. The second is the idea of becoming who one *is* as opposed to who one *is not,* the idea of becoming an authentic rather than inauthentic self. It is this second aspect that is emphasized in section 335 of *The Gay Science*: we who "want to become those who we are [*wollen die werden, die wir sind*]," who want to "create" ourselves as beings who are "new, unique, incomparable, who give themselves laws," must acknowledge everything that is "necessary," *given* in the world. "Therefore: long live physics! [clearly a metaphor, here, for comprehensive, exhaustive, hard, and unromanticized knowledge of the given] And even more that which *compels* us to turn to physics – our honesty!"

So the idea seems to be that though in a sense created, the self that figures in the Dionysian solution to the riddle is an honestly created and in *that* sense authentic self: none of the deceptions and fabrications which help to create the Apollonian self are employed.[10]

How does the construction of this authentic self proceed? And how does that construction help to solve the problem of the riddle? To understand this we need to understand the intimate relations that exist in Nietzsche's thought between three things: becoming who you are, *amor fati* (love of fate), and willing the eternal recurrence.

14 It is by now widely accepted that the thought of the eternal recurrence is not, certainly not primarily, intended as the for-mulation of a cosmological doctrine. It occurs rather in a test for, as Nietzsche conceives it, the ideal relationship in which one can stand to the world. More exactly, it occurs in a test for the ideally *healthy* stance towards the world: in *Zarathustra* its hero is called a "convalescent" on account of his inability yet to will the eternal recurrence (*Z* iii, 13). The test, in its first formulation (*GS* 341), is this: can you bring yourself to will the eternal recurrence of everything in your life *down to the last detail*? More precisely, can you bring yourself to "crave *nothing* more fervently" than that, to be in a condition such that there is *no* future life you would prefer to the repetition of your exact life just as it is.

As such, the injunction to bring oneself to will the eternal recurrence is the same as the injunction to "love fate," an injunction which also receives its first formulation in *The Gay Science*:

For the new year... Today everybody permits himself the expression of his wish and his dearest thought; hence I, too, shall say what it is that I wish from myself today... I want to learn more and more to see as beautiful what is necessary in things beautiful. *Amor fati*: let that be my love henceforth! I do not want to wage war against what is ugly. I do not want to accuse; I do not even want to accuse those who accuse. *Looking away* [after the fashion of the profoundly superficial] shall be my only negation. And in its totality and greatness [*alles in allem und grossen*]: some day I wish to be only a yes-sayer. (*GS* 276)

Since all of the past is "necessary," unalterable, the doctrine of *amor fati* entails loving, that is being able to will the eternal recurrence of everything that (to one's knowledge) has happened. This becomes even clearer in a later formulation of *amor fati*: "my formula for greatness in a human being is *amor fati*: that one wants nothing to be other than it is, not in the future, not in the past, not in all eternity. Not merely to endure that which happens of necessity, still less to dissemble it [after the fashion of the profoundly superficial]... but to *love* it" (*EH* II, 10). That eternal recurrence and *amor fati* are equivalent formulations of the same injunction is not merely implicit in this quotation but is made quite explicit by Nietzsche's habit of referring indifferently to each as the "highest," "Dionysian relationship to existence," the "formula for greatness" (*WP* 1041; *EH* II, 10).

15 How can one possibly come to love, will the recurrence of, *everything* that has happened? Section 276 of *The Gay Science* (quoted in sec. 14 above) starts to tell us: one is "to see as beautiful what is necessary in things." The following section continues the thought. Though there is no divine providence in the world we are to seek to put in its place the vision of a "wonderful harmony," a "personal providence." We are

to see how palpably always everything that happens to us turns out for the best. Every day and every hour, life seems to have no other wish than to prove this proposition again and again. Whatever it is, bad weather or good, the loss of a friend, sickness, slander, the failure of some letter to arrive, the spraining of an ankle, a glance into a shop, a counter-argument, the opening of a book, a dream, a fraud – either immediately or very soon after it proves to be something that "must not be missing": it has a profound significance and use precisely for *us*. (*GS* 277)

Nietzsche, it seems, was strongly influenced in his development of the idea of *amor fati* and of how it is to be achieved by Ralph Waldo Emerson [an initially surprising conjunction between the Unitarian minister and the self-styled "Antichrist"] whom he had loved since boyhood, continued to love until the end of his productive life, and was rereading as he wrote *The Gay Science*.[11] The first edition carried a quotation (slightly mistranslated into German) from Emerson, on the title page: "To the poet, to the philosopher, to the saint, all things are friendly and sacred, all events profitable, all days holy, all men divine."[12] Emerson actually called himself "a Professor of the Joyous Science" meaning among other things thereby "a detector and delineator of occult harmonies and unpublished beauties."

Seeing a personal providence in one's life is, says Nietzsche, a matter of "practical and theoretical skill in interpreting and arranging events" (*ibid.*). One is, that is, to discover all events in one's past including apparent evils, apparently harmful events, to be not evils at all but rather "for the best," benefits, means to subsequent goods. Nietzsche constantly stresses this as a way of coming to love one's fate. Rather than seeking revenge for a wrong, he says in *Zarathustra*, one should show that one's enemy has actually done one some good (*Z* 1, 18). And in *Ecce Homo*, in the course of demonstrating the alleged (see the Epilogue below) fact that "*amor fati* is my inherent nature" (*EH* XIII, 4), he says, speaking in a homeopathic vein, that though Wagner is a "poison," he himself is "strong enough to turn even the most questionable and most perilous things to [his]...own advantage and thus to become stronger." Thus he says, "I call Wagner the great benefactor of my life" (*EH* II, 6).

This, it must be emphasized, is by no means Nietzsche's only technique for accommodating the "questionable" (*GS* 370): another consists in exhibiting problematic attributes and events not as *means to* but rather as *parts of* the good. The giving of "style" to one's character, for example, is, he says, an "art" that is "practiced by those who survey all the strengths and weaknesses of their nature and then fit them into an artistic plan until every one of them appears as art and even weaknesses delight the eye" (*GS* 290). So, for example, one might see a character trait that in isolation one might regard as a vice as, in the context of one's personality as a whole, having the necessary function of softening, taking the hard edge off one's virtues, humanizing one's character. Or one might come to view a period of slavish discipleship to Schopenhauer and Wagner as having the aesthetically necessary function of highlighting the courage and originality of one's later career. This, as I suggested (ch. 2, sec. 2), is one of the strategies Nietzsche employs for accommodating that problematic aspect of his own career.

A further technique that applies to only one – but a very important – phenomonon, the phenomenon of death, is to see its occurrence at a given time as demanded by the pleasingness of one's life as a whole, in the way in which the inner logic of a play or piece of music demands that at a certain point it should stop. In "On free death" (Z I, 2I) Zarathustra enjoins: "Die at the right time!" One should, he says, "cease letting oneself be eaten when one tastes best" and not, like a wizen apple, hang upon the branch for too long.

A still further technique (though strictly "technique" is not the right word here) is not taking things seriously, forgetting about them:

> to be incapable of taking one's enemies, one's accidents, even one's misdeeds seriously for very long – that is a sign of strong, full natures in which there is an excess of power to form, to mould, to recuperate, and to forget (a good example is Mirabeau who had no memory for insults and vile actions done him and was unable to forgive simply because he forgot). (*GM* I, 10)

(Notice that there is all the difference in the world between repressing the memory of an event – on account of its extreme significance – and forgetting it on account of its utter triviality. *Amor fati* is not a test of the memory: one is allowed to forget providing the forgetting is genuine.)

16 The important thing to notice about all of these techniques for coming to terms with *prima facie* evils in one's life (in the case of past evils Nietzsche calls the process one of "redemption" – "recreat[ing] all 'it was' into a 'thus I willed it'" [Z II, 20]) is that one cannot do it without knowing, that is, for Nietzsche, *choosing* who you are: deciding, that is, what your dominant desires, character traits, emotions, goals, and values are. I cannot view a weakness as contributing to the overall attractiveness of my nature unless I know

the "artistic plan" of that nature as a whole. Neither can I view, let us say, the mental damage that terminated my career as a mathematical logician and turned me to the life of philosophy nor the "counterargument" that turned me from a philosopher into a peace activist as a benefit unless I have decided that being a philosopher or a peace activist is what, fundamentally, I want to be. To decide that some past event was a benefit presupposes and commits me to certain views as to who I am, what my dominant desires and goals are now. Thus the process of coming to love fate, coming to will the eternal recurrence, demands, and incorporates the construction of the self – the construction of an authentic, truth-embracing self: becoming, in other words, who one is.

Notice that the process of creating this self is an *artistic* process,[13] a task of ordering the events in one's life that in some respects is analogous to the writing of a *Bildungsroman*,[14] a story of the growth of personality from naivety to maturity, and in other respects is analogous to the task of constructing a character that will engage the esteem and attention of the reader. And notice, too, that in a clear sense the creation of this self is *more* artistic (see sec. 11 above), more of an artistic *tour de force* than the creation of an inauthentic self. For as we think of one scientific theory as better than another if it comprehends a greater range of observational "data" it makes sense to think of art as more or less consummate according to the richness of the "data" that it accommodates.

Of course, the construction of a self such that all its past deeds and experiences add up to the life of an attractive, fortunate self – a self we can "esteem," "desire," view with "pleasure" (*GS* 78), "attain satisfaction" with (*GS* 290), a self we like, indeed love being – is not the only self one could construct. One could construct out of the same set of facts an equally clear coherent and honest self that is the victim of misfortune. ("The world of the happy person is a different one from the world of the unhappy person," writes Wittgenstein. But it is not the "facts" that are different only the "limits" [*Tractatus*, 6.43].) That way, however, lies the path to "nausea and suicide." The construction of a self that we love to be is the one we need because in it we find the solution to the problem of the riddle.

17 It might be wondered, however, just what being able to will the recurrence of one's own life in all its remembered detail has to do with solving the riddle. That, after all, which threatens to be an

object of nausea is nothing so trivial as *my life*. It is, rather, *existence as such*. "Nausea," that is, is no mere sense of personal failure or misfortune but is, rather, a *metaphysical*, almost dignified condition, something that afflicts only those of deep and knowledgeable perspectives. Yet could not one perhaps will the recurrence of one's own life yet find being as such deeply nauseating? Could one not be thoroughly content with one's own life yet find, for example, the death of Jacqueline du Pré from multiple sclerosis or the massacre in Tianamen Square to be inescapable and unredeemable objections to being as such? One would then be in the position of regarding one's own life as a lucky exception to the generally problematic character of existence.

Nietzsche formulates the thought of the eternal recurrence indifferently in terms of individual life (*GS* 341) and in terms of world history (Z III, 2). Sometimes, as in section 56 of *Beyond Good and Evil*, where the "world-affirming man" calls out "da capo" to "the whole piece and play," it is quite vague as to just what it is that is to recur. This indifference and vagueness indicates, I think, that Nietzsche believes one can will the recurrence of one's life if and only if one can will the recurrence of the world. The wording of section 341 in *The Gay Science* explains, I think, why. Here, the thought of eternal recurrence is formulated as follows:

This life as you now live it and have lived it, you will have to live once more and innumerable times more; and there will be nothing new in it, but every pain and every joy and every thought and sigh and everything unutterably small and great will have to return to you, all in the same succession and sequence – even this spider and this moonlight between the trees.

Notice that the spider and the moonlight are treated here as, like my pains and joys, parts of my biography. This can only be a shorthand way of saying that the *experience* of the spider and of the moonlight is part of my biography. If, then, I am to will the recurrence of not just my life but of my *exact* life, I must will the recurrence of all of my knowledge of world history. But if there are any world-historical events I cannot will to recur then I cannot will the recurrence of my knowledge of them. To will, then, the recurrence of my exact life I must be able to will the recurrence of all those events in world history I know about. The thought of the recurrence of my life and of the world as seen from my perspective are equivalent. It follows that bringing oneself to will the recurrence of one's exact life requires the redemption not just of problematic events that belong to one's biography, but of those too which do not. The artistic techniques by means of which one discovers a personal providence must be extended to embrace world history as a whole.[15]

18 This, then, is the Dionysian solution. The riddle posed by the existence of absurd, pointless, nauseating suffering is to be solved by achieving the world-view of Emerson's "joyful scientist," according to which *there is, in fact, no such suffering at all. "The riddle"*, in Wittgenstein's words (and with, I believe, essentially his senti-ments[16]) "does not exist" (*Tractatus*, 6.5). In this respect the Dionysian and Apollonian solutions are the same. They differ only in their methods: the Apollonian denies all knowledge of the "questionable" in life. The Dionysian acknowledges it but, as it were, *answers the question* by attaining to a view of the world "that sanctifies and calls good even the most terrible and questionable qualities of life" (*WP* 1050), by performing, that is, a kind of atheistic theodicy.

The Gay Science, as we now see, contains not just the Apollonian but also the Dionysian solution to the Schopenhauerian riddle: a prescription for a genuine cure rather than a brief evasion of the problem, a recipe for a genuine, truth-accepting, lasting, Emersonian cheerfulness. But why then is the forced uncertain, febrile gaiety of the Apollonian solution the dominant tone in the work? Why, when the text contains the Dionysian solution, does the Preface – *which must have the last word since it was written last* – offer us only the Apollonian?

Because, Nietzsche holds, "Nobody yet has the strength to will the eternal recurrence" (*GS* 285). Section 370 makes the same point: "Dionysian pessimism" – Nietzsche's paradoxial name for that profoundly *un*pessimistic view of the world which acknowledges all of the questionable in life yet finds it to be justified – is a "pessimism of the future," achievable not by ordinary mortals but only by the "Dionysian god and man." In other words, the *Übermensch*. What we lack is the strength and more particularly the spiritual *health* to will the eternal recurrence. We cannot do so because, like Zarathustra, we are still "convalescents" (*Z* III, 13).

19 What has health or its lack got to do with coming to a view of the world in which the questionable is redeemed, the appearance that

life is a pit of reasonless pain dispelled? What, in other words, does the *Übermensch* have that we lack?

Nietzsche's answer is: "energy." A "fullness," an "*over-fullness of life*," an "overflowing energy that is pregnant with future." It is this which brings it about that "The Dionysian god or man, cannot only afford the sight of the terrible and questionable but even the terrible deed and any luxury of destruction, decomposition, and negation. In his case what is evil, absurd and ugly seems, as it were, permissible, owing to an excess of procreating, fertilizing energies that can still turn any desert into lush farmland" (*GS* 370). We, however, suffer, to one degree or another, from "*impoverishment of life*" (*ibid.*). In the *Geneaology of Morals* this is said to be a physiological state associated with a coolness of the "affects," a slowness in the "tempo of life," and the absence of "certainty of life and of the future" (*GM* iii, 25).

Why should energy be the key to willing the eternal recurrence? And why should it be connected in some important way with the future? What Nietzsche is confronting here, I believe, are the limits to any redemption of the past which does not embrace the future. There are, I think he is prepared to concede, atrocious events that can be redeemed by nothing that is discoverable in past or present experience. And for ordinary mortals that is the end of the matter: the future is dark, and while it is not, perhaps, *inconceivable* that some pattern in future history might present materials for the redemption of those events, that is something of which we lack all "certainty." Dionysian man, however, is different: he possesses such certainty.

What has this certainty, or its lack, to do with energy levels? Nietzsche is pointing out, it seems to me, that with regard to certain beliefs about the future it is inappropriate to regard them as based on evidence or to demand that they should be thus based. Rather, they are to be treated as aspects of a general orientation towards the world that is a symptom of one's level of psychic energy. If, that is, one's energy level is high one will feel not merely equal to whatever exigencies may be thrown at one by fate but possessed of a surplus of energy with which to master fate, mold it to one's will. One will then be likely to subscribe to a set of beliefs expressing confidence in a congruence between one's future and one's will. And by an extension of confidence one will be likely to subscribe to a set of more-or-less ungrounded beliefs concerning events over which, in the normal sense, one has no personal control. A highly ebullient Russian, for example, might (at least at the time of writing) be expected to be confident of both an orderly transition to liberal democracy and of the continued integrity of the Soviet Union.

Those of low psychic energy, on the other hand, will feel unequal to what fate is liable to throw at them and their vision of the future will be (equally groundlessly) full of foreboding. Since they expect no consolation in the future for present ills they will turn instead, in one form or another, to *other* worlds. They will become "romantic" rather than "Dionysian" pessimists and will seek "rest, stillness, calm seas, redemption... through art... or intoxication, convulsions, anesthesia and madness" (*GS* 370).[17] Or else, we might add, through profound superficiality.

The *Übermensch* is an extreme case of the person of high energy. So "overflowing" is she with energy that she is certain of the redemption of presently unredeemed evils. Though she cannot always see what these redemptions are, she has absolute faith that they will occur, an absolute faith that enables her to "at last cry [using Goethe's line]: 'life however it may be is good!'" (*HH* I, 222). We, however, have lived under the shadow of God for so long that we possess still a theological cringe (see *GS* 285), a culturally transmitted taint of "guilt" and "depression" (*HH* I, 133). We lack a sense of our own worth and power, we lack "self-love" and "self-valuation" (*HH* I, 134), and cannot therefore believe in the future redemption of, as yet, unredeemed events: because of our guilt we feel that there *cannot* be redemption, that existence *must* be eternal "punishment" (*Z* II, 20). As "convalescents," therefore, the only recourse for us is profound superficiality, the remedy for convalescents. Only that can rescue *us* from the riddle.

20 It may be observed at this point that someone conspicuously unable to believe in future redemption is Nietzsche himself. In section 343 of *The Gay Science*, as Schacht in the quotation with which we began this chapter says, Nietzsche records his personal excitement at "the news that 'the old god is dead,'" the excitement of any empty "horizon," of preparation for a voyage into "open sea." What Schacht fails to mention, however, is that in the same section Nietzsche *criticizes* himself for this excitement, suggesting that he is "too much under the impression of the *initial consequences* of this event, the consequences for *ourselves*," too uninvolved in the "shadows that must soon envelop Europe." When we take into account how much was based on the Christian God, "for example,

the whole of our European morality," we cannot fail to confront "the long plenitude and sequence of breakdown, destruction, ruin, and cataclysm that is now impending ... an eclipse of the sun whose like has probably never yet occurred on earth." It is remarks of this order (see also sec. 347) – remarks which it must be legitimate to regard as premonitions of the First World War, just twenty-seven years away – which set the dominant tone of book v of *The Gay Science*. Not Schacht's "joyful affirmation of life" but rather a sense of Spenglerian doom envelops it. Nietzsche has no optimism about the visible future – is conspicuously unable to believe that events must "either immediately or very soon after" turn out "for the best" (*GS* 277) – and is quite silent with respect to the invisible future. As disgust at the being and doings of the "small man" prevent Zarathustra willing the eternal recurrence (*Z* III, 13), so in *The Gay Science* it prevents Nietzsche. At least part of what, in the Preface, he finds refuge from in profound superficiality is that disgust.

21 Why does Nietzsche not entertain the possibility of a *third* kind of solution to the riddle, distinct from both the Apollonian and Dionysian solutions, which consists in, though acknowledging, the existence of unredeemed and unredeemable evil, setting it in the context of existence as a whole which, as a whole, is seen as desirable and worth living? Why cannot life be loved warts and all, affirmed, that is, as a lovable whole *in spite* of its faults? Why cannot it be affirmed without whitewashing of those faults, without the effort to "call ... good even the most terrible and questionable qualities of life" (*WP* 1050), to pretend, that is, that they are not really faults at all? Why, in short, is it not a sufficient response to the riddle to be, while not able to will the recurrence of absolutely everything, yet able to will the recurrence of *most* of one's life and of what one knows of the world?

Alexander Nehamas (*Nietzsche*; see ch. 5 [which presupposes ch. 3]) explains this by attributing to Nietzsche the metaphysical view that every feature of an object or event, whether intrinsic or relational, is essential to it. From this it follows, since everything is related to everything, that if anything at all were to recur everything would have to. Hence to will the recurrence of anything one must will the recurrence of everything.

Apart from the fact that Nehamas attributes this thesis to

Nietzsche almost entirely on the basis of unpublished material (the one exception to this, a passage from *Zarathustra*, I shall return to in a moment), I view this interpretation with disfavor because it implicitly attributes to Nietzsche an intensional fallacy and thereby renders his view of spiritual health the uninteresting result of inferential error. Nehamas, that is (see p. 156), represents Nietzsche as arguing that if (1) a person S wills the recurrence of an event E then since (2) if E recurs then every event recurs it follows that (3) S wills the recurrence of every event. But one might not *know* that nothing can recur unless everything does. Or one might not believe it. As a matter of fact *I* do not believe it: it strikes me as metaphysically bizarre to suppose that if someone drops a bus-ticket in Red Square just as I eat my dinner then the event of the eating could not but have had the property of being contemporaneous with the dropping of the bus-ticket. Hence I at least *can* will the recurrence of some without willing the recurrence of every event.

Nietzsche may have toyed in private moments with the idea Nehamas suggests. He may even, at some stage, have believed it. But I do not think the idea is at all relevant to our question. For it seems to me clear that the source of Nietzsche's view that to stand in the ideal relationship to the world is to love, will the recurrence of, everything about it lies not in his metaphysics but in, rather, his concept of love, his conception of what it is to accept, love, *joyfully* to affirm something.

This is really made quite clear in the one published passage Nehamas does quote (*Nietzsche*, p. 155) in support of his interpretation. Nietzsche does indeed say, in the penultimate section of *Zarathustra*,[18]

Have you ever said Yes to a single joy? O my friends, then you have said yes to *all* woe. All things are entangled, ensnared, enamoured: if ever you wanted one thing twice, if ever you said, "You please me, happiness! Abide moment!"[19] Then you wanted it *all* back. All anew, all eternally, all entangled, ensnared, enamoured.

But what he immediately goes on to say (a continuation not quoted by Nehamas) is:

oh, then you *loved* the world. Eternal ones, love it eternally and evermore; and to woe too, you say: go but return! For *all joy wants – eternity.*

All joy wants the eternity of all things, wants honey, wants dregs, wants drunken midnight, wants tombs, wants tomb-tears' comfort, wants gilded evening glow.

The focus of the passage is thus not metaphysics but the concept of joy. If, Nietzsche is saying, you stand in the ideal relationship to the world then you perceive all things to be interconnected not because they *are*, of metaphysical necessity, so interconnected but rather because standing in that relationship is a matter of accepting the totality of things as constituting a beautiful, "perfect" (*ibid.*) whole of which everything is an organic part and in which problematic events stand in redemptive relationships to ones which are not problematic. If, Nietzsche is saying, you ever "say Yes" to anything you must "say Yes" to everything – not on account of the *metaphysical* interconnectedness of all things but simply because if you do not "say Yes" to *everything* then it is not, *in Nietzsche's sense*, "Yes" that you say. "Joy," he writes, "wants everything eternally the same" (*ibid.*). If that is not what one wants then one's "Yes" to life (the cautious, qualified discerning "Yes" of, as Nietzsche would be likely to say, the scholar) is not the joyful "Yes" that Nietzsche seeks.

The search for such a "Yes" is manifested not just in the dithyrambic *Zarathustra* but in *The Gay Science* too. Most people, he complains in section 288, do not believe in "elevated moods" (*hohe Stimmungen*). At best they believe in their lasting for a few moments, "at most a quarter of an hour." To be "a human being with one elevated feeling – to be a single great mood incarnate" has up to now been considered "a mere dream and delightful possibility." Yet might not history, Nietzsche speculates, one day give rise to such beings, beings whose perpetual state is, as it were, "a continual ascent as on stairs and at the same time a sense of resting on clouds"?

To achieve, then, the status of *Übermensch* is to achieve and sustain a condition of *ecstasy* (*Rausch*) – to be, as we used to say in the 1960s, on a "permanent [and apparently ever-ascending] high." Now it seems to me that Nietzsche is quite right that ecstasy is, by definition, unqualified and unconditional. If one affirms something *ecstatically*, if one loves someone or something ecstatically, then one does not love it *in spite of* but rather *because of* its faults. Its faults, that is, to the extent that one is aware of them, are seen as part of what one loves about it – which is to say that they are not really faults at all but necessary contributors to the "desirability" (*WP* 1041) of the whole. The reason, therefore, that Nietzsche demands the willing of the recurrence of *everything* about the world is that it alone expresses the condition of ecstasy; and *ecstasy is what he regards as the ideal relationship to reality*.[20]

22 It may be noticed, *en passant*, that it is on account of this ideal that, given that *we* are unable to achieve the Dionysian solution to the riddle, the *only* alternative considered by Nietzsche is the Apollonian. The stance of profound superficiality, that is, *also* yields an ecstatic state. (As we observed earlier, Nietzsche describes not merely Dionysian joy but also his own convalescent gaiety as a state of "intoxication" [*GS*, Preface, 1].) For *qua* inhabitant of the condition of profound superficiality, one affirms, like Dionysian man, *everything* in one's world; one loves one's fate. The only difference between this and the Dionysian state is that what one loves is a fake fate. Nietzsche's valuation of ecstasy is thus so high that, so he believes, if one is unable to affirm everything, the only viable response is to eliminate the irremediably unlovable from one's world. *La gaya scienza* is a kind of parody of willing the eternal recurrence.

23 *Why* does Nietzsche believe ecstasy to be the ideal relationship to the world? Because, in a word, he wants something to *worship* and is aware once again, as he was in *The Birth of Tragedy* (see ch. 2, sec. 14), that a sense of the holy, of the sacred is a fundamental human need. If the old God is dead then nature herself must be made divine, "perfect" (*Z* IV, 19). The non-ecstatic affirmation of life holds no interest for Nietzsche since it has no bearing on *his* problem; the problem of proving that God, after all, exists. Less provocatively: the problem of achieving a state of mind, "feel[ing] oneself 'in heaven,'...'eternal'" (*A* 33), in which a naturalized object is the target of all those feelings and attitudes that used to be directed towards the (no longer believable) transcendent.[21]

24 Suppose one were to dispute Nietzsche's claim that his Dionysian "pantheism" (*WP* 1050) constitutes the ideal stance towards the world. He would reply that what makes it the ideal stance is that it is the stance you would adopt if you did not suffer from diminished psychic energy. It is, he would claim, the ideal relationship to the world because it is that relationship we would adopt if we were fully healthy. Ecstatic affirmation is the ideal because it is the expression of the ideal of spiritual health.

Here, however, it needs to be pointed out that the idea that the person of "overflowing" energy will have faith in the future redemption of *all* events which are, to date, unredeemed is, as so

often with Nietzsche, an *exaggeration* of a genuine insight. For while
it is true that the energetic, healthy person will tend to subscribe to
a set of beliefs that express her excitement about and confidence in
the future, there is no reason at all to demand that this set should
include anything as comprehensive as the redemption of each and
every hitherto unredeemed event. One can, in Nietzsche's language,
be full of an overflowing desire for "destruction, for change, for
future, for *becoming*" (*GS* 370) without (unless one has, like Nietzsche,
a religious need to satisfy) at all believing in the redemption of all of
the past. It is a truism that many people look forward to the future
precisely because they believe that many of the unacceptable aspects
of the past will be, not redeemed, but rather eliminated. Nietzsche
tries to suggest that if a desire for becoming is of this character then
it expresses "the hatred of the ill-constituted, disinherited, and
under-privileged who destroy, *must* destroy, because what exists,
indeed all existence, all being, outrages and provokes them" (*ibid.*).
But, again, while this psychology of socialism is penetrating, it is also
exaggerated. One *can* deplore absolutely certain states of affairs and
hope for (and believe in) their elimination from the future without
necessarily being consumed by sick-making resentment towards the
perpetrators of those conditions.

25 To summarize: Nietzsche suggests, it appears, that failure to will
the eternal recurrence, failure to believe in the future redemption of
all that appears at present as unredeemed evil, indicates a lack of
psychic energy and constitutes, therefore, a critique of one's state of
spiritual health. Against this, however, I have suggested that there
is no reason to suppose that that general confidence in the future
which, in normal circumstances, plausibly *is* implied by a high level
of psychic energy must include faith in the future justification of
every "questionable" aspect of the past. We have therefore no
reason to accept the capacity to will the eternal recurrence as a
condition of spiritual health. Neither, therefore, do we, lacking that
capacity, have a motive to seek a surrogate in the life of profound
superficiality. We are not, in short, compelled to accept the equation
of psychic health with ecstasy. The psychology of the non-ecstatic
life affirmer may be dull. But there is no reason to accept that it must
be diseased.

CHAPTER 5

Twilight of the Idols

1 Nietzsche's final year of sanity, 1888, was a time of extraordinary productivity. In it he wrote four major works, *The Case of Wagner*, *Twilight of the Idols*, *The Anti-Christ*, and *Ecce Homo*, as well as compiling *Nietzsche Contra Wagner* out of earlier writings[1] and producing a large amount of the *Nachlass* material published posthumously as *The Will to Power*. He must have written, even more than in previous years, in an extraordinary frenzy of productivity. The portrait of the artist as creating out of a state of frenzy (*Rausch*) painted, as we will see, in *Twilight of the Idols*, must be amongst other things a self-portrait.

The works of 1888 hang together in a closely coherent way so that collectively they can be taken to constitute Nietzsche's final thoughts about art and about its relation to life. The unity which they form is, it seems to me, one that is separate from that constituted by *The Gay Science* and the works discussed with it in the last chapter. Though it would be aesthetically pleasing for Nietzsche's output to fall, like Gaul, into three parts (early, middle, and late), actually, it seems to me, it falls into four. In a way, though, the tripartite structure is preserved since, so I shall argue, Nietzsche's final account of the relation between art and life constitutes a return to his first.

2 Two contrasts in particular separated the works of 1888 from *The Gay Science*. First, a renewed sense of the ultimate importance of the artist and of art: the "art of works of art," as much as that which has one's life as its product. None of the antagonism to the former expressed in the "positivistic" period and still preserved to some extent in *The Gay Science* ("we should learn from artists while being wiser than they are in other matters. For with them [their] ... subtle power usually comes to an end where art ends and life begins; but

we want to be poets of our lives" [*GS* 299]) is present in the works of 1888. Instead art, literal art, is seen as the "great stimulus to life" (*TI* IX, 24) and a cause of health (*CW* 3), while the "psychology of the artist" is seen as the epitome of healthy life-affirmation (*TI* IX, 8–9, X, 4–5). That artists are by *our* standards typically "sick" is viewed, in *The Will to Power*, as a criticism not of the artist but of our criteria of health (812).

The fact is that in 1888 art and its creators are restored to their former glory: the glory they possessed in *The Birth of Tragedy*. It seems to me completely wrong to suggest, as does Michael Tanner,[2] that Nietzsche spent the rest of his life regretting his characterization of art in *The Birth of Tragedy* as "the highest task and truly metaphysical activity of this life" or to suggest, as does Richard Shacht, that "Nietzsche's enthusiasm for art in *The Birth of Tragedy* was so great that further reflection could only have tempered it – as it in fact did."[3] After *The Birth* Nietzsche did indeed have, as Schacht suggests "second thoughts about art" (*ibid.*). But he also had third and fourth thoughts, and the fourth ones return, in their esteem for art, to the first. To be sure, it is no longer Wagner who sits upon the throne of art. But the throne remains, occupied now by the likes of Hafiz, Raphael, Rubens, Goethe, Bizet, and, once again, the Greek tragedians.

The second and connected contrast is that the "Dionysian" attitude to life, regarded in *The Gay Science* as beyond the power of ordinary mortals, is viewed in 1888 as achievable, indeed achieved, by at least the artist (*TI* IX, 8, X, 5). The sense of *The Gay Science* that we are all "convalescents" disappears in Nietzsche's final year. (In fact, however, this apparently optimistic turn in Nietzsche's thought is an illusion; for, so I shall argue, the only reason the Dionysian condition is viewed as achievable is that, without Nietzsche properly noticing it, the concept of what constitutes it has altered.)

3 According to Kant, aesthetic pleasure is "disinterested." The beautiful, he says, is that which gives pleasure "apart from any interest" (*Critique of Judgment*, sec. 5). Schopenhauer, as we saw in chapter 1, takes over this idea and interprets it in his own way. Disinterestedness (or "objectivity," as he also calls it), while for Kant a necessary *mark* of aesthetic pleasure, is not its object. The object, that in which we take pleasure, is a kind of "free" orderliness, the kind of orderliness we recognize in an object of perception when

we bring it under a concept but which, in the case of the beautiful, is perceived without bringing the object under any concept. For Schopenhauer, however, the *object* of pleasure is one's own state of disinterestedness. In the aesthetic state what one takes pleasure in[4] is one's freedom from the "vile [*schnöde*] pressure of the will." One's pleasure consists in experiencing the "Sabbath of the penal servitude of willing" (*WR* I, 196). The significance of this pleasure, for Schopenhauer, is that it is a brief intimation of "how blessed must be the life of a man in whom the will is silenced not for a few moments, as in the enjoyment of the beautiful, but for ever" (*WR* I, p. 390). Art, in other words, is an intimation of, a pointer towards, the "correct" stance to life and the world, asceticism: the denial of the will and the world.[5]

Nietzsche refers to Schopenhauer's account of the aesthetic state in sections 21–2 of the part of *Twilight of the Idols* called "Skirmishes of an untimely man" – his last sustained (published) discussion of art and the heart of the material we will consider in this chapter. He speaks of Schopenhauer's "melancholy fervor" in describing the beautiful, observing correctly that Schopenhauer sees it as "a bridge on which one will…develop a thirst to go further…a momentary redemption from the 'will' – a lure to eternal redemption" (*TI* IX, 22).

Schopenhauer's representation of art as a pointer to asceticism provides the motive for Nietzsche's attack upon the Kant–Schopenhauer (but mainly Schopenhauer) account of "the aesthetic state" (*WP* 801). Art, he holds, far from serving "the ascetic ideal," is its fundamental opponent (*GM* III, 25). Schopenhauerian aesthetics is a "maliciously ingenious" attempt to stand the truth on its head, to "adduce in favour of a nihilistic total depreciation of life" precisely the great "counter-instance," the great self-affirmation of the "will to live," life's form of exuberance (*TI* IX, 21). The defense of this latter thesis – the essentially life-affirming character of art – is the fundamental concern of Nietzsche's philosophy of art during his final productive year and constitutes the central topic of this chapter.

4 Nietzsche's attack upon the attempt to link disinterestedness to the aesthetic state goes back to *Zarathustra* and *The Genealogy of Morals*. In the latter he attributes the creation of the "fat worm of error" which is the disinterestedness theory to the fact that Kant "like all

philosophers instead of envisaging the aesthetic problem from the point of view of the artist (the creator), considered art and the beautiful purely from that of the 'spectator,' and unconsciously introduced the 'spectator' into the concept 'beautiful'" (*GM* III, 6). No *artist*, Nietzsche continues, could possibly have done this. Take, for example, Stendhal, who calls the beautiful "a promise of happiness." To him, far from Schopenhauerian will-lessness, "the fact seems to be precisely that the beautiful *arouses the will* ('interestedness')" (*ibid.*).

A question that needs to be raised at this point, is why, in Nietzsche's view, aesthetics must be done *only* from the artist's point of view. Why should it not be done from *both* perspectives? Why should there not be both a spectator's aesthetics and a creator's so that Kant and Stendhal could both be right about their respective subject-matters?

The answer is that, according to Nietzsche, that state which is, properly, the product of art is identical in kind with the state that produces it. This assumption is implicit in the reference to Stendhal as a "genuine spectator and artist" (*ibid.*) – Kant, he says, lacking the nature of the latter, lacking "personal...vivid authentic experiences, desires, surprises, and delights in the realm of the beautiful" (*ibid.*), fails to count as the former – and is explicit in various remarks in *The Will to Power*. In section 801, for example, he writes that "the aesthetic state" cannot appear in "the sober, the weary, the exhausted, the dried up (e.g. scholars)." They, he continues, "can receive nothing from art because they do not possess the primary artistic force...whoever cannot give also receives nothing." And in section 821, even more explicitly, he claims that "the effect of works of art is to excite *the state that creates art*."[6] There is, in short, a psychological condition that is uniquely identifiable as "*the* aesthetic state," a state that is common to the creator of art and the "genuine" spectator. The question of its nature constitutes "*the* aesthetic problem."

5 Nietzsche's claim is that if we examine "the aesthetic state" from the correct, that is the creator's, viewpoint we will see that it cannot possibly be a state of disinterestedness. Why not? Nietzsche tries to explain this in the somewhat labored section of *Zarathustra* called "On Immaculate Perception" (*Z* II, 15). Here he makes two claims. First, that "pure perceivers" are secret "lechers." Their "spirit" has

been persuaded that "to look at life without desire and not, like a dog, with one's tongue hanging out" is best; but not their "entrails." They are, therefore, "sentimental hypocrites...lechers" who lack "innocence" in their desire for immaculate perception, their desire to be "nothing but a mirror." This surely, is another presentation of the psychoanalysis of Schopenhauer (see n. 5 above), the theory that his "interest" in disinterested is in using it "like lupulin[7] or camphor" (*GM* III, 6) as an antidote to the "vile urgency" of sexual desire.

Nietzsche's second claim is that pure perceivers are barren. It is not as "creators," not as the sun but rather as the moon, that they "love the earth": they will never "give birth." To think that their emasculated leer constitutes the experience of the beautiful, continues Nietzsche, is a travesty. Where really is beauty? "Where I must will with all my will: where I must love and perish that an image may not remain a mere image." A similar connecting of the beautiful with sex and reproduction occurs in *Twilight of the Idols*: "beauty," he says there, "incites procreation" (*TI* IX, 22).

Nietzsche's objection to the disinterestedness theory is, it seems to me, a simple one: disinterested, will-less contemplation is not a state out of which anything is created. Yet art, the state which produces it, essentially *is* creative. Hence "objectivity, mirroring, suspended will" are "inartistic states" (*WP* 812). Art, in short, is not contemplation but *action*. Nietzsche's activist vocabulary for talking about artists – he refers to them as *creators, makers, doers, violators* and as *rapists* (*TI* IX, 8) – continually emphasizes this. And it is this perspective on the artist that provides the basis for the inclusion of conquerors and builders of states and empires among the ranks of "artists": men possessed of the artist's "terrible...egoism," artists of "violence" (*GM* II, 17).

6 One might offer, on Schopenhauer's behalf, the following kind of defense of the role of immaculate perception in the genesis of art. *Of course*, one might say, artists are doers; for art essentially involves the production of artworks and that of course demands action and the will. This much is obvious. But these truisms, one might continue, pertain only to the *executive* phase of the process that leads to the birth of the artwork. Distinct and separable from this in the process that is the creation of (at least good) art is a *contemplative* phase. It is this, and this alone, that is claimed to be disinterested. Moreover, if the

aesthetic state is held to be common to both artist and audience then, since (typically) the audience is not prompted by the artwork to the production of further artworks, we ought to restrict the application of that phrase to the contemplative phase of the productive process.

To understand the kind of reply Nietzsche would give to this defense of disinterestedness we need to recall (see ch. 1, sec. 6 above) that in Schopenhauer's account the aesthetic state is a condition of pure passivity. This conception is implicit in Schopenhauer's very methodology for elucidating the character of the aesthetic state. In ordinary perception, as he describes it, the mind is active, constantly selecting information that is of interest to the will, rejecting that which is not. And our emotions, too, are continually at work "colouring" perception – in bright hues when things go well for the will, in dark ones when they go badly. The aesthetic state is conceived, negatively, as the cessation of all this activity. One escapes the perception-molding (*creative*, let it be noted) effects of the will and exists as a "pure," "objective," "clear mirror" of the object (*WR* I, 178–9). The mind becomes, as it were, a reflecting *tabula rasa* that registers without any distortion, selection, or comment that which is objectively given. One might compare Schopenhauer in his conception of the aesthetic state to the Counter-Reformation Pyrrhonists such as Erasmus who used the arguments of classical skepticism as a technique for clearing the mind of human pride and pretension so that it could become receptive to the implantation of true knowledge by God. This comparison is by no means fanciful since Schopenhauer says of that insight into the true nature of the world that comes with the aesthetic state that it is "independent of free choice...not to be forcibly arrived at by intention or design but comes suddenly as if flying in form without...[as it were an] *effect of grace*" (*WR* I, p. 404).

On the other hand, however, Schopenhauer also holds, as we saw (ch. 1, sec. 7), that in the aesthetic state we experience the object as "Idea," as beautiful, and that this is a matter of experiencing the "significant form," that which is essential and universal in a particular individual. And this, it seems clear, is inconsistent with the idea of the aesthetic subject as pure receptivity, or mere mirror. For what it demands of the subject is *activity*; selecting a particular *Gestalt* upon an object, sorting things into figure and ground and so on. This inconsistency manifests itself in a tension between Schopenhauer's view that (1) art deals in essences, that the "Platonic Idea" is the content of art, the artist's vision pared down to just that which is universal in an object and (2) his account of the unparaphrasability of the content of art – "we are entirely satisfied by the impression of a work of art only when it leaves behind something...we cannot bring down to the distinctness of a concept" (*WR* II, pp. 408–9) – in terms of the idea that the mirror-like quality of the aesthetic mind means that the content of aesthetic vision is as infinitely rich in aspect and detail as is the object itself (*ibid.*).

Nietzsche's thoughts about art and the beautiful are consonant with his second strand in Schopenhauer's thought. The beautiful, he insists, is made, not discovered. "Beauty in itself" is, he says, an empty phrase (*TI* IX, 19): one *makes* things beautiful by "enriching everything out of one's own fullness," "transforming things until they mirror... [one's own] perfection" (*TI* IX, 9). "This *having* to transform into perfection is – art" (*ibid.*). Out of one's "fullness"

one lends to things, one *forces* them to accept from us, one violates them – this process is called *idealising*. Let us get rid of a prejudice here: idealising does not consist, as is commonly held, in subtracting or discounting the petty and inconsequential. What is decisive is rather a tremendous drive to bring out the main features so that the others disappear in the process. (*TI* IX, 8)

The point here, in the last two sentences, is the rejection of the notion that the experience of the beautiful can be divided up into (1) a phase of pure receptivity and (2) a will-governed phase in which one subtracts, erases, that which obscures or is irrelevant to "the main features." If, as both Nietzsche and Schopenhauer agree, experiencing the beautiful is experiencing "significant form," then being significantly structured is how one's experience is from the start. If, to employ an analogy, one sees one's lover across a crowded room one does not observe first a sea of faces and then attach the predicate "nonlover" to all but one. Rather one sees the lover and simultaneously all the other faces simply disappear from consciousness. The lover becomes in Wittgenstein's phrase (*Notebooks 1914–16*, p. 83) the whole of "my world."

Nietzsche is certainly right that "mirroring" in the sense of pure passivity is an "inartistic state." Conceived as pure passivity the aesthetic state is a fiction. In fact, as Kant pointed out, there is no consciousness of *any* kind with respect to which the mind is a *tabula rasa*. The subject of aesthetic experience, whether it be the creator of art or the spectator (who must also, though perhaps with *help* from the artwork, impose a construction upon the object of experience), must always "do" things to, "act" upon the object.

But does this mean that the will, *interestedness* in Schopenhauer's sense, is necessarily involved in the state out of which art grows? Let us remind ourselves, firstly, of what Schopenhauer means by saying that in the aesthetic state we cease to view objects "in relation to the will" (see ch. 1, sec. 6). In ordinary perception, he holds, we cannot but view objects as potential satisfiers or else frustrators of our desires, promoters or threats to our well-being. Such "interestedness" is not a view of things that is *added* to one's initial perception but is, rather, built into ordinary perceptual experience itself. Ordinarily, we perceive objects under concepts that relate them immediately to our "subjective" interests:

In the immediate perception of the world and of life we consider things as a rule...according to their relative...essence and existence. For example, we regard houses, ships, machines, and the like with the idea of their purpose and their suitability therefore; human beings with the idea of their relation to us, if they have any, and then according to their position and vocation, perhaps judging their fitness for it, and so on. (*WR* II, p. 372)

Ordinarily, in short, we are aware of objects only under "subjective" concepts – "hammer," "boss," "servant," "real estate," "tornado," "war," and so on – concepts that relate them to our own practical needs. And we perceive in objects only that which so relates them: to the traveler in a hurry the beautiful Rhine bridge appears as little more than a dash intersecting with a stroke (*WR* II, 381).

In describing aesthetic perception as disinterested Schopenhauer means that in the aesthetic state these normal categories of perception are suspended, thereby enabling us to become alive to usually unnoticed aspects and construals of objects: in Nietzschean language, the object undergoes "transfiguration." And this, surely, *is* essential to (good) art. Schopenhauer says that the concept, in art, is "eternally barren and unproductive" (*WR* I, 235), that art which has a conceptual origin is always stiff, lifeless, and second-rate. This does not seem to me quite correct. If I become aware of the light from the street-lamps in the snow-thick night air as a double row of imposing, semi-transparent pyramids then my normal account of what I see – my normal account of figure and ground, of what are the "things" in my field of vision – has been dislocated; but it is not the case that my experience has become nonconceptual. It is rather that tired old routines, the clichés of vision, have been replaced by new concepts, by a novel – and hence pleasurable – conceptualization of the situation. Still, Schopenhauer's main point, the demand for the dislocation of the normal, interested categories of perception, is surely correct. It constitutes, I think, the core of truth in the much-abused notion that art requires an "innocent eye."

It seems to me, therefore, that Schopenhauer's central point is correct. Though wrong to regard the aesthetic state as a condition of absolute passivity, he is correct in seeing that art demands the suspension of our normal, interested categories of perception. And this suspension does, in fact, entail a kind of passivity, for the suspension of interested concepts means, of course, the suspension of our normal anxious, planning, scheming, manipulative stance to the world. In the aesthetic state one does not will. Though one is active, one does not act.

7 Nietzsche, then, though his objections to the picture of the aesthetic perceiver as in a condition of absolute passivity are well taken, is mistaken in thinking that the correct, activist view invalidates Schopenhauer's point that aesthetic perception is disinterested. In a way, however, this mistake does not matter to the overall structure of his argument for the life-affirming character of art. For the next stage in the argument presupposes only the falsity of the absolute passivity account of the aesthetic state. Given, that is, the creative role of the perceiver in the transfiguration of the object of aesthetic perception, it becomes appropriate to inquire into the kind of conditions in the perceiver that brings this transfiguration about. What, Nietzsche asks, constitutes the "psychology of the artist" (*TI* ix, 8)?

"If there is to be art," he replies, "any aesthetic doing and seeing, one physiological condition is indispensable": *Rausch*, "intoxication" or, as Kaufmann in this passage in which Nietzsche is concerned to emphasize the *active* character of art rather better translates it, "frenzy" (*ibid.*). What is essential in this frenzy, Nietzsche continues,

is the feeling of increased strength and fullness. Out of this Feeling one lends to things, one *forces* them to accept from us, one violates them – this process is called *idealising*. Let us get rid of a prejudice here: idealising does not consist, as is commonly held, in subtracting or discounting the petty and inconsequential. What is decisive is rather a tremendous drive to bring out [*ein ungeheures Heraustreiben*] the main features so that the others disappear in the process. (*ibid.*)

In sections 10 and 11 of "Skirmishes of an untimely man"

Nietzsche makes an important revision to the conception of the Apollonian–Dionysian distinction as presented in *The Birth of Tragedy*. There, as we saw, "intoxication" was associated exclusively with the Dionysian and was opposed to Apollonian "dreams" (see ch. 2, sec. 7). Now, however, *both* are to be "conceived as kinds of *Rausch*" (*TI* ix, 10). The difference, now, is only that in the Apollonian state *Rausch* "excites above all the eye so that it gains the power of vision," whereas in the Dionysian state "the whole affective system is excited and enhanced: so that it discharges all its means of expression at once and drives forth the power of representation, imitation, transfiguration, transformation[8] and every kind of mimicking and acting" (*ibid.*). Music is still given a special association with the Dionysian, being conceived as an immobilization of all the manifestations of Dionysian intoxication save for song: a kind of repressed dance or, more exactly, *Gesamtkunstwerk*. The importance of this recasting of the Apollonian–Dionysian dichotomy as different in species (of *Rausch*) rather than in kind is that it enables Nietzsche to inquire into the psychology of the artist, to give a unified account of the genesis of all (good) art. The view of art as growing out of *Rausch* gains comprehensiveness.

8 What kind of *Rausch* is it that constitutes the art-generating state? In the *Genealogy of Morals* (*GM* iii, 6), spurred on by the desire to adopt a position "antipodal" to that of Schopenhauer (whom, remember, Nietzsche psychoanalyses as finding in the aesthetic state an escape from the guilty torments of the *sexual* will), he flirts in a rather indistinct way with the idea that specifically *sexual* intoxication is the ground of art: Pygmalion, he suggests, was not an "unaesthetic man," and the "sensual" Stendhal's view that "the beautiful promises happiness"[9] is intimated by Nietzsche to be the view that the beautiful is a promise of *sexual* happiness.

In *The Will to Power* he is much more direct: "without a certain overheating of the sexual system a Raphael is unthinkable" (800); and again: "The demand for art and beauty is an indirect demand for the ecstasies of sexuality" (805). In *Twilight of the Idols* he returns to a more indistinct, flirtatious position, inviting us to embrace the idea that art is universally sexual in origin without actually affirming it. He reports Plato as saying that if there had been no beautiful youths in Athens there would have been no Platonic philosophy. The art-form constituted by the Platonic dialogues as well as the culture of classical France at least, he suggests, "grew on the soil of sexual interest." He also asks us to consider the function of "beauty in tone, colour, fragrance [and]...rhythmic movement in nature" (*TI* IX, 22, 23).

Nietzsche does not, of course, maintain that art is the *natural* expression of sexual excitement. The idea he entertains, rather, is that it is its *sublimated* or, to use his favored term, "spiritualised" (*TI* v, 2) expression. He quotes with approval Plato's remark that "all beauty incites procreation from the most sensual up to the most spiritual" (*TI* IX, 22), suggesting, obviously, that art belongs at the spiritual end of this continuum. In *The Will to Power* again the sublimation thesis is expressed in a much more direct and unequivocal way: "The force that one expends in artistic conception is the same kind as that expended in the sexual act: there is only one kind of force. An artist betrays himself if he succumbs *here*, if he squanders himself here" (*WP* 815); and again: "Making music is another way of making children; chastity is merely the economy of the artist" (*WP* 800).

9 What is it that inclines Nietzsche to the view that art is sublimated sexuality? To understand this we need first to remember that the central, all-important thesis Nietzsche wishes to establish in his final meditations upon art is that it is of its essence to affirm, "say Yes to," life. Art, he says in *Twilight of the Idols*, is "transform[ing things] into perfection" (*TI* IX, 9). In *The Will to Power* he writes, more expansively:

What is essential in art remains its perfection of existence, its production of perfection and plenitude: art is essentially *affirmation, blessing, deification of existence*. What does a *pessimistic art signify*? Is that not a contradiction? – Yes. – Schopenhauer is *wrong* when he says that certain works of art serve pessimism. (*WP* 821)

And in a similar vein he describes "the ugly" as "the contradiction to art, that which is excluded from art" (*WP* 809). In *Twilight* this view of art is turned into a critique of the Aesthetic Movement:

L'art pour l'art. The fight against purpose in art is always a fight against the moralizing tendency in art, against its subordination to morality. *L'art pour l'art* means, "The devil take mortality!" But even this hostility still betrays the overpowering force of the prejudice. When the purpose of moral preaching and of improving man has been excluded from art, it still does not follow by any means that art is altogether purposeless, aimless, senseless – in short, *l'art pour l'art* a worm chewing its own tail. "Rather no purpose at all than a moral purpose!" – that is the talk of mere passion. A psychologist, on the other hand, asks: what does all art do? does it not praise? glorify? choose? prefer? With all this it strengthens or weakens certain valuations. Is this merely a "moreover"? an accident? something in which the artist's instinct has no share? Or is it not the very presupposition of the artist's ability? Does his basic instinct aim at art, or rather at the sense of art, at life? at a desirability of life? Art is the great stimulus to life: how could one understand it as purposeless, as aimless, as *l'art pour l'art*? (*TI* ix, 24)

Notice that in this passage the essentially affirmative character of art stands revealed as a *normative* thesis: the artist's basic instinct *must* "aim at life," otherwise he is not, properly speaking, an artist at all. Of course, says Nietzsche, history is rich in examples of, in the descriptive sense, art produced out of the "opposite state," a life-denying psychology: all art, for example, produced by the "genuine Christian." Normatively speaking, however, what such people produce is not art but rather "anti-artistry." Let us not, he adds, be "childish" and offer Raphael as a counterinstance. "Raphael said Yes, Raphael did Yes: consequently Raphael was no Christian" (*TI* ix, 9).

Now one of Nietzsche's central techniques for persuading us of the life-affirmative character of all (good) art – this is what prompts his interest in the "psychology of the artist" – is to present what we are to recognize as a paradigm of the psychological state out of which the truly great artist creates. That paradigm state is *Rausch*. But in such a state Nietzsche, as we have seen, claims, one idealizes, perfects, glorifies, deifies, beautifies. Hence art affirms.

But why should we accept that the world perceived in a state of *Rausch* is necessarily a world perfected? It is in answer to this question that the idea that the artist's *Rausch* has a specifically sexual character proves attractive. No doubt reflection upon his own sources of creativity had something to do with giving the idea a certain plausibility for him. Nietzsche's suggestion that "an artist betrays himself" if he squanders his energy in the sexual act (*WP* 815) has an unmistakable air of self-justification, of compensating for his own limited and unhappy excursions into the domain of real sex. But mainly it seems that it is the appropriateness of the idea of a sexual genesis to Nietzsche's conviction as to the essentially affirmative character of art that attracted him to the hypothesis. That is, art, Nietzsche believes, essentially transfigures, perfects, beautifies, idealizes. But this is just what sexual love does:

On the genesis of art. – That making perfect, seeing as perfect which characterises the cerebal system bursting with sexual energy (evening with the beloved, the smallest chance occurrences transfigured, life a succession of sublime things, "the misfortune of the unfortunate lover worth more than anything else"). (*WP* 805)

And again:

sensuality in its disguises… (3) in *art*, as the "embellishing" power: as man sees woman and, as it were, makes her a present of everything excellent, so the sensuality of the artist puts into one object everything else that he honours and esteems – in this way he *perfects* an object ("idealises" it). (*WP* 806)

Thus, such seems to be the idea to which Nietzsche is attracted, the notion that art is sublimated sexuality is true because it accounts for its essentially transfiguring, affirmative character.

10 But of course an argument of this character renders Nietzsche's position implicitly circular. That is, art, we are asked to believe, paradigmatically idealizes reality because it is the product of sexual intoxication. But when we ask why we should believe art to have such an origin all we are offered is the claim that art idealizes and that the postulation of a sexual origin provides a plausible explanation of this phenomenon. It should be noticed that, apart from autobiographical and anecdotal reflections (highly *suspect* reflections – Bach produced not only a large number of cantatas but also twenty-three children), Nietzsche provides no argument for the hypothesis of the sexual origin of art other than its power to explain its supposed idealizing character.

It is important to observe here that the resemblance between the Nietzschean view we have been considering and that of Freud is only superficial. Freud, that is, the earlier Freud at least, held the theory that sexual energy is the only kind of energy there is so that, for him, *any* nonsexual act is a sublimation. That art is sublimated sexuality is just a special case of the view that *everything* is sublimated sexuality. But this is not Nietzsche's view. In spite of *The Will to Power*'s "The force that one expends in the artistic conception is the same as that expended in the sexual act: there is only one kind of force" (*WP* 815), the published works of the later Nietzsche acknowledge a *multiplicity* of primal drives.[10] In *Twilight*, for example, whereas "love" is a "spiritualisation of sensuality," "another triumph is our spiritualisation of *hostility*" into, for example, politics (*TI* v, 3). Unlike Freud, therefore, Nietzsche has no *general* theory of behavior of which the sexual origin of art is a specific application. The sole argument for such an origin rests on Nietzsche's claim that art idealizes its content. This is what threatens the circularity in Nietzsche's thought.

It is doubtless the recognition of this threat which, in the published works, leads Nietzsche to flirt with, rather than to embrace, the thesis of the exclusively sexual origin of art (though he is not above using the suggestion of such a thesis, rhetorically, to manipulate us into accepting the life-affirming paradigm for art). And actually, when he comes to consider the "psychology of the artist" as such, he rejects the thesis allowing a *multiplicity* of types of *Rausch* to find sublimated expression in art:

If there is to be any aesthetic doing and seeing, one physiological condition is indispensable: frenzy. Frenzy must first have enhanced the excitability of the whole machine; else there is no art. All kinds of frenzy, however diversely conditioned, have the strength to accomplish this; above all, the frenzy of sexual excitement, this most ancient and original form of frenzy. Also the frenzy that follows all great cravings, all strong affects; the frenzy of feasts, contests, feats of daring, victory, all extreme movement; the frenzy of cruelty; the frenzy in destruction; the frenzy under certain meteorological influences, as for example the frenzy of spring; or under the influence of narcotics; and finally the frenzy of an overcharged and swollen will. (*TI* ix, 8)

11 What then remains of the thesis of the life-affirming character of art? It seems to me, first of all, that Nietzsche is quite right in holding *Rausch*, psychic frenzy, to be the essential psychological condition of the creation of art; for it is this that generates the energy necessary to disrupt and dislodge the routine clichés of "interested" perception. And, in a sense, it seems to me that Nietzsche is also correct to insist that *Rausch* "idealises," that is "brings out the main features" (*ibid.*), in the object of perception. But once we acknowledge the truth that not merely sexual but many other kinds of emotional excitement can produce a transformation of perception, the thesis that *Rausch*, and hence art, idealizes *in Nietzsche's sense according to which idealization is equivalent to beautification or perfecting*, becomes extremely problematic. In states of anger, cruelty, or fear for example, a particular *Gestalt* upon the world is constructed –

confronting a maniac, our focus is likely to contract to little more than the knife gleaming in his hand (cf. Schopenhauer's remarks on how the will "colours" the world quoted in section 6 above) – but there seems no reason to suppose that *beautification* of the object of perception will occur in these cases. I conclude that Nietzsche offers no compelling argument that will take us from contemplation of the psychological origin of art to the conclusion that it is essentially life-affirming.

12 Nietzsche has, however, a different way of defending the thesis: the demonstration that *prima facie* difficulties for the thesis are not really difficulties at all. With somewhat uncharacteristic circumspection he recognizes that such difficulties do indeed exist. Art, he says, is "the great stimulus to life." Yet

one question remains: art also makes apparent much that is ugly, hard and questionable in life: does it not thereby spoil life for us? And indeed there have been philosophers who attributed this sense to it: "liberation from the will" was what Schopenhauer taught as the overall end of art; and with admiration he found the great utility of tragedy in "evoking resignation." But this, as I have already suggested, is the pessimists' perspective and "evil eye." (*TI* ix, 24)

Nietzsche acknowledges two kinds of art that might appear to "spoil life": "naturalism" in the sense of the term introduced by Zola and, as just mentioned, tragedy.

In section 809 of *The Will to Power*, as we saw, Nietzsche describes ugliness as "the contradiction of art." "All art," he claims, "works tonically." But the effect of the ugly is "depressing." In section 802, however, the ugly is, more plausibly, allowed a certain place in art. It is allowed a place because Nietzsche perceives that in certain cases even ugliness can work as "an enhancement of the feeling of life, a stimulant to it." He distinguishes two such cases: ugliness can be a stimulant "insofar as it...communicates something of the artists' victorious energy which has become master of this ugliness and awfulness; or insofar as it mildly excites in us the pleasure of cruelty." In general terms, it may be said that Nietzsche seeks to accommodate tragedy and naturalism to his thesis of the life-affirming character of art by exhibiting tragedy as a case of the former kind of "stimulating" ugliness, naturalism as a case of the latter. I turn first to his discussion of naturalism.

13 How is Zola's ugliness, his portrait of urban squalor and destitution, to be seen as life-affirming? Nietzsche writes: "Art affirms. Job affirms. – But Zola? But the Goncourts? – The things they display are ugly: but *that* they display them comes from their *pleasure in the ugly*" (*WP* 821). Since "the effect of works of art is to excite the state that creates art" (*ibid.*), it follows that, in Nietzsche's view, such pleasure not only produces but is produced by the novels of naturalism.

What is "pleasure in the ugly"? Presumably, it is the same as "the pleasure of cruelty" mentioned in the previous section and the "frenzy of cruelty" which appeared in section 10 as one of the forms of *Rausch* whose sublimation can be art. Nietzsche in his reflections on naturalism is reminding us, as he did in the second essay in the *Genealogy of Morals*, that *Schadenfreude*, the taking of pleasure in the sight of the suffering of others (and even, on occasion, of one's own), is a primal element in human nature. In the old days, he there claims, before men became ashamed of their cruelty, suffering was seen as "an enchantment of the first order, a genuine seduction to life":

With what eyes do you think Homer made his gods look down upon the destinies of men? What was the ultimate meaning of the Trojan Wars and other such tragic errors? There can be no doubt whatever: they were intended as *festival plays* for the gods; and insofar as the poet in these matters was of a more "godlike" disposition than other men, no doubt also as festival plays for the poets. (*GM* II, 7)

Thus Homer and now, Nietzsche claims, Zola too. Zola's joy in creation is the joy of his surrogate satisfaction of the impulse to cause and witness pain. And of such a character, too, is the satisfaction we derive from reading Zola.

14 Is Zola really thus pornographic; a pulp, sex-and-violence novel given a veneer of respectability by the Penguin on the outer cover? This, surely, is a misrepresentation of absurd proportions. (As not infrequently happens, Nietzsche's enthusiasm for a theory has temporarily blinded his normally acute perception of literary reality.) What he has willfully blinded himself to is the fact that Zola, like the Goncourts or Dickens, was a social reformer, a socialist. *His* response to the "ugly" was not – not, at least, *qua* artist – pleasure but outrage (his novels were criticized by Marx and Engels as *too*

overt, too unsubtle, a species of socialist propaganda), and that, of course, is the response he intends to evoke in the reader.

It is instructive to note that Nietzsche not only produces this really quite stupid account of Zola (though he did not, it must be remembered, publish it) but has, at his disposal, a theory of art which fits the case of Zola perfectly. I have in mind here the "signposting" theory of his "positivistic" period (see ch. 3, secs. 14–16), the view of the artist as someone who seeks to help "create the future" by constructing "images of man." In Zola's case, of course, the image possesses not a beauty designed to excite "envy and emulation," but rather an ugliness designed to provoke outrage and the impetus to reform. But that is no reason at all why the signposting theory should not acknowledge and embrace this kind of future-shaping art.

Notice that the signposting theory not only provides a correct account of the art of Zola but also, in an obvious way, exhibits it as *life-affirming*. The naturalist, Nietzsche could point out, by providing a critique of the condition in which life is actually lived (by some) together with an implicit account of the oppressive social structures responsible for this condition commits himself (and us) to the suggestion that life is potentially a wonderful and beautiful phenomenon. The demand is that we remove those structures which prevent this beauty from flourishing.

Why does Nietzsche fail to consider this obvious way of reconciling the art of naturalism with his thesis of the life-affirming character of art? The answer is that to adopt it would be to acknowledge the varieties of socialist art as constituting a legitimate and valuable species. But socialism, Nietzsche considers, is nothing but "the hatred of the ill-constituted, disinherited, and underprivileged who destroy, *must* destroy, because all existence, all being, outrages and provokes them" (*GS* 370). But why *must* this be so? Why *must* socialist talk be mere resentment-driven cant? Why cannot a socialist, a socialist artist, genuinely and constructively believe in the possibility of a "better future"? The answer is that Nietzsche believes once again, as he did in *The Birth of Tragedy*, that suffering is inseparable from life. This is so because life, he holds, is essentially change, becoming, and, like the becoming of child-birth, "all becoming...involves pain" (*TI* x, 4). It follows that though there are various responses, perhaps, which one might usefully make to the pain of existence, the one thing one cannot do is to eliminate or even, it seems, ameliorate that pain by means of social engineering. Schopenhauer claims that the most that can be achieved by social engineering is an alteration in the *form* of suffering (*WR* I, 315): pain is always conserved, its quantum can be neither increased nor diminished. In a similar vein Nietzsche writes that "decadence" is inseparable from life:

> one is in no position to abolish it...It is a disgrace for all socialist systematizers that they suppose there could be circumstances – social combinations – in which vice, disease, prostitution, distress would no longer grow...A society is not free to remain young. And even at the height of its strength it has to form refuse and waste materials...Age is not abolished by institutions. Neither is disease. Nor vices. (*WP* 40)

Therefore, if art, good art, is to be of "service to life" – the one view Nietzsche always holds – it follows that it *cannot* be more or less overt propaganda on behalf of socialist reform. And Zola was a good artist. So let us not be "childish" about this. Zola was a good artist: consequently Zola was no socialist.

15 If life and pain are inseparable and if art is to be of service to life then there exists an obvious motivation for Nietzsche's inclination to insist that good art *must* be a beautification or transfiguration of life, why it must act as a "tonic" or "stimulus," a "stimulant" of, and "seduction" to, life (see *WP* 853). "Truth," says Nietzsche, "is ugly." ("For a philosopher to say, 'the good and the beautiful are one,' is infamous; if he goes on to add 'also the true,' one ought to thrash him. Truth is ugly" [*WP* 822].) That is to say – except for those special cases where the ugly acts as a stimulant – depressing: "The effect of the ugly is depressing: it is the expression of a depression. It takes away strength, it impoverishes, it weighs down" (*WP* 809). "Truth is ugly. We possess *art* lest we *perish of the truth*" (*WP* 822). In other words, art must represent life as beautiful, as affirmable, precisely because life is *not* beautiful. Life truthfully known, it is implied by Nietzsche's demand that art must be an idealization and stimulant, is unaffirmable.

Notice how these observations absorb us, once more, back into the world of *The Birth of Tragedy*. As in *The Birth*, being is again held to be incapable of "correction." Consequently, just as there was no place in *The Birth* for "Socratism," so there is now no place for naturalism, the art of socialist reform. What we need rather is the redemptive power of illusion. What Nietzsche offers us, in short, in his final year, is once again the Apollonian solution to the horror and terror of existence:

The antithesis of a real and apparent world is lacking... there is only *one* world and it is false, cruel, contradictory, seductive without meaning – A world thus constituted is the real world. *We have need of lies* in order to conquer this reality... "Life ought to inspire confidence": the task thus imposed is tremendous. To solve it man must be a liar by nature, he must be above all an *artist*... Art and nothing but art! It is the great means of making life possible, the great seduction to life, the great stimulant of life. (*WP* 853)[11]

16 The second apparent difficulty for the thesis that art affirms life acknowledged by Nietzsche is provided by the case of tragedy. It is, I think, of considerable significance that tragic art, the starting-point of Nietzsche's philosophy but absent from his thought ever since its dismissal as a serious phenomenon in *Human, All-too-human* ("the realm of inescapable, implacable destiny is growing narrower and narrower," a "bad lookout for writers of tragedy" [*HH* I, 108]), reappears at its terminus. (Tragedy does make a brief appearance in *The Gay Science*, but because it suits Nietzsche's theoretical purposes of the moment is represented, quite scandalously *mis*represented, as a species of *Apollonian* art. The Athenian went to the theater, Nietzsche there claims, not to experience strong sentiments but "*in order to hear beautiful speeches. And beautiful speeches were what concerned Sophocles: pardon this heresy!*" [*GS* 580]. Certainly not, one wishes to respond.)

Does the tragic artist's display of the "ugly" "spoil life" for us? There have indeed been philosophers, writes Nietzsche, who thought so:

"liberation from the will" was what Schopenhauer taught as the overall end of art; and with admiration he found the great utility of tragedy in its "evoking resignation." But this... is the pessimist's perspective and "evil eye." We must appeal to the artists themselves. What does the tragic artist communicate of himself? Is it not precisely that state *without* fear in the face of the fearful and questionable that he is showing? This state itself is a great desideratum; whoever knows honours it with the greatest honours. He communicates it – *must* communicate it, provided he is an artist, a genius of communication. Courage and freedom of feeling before a powerful enemy, before a sublime calamity, before a problem that arouses dread – this triumphant state is what the tragic artist chooses, what he glorifies. (*TI* IX, 24)

What is this "courage and freedom of feeling before a powerful enemy" (this "mastery of ugliness and awfulness," as section 802 of *The Will to Power* puts it [see sec. 12 above])? And – a supplementary question we may bear in mind – does it amount to *real* courage? Nietzsche's answer is given in the following passage – a passage he clearly thought highly of since it is quoted, in part, in *Ecce Homo* (*EH* IV, 3):

The psychology of the orgiastic as an overflowing feeling of life and strength, where even pain still has the effect of a stimulus, gave me the key to the concept of *tragic* feeling, which had been misunderstood both by Aristotle and, quite especially, by our modern pessimists. Tragedy is so far from proving anything about the pessimism of the Hellenes, in Schopenhauer's sense, that it may, on the contrary, be considered its decisive repudiation and counter-instance. Saying Yes to life even in its strangest and hardest problems, the will to life rejoicing over its own inexhaustibility even in the very sacrifice of its highest types – *that* is what I called Dionysian, that is what I guessed to be the bridge to the psychology of the *tragic* poet. *Not* in order to be liberated from terror and pity, not in order to purge oneself to a dangerous affect by its vehement discharge – Aristotle understood it that way – but in order to be *oneself* the eternal joy of becoming, beyond all terror and pity – that joy which included even the joy in destroying. And herewith I again touch that point from which I once went forth: *The Birth of Tragedy* was my first reevaluation of all values. Herewith I again stand on the soil out of which my intention, my *ability* grows – I the last disciple of the philosopher Dionysus – I, the teacher, of eternal recurrence. (*TI* X, 5)

The answer here is clear: one experiences "courage and freedom before a powerful enemy," courage in the face of, in other words, the "horror and terror of existence," one is able to "say Yes to life even in its strangest and hardest problems" because, in the experience of tragic art, one shares in the artist's "Dionysian," "orgiastic" transcendence of individuality; one identifies not with any of the individuals who are vulnerable to pain and death but becomes, rather, "oneself the eternal joy of becoming, beyond all terror"; one loses one's identity as an individual and identifies instead with "the will to life rejoicing over *its* own inexhaustibility" (my emphasis). The tragic effect, in short, is, as it was in both *The Birth of Tragedy* and in Schopenhauer's account of tragedy, identified as the feeling of the *sublime*. As in *The Birth*, what tragedy does for life is to bring one the "metaphysical comfort" of feeling oneself to be at one with the "primal unity," or as Nietzsche says, "the will to life." (Notice how as, at the end of his work, his thought returns to its Schopenhauerian starting-point, Schopenhauer's vocabulary starts to replace his own. In *Zarathustra* he had been exercised to reject "will to life" as a fundamental metaphysical concept in favor of his own "will to power." Now Schopenhauer's phrase is preferred to his own.) What, therefore, Nietzsche offers us at the end of his life is once again "the point from which I once went forth" – the Dionysian solution to pessimism (see ch. 2, sec. 13).

17 At the end of the section from *Twilight of the Idols* that we have been discussing, Nietzsche seems to indicate that he perceives some connection between the experience of tragic feeling and willing the eternal recurrence ("I, the last disciple of the philosopher Dionysus, I, the teacher, of eternal recurrence"). The preceding section explains the connection he believes to obtain. Goethe, he claims, excluded the orgiastic from his understanding of the Greek soul:

Consequently Goethe did not understand the Greeks.[12] For it is only in the Dionysian mysteries, in the psychology of the Dionysian state, that the *basic fact* of the Hellenic instinct finds expression – its "will to life." What was it that the Hellene guaranteed himself by means of these mysteries? *Eternal* life, the eternal return of life; the future promised and hallowed in the past; the triumphant Yes to life beyond all death and change: *true* life as the over-all continuation of life through procreation, through the mysteries of sexuality. For the Greeks the *sexual* symbol was the venerable symbol par excellence, the real profundity in the whole ancient piety. Every single element in the act of procreation, of pregnancy, and of birth aroused the highest and most solemn feelings. In the doctrine of the mysteries pain is pronounced holy: the pangs of the woman giving birth hallow all pain: all becoming and growing – all that guarantees a future – involves pain. That there may be the eternal joy of creating, that the will to life may eternally affirm itself, the agony of the woman giving birth *must* also be there eternally.

All this is meant by the word Dionysus: I know no higher symbolism than this *Greek* symbolism of the Dionysian festivals. Here the most profound instinct of life, that diverted towards the future of life, the eternity of life, is experienced religiously – and the way to life, procreation, as the *holy* way. (*TI* x, 4)

This passage suggests, among other things, that to be in the

Dionysian state – *as that is conceived in Twilight of the Idols* – is to will the eternal recurrence. But this is deeply confused – or at the very least confusing.

In *The Gay Science* and in *Zarathustra*, that which – if I am a nonconvalescent, fully healthy, Dionysian *Übermensch* – I will is the eternal recurrence of *my* life: the totality of the deeds and experiences which constitutes my exact life as an individual human being. The fate I love is the fate I experience as an individual *within* the world of becoming and pain. Such love and affirmation, if I achieve it, manifests *genuine* courage, for, as we saw, if I really will the eternal recurrence of my life (rather than some falsified, "profoundly superficial" account of it) then I face the world "honestly": I acknowledge its horrors and terrors, I acknowledge that pain and ultimately death are part of *my* inexorable lot. What, however, Dionysian man as conceived in *Twilight of the Idols* wills to recur is just *life*: he wants "eternal life, the eternal return of [not, notice, *to*] life," "*true* life as the overall continuation of life through procreation, through the mysteries of sexuality." The only sense it makes to speak of him willing his own return is if he identifies himself with a transindividual entity that lives on in his children and in the human species. In his later conception, in short, Dionysian man says "Yes" to life only by identifying with something outside of individual human life: the "will to life" or "eternal becoming." (Compare "The word *Dionysian* means: an urge to unity, a reaching out beyond personality, the everyday, society, reality, across the abyss of transitoriness" [*WP* 1050].) But to affirm life from the point of view of this identification is entirely consistent with the saying of an emphatic "No" to one's life as an individual.

Another way of describing the tremendous difference of outlook between *The Gay Science* and *Twilight of the Idols* that is disguised (disguised, it would seem, from Nietzsche too) by a similarity of phraseology is to observe that in *Twilight* Dionysian man (or man in the Dionysian state) has transformed himself into, in Nietzsche's terminology, a *being*. The problematic character of our life, that is, its terror and horror, is, we have seen, attributed by Nietzsche to the fact that the world we inhabit is a world of "flux," of *becoming*: being subject to change inexorably entails, Nietzsche holds, being vulnerable to pain and death. This is why becoming is the object of our deepest dread, why we yearn above all for a state, a world of being (cf. *GS* 109). In *The Gay Science* Dionysian man is conceived as loving his fate *as* an inhabitant of the realm of becoming. In *Twilight*, however, in the Dionysian state, one escapes becoming by transforming oneself, by becoming "oneself the eternal joy of becoming." Dionysian man, in other words, identifies himself with the whole eternal process of becoming and, as such, achieves immunity to the penalties of being *part* of that flux. He has, in short, become a *being*. Whatever the merits of achieving this state, to do so is not to show the courage that is involved in *facing* one's habitation of the world of becoming. If one conceives oneself as identical with the process of becoming and as such "beyond all death and change" (*TI* x, 4), then one's "freedom of feeling before a powerful enemy, before a sublime calamity" (*TI* ix, 24) does not really constitute "courage" at all. For the "enemy" is not experienced as an enemy. This is what makes the experience "sublime."

18 In *The Gay Science* and in *Zarathustra* Nietzsche made an heroic attempt to affirm (ecstatically – the only kind of affirmation he acknowledges) his habitation of the human world, the world of human individuality: in the language of *The Birth of Tragedy* the world of the *principium individuationis*. But in the end he failed. Though *Zarathustra* ends on a note of optimism (the appearance of the laughing lion at its end symbolizes Zarathustra's proximity to the child state, the final metamorphosis into *Übermenschlichkeit*, and with Zarathustra Nietzsche *sometimes* felt himself to be identical), by the time he came to write the preface to *The Gay Science* he could see no solution to the pain of existence other than profound super-ficiality. Here, profound superficiality is not a merely temporary solution for those *en route* to the health of *Übermenschlichkeit* but rather *the* solution for human beings.

   In the final months of his thought about art and its relation to life Nietzsche offers us a *choice* of solutions: on the one hand, we are offered the redemptive power of Apollonian illusion – profound superficiality, in other words; on the other, the redemptive power of Dionysian sublimity. But the latter too is, as he points out in *The Birth* (*BT* 18), a species of illusion, an evasion of the actuality of our human existence. What we are offered, therefore, is a choice between two forms of dishonesty: human life is to be made bearable either by telling ourselves beautiful lies about it or else by pretending to belong to an order of being other than that of human individuality. The implication of this is clear: life, real life, is unaffirmable. The

wisdom of Silenus is true. We possess art, whether Apollonian or
Dionysian, lest we perish of this truth. In the end, therefore,
Nietzsche ends up with a view of the human condition indis-
tinguishable from that expressed in *The Birth of Tragedy*. And, despite
his many protestations of the antipodean character of their
philosophies, it is a view as afflicted as is that of Schopenhauer.

19 A third kind of art, the existence of which Nietzsche recognizes
as being in *prima facie* conflict with his thesis that all (good) art
affirms life, is, as he calls it, "romantic" art. Here he employs a new
strategy. With respect to naturalism and tragedy the thesis was
defended *via* the demonstration that, contrary to appearances, both
the naturalist and the tragedian really do affirm life. With regard to
romanticism, however, the strategy is to deny that it constitutes good
art: romantic art is bad, "decadent" (*CW*, Epilogue; *EH* II, 5) art.
    What, to repeat Nietzsche's own question (*GS* 370), is ro-
manticism? First, some of Nietzsche's examples: Wagner (particularly the Wagner of the post-*Tristan* period, above all the
Wagner of *Parsifal* [*GS* 370; *CW passim*]), Schopenhauer considered
as art (*GS* 370), Brahms, Goldmark (*CW* Second Postscript),
Delacroix, Berlioz, Baudelaire (*EH* II, 5). And, more startlingly,
Ingres (*WP* 105), authentically Christian art (*GS* 370; *TI* IX, 9), *all*
music since the Renaissance (*WP* 842).
    What is it that links these examples together? Romanticism, says
Nietzsche, is the product of alienation: it is the art of "homesickness"
(*WP* 419), art which "looks away, looks back from... [the artist's]
self and from his world" ("yearning" is all that is distinctive of
Brahms [*CW*, Second Postscript]), art which longs for "rest, stillness,
calm seas, redemption from... self" (*GS* 370), such longing being the
product of a "great dissatisfaction" (*WP* 844) with, a hatred for,
vengefulness against (*NCW*, "We Antipodes") one's self and one's
world. This art of "dissatisfaction with reality" has as its antipode
the "art of apotheosis," art which expresses "gratitude for happiness
enjoyed," the art of Homer, Hafiz, Rubens, and Raphael (when we
realize that his Christian iconography is a mere vehicle for the
expression of a quite un-Christian stance towards life) (*WP* 845; *GS*
370).
    At a deeper level of analysis, romantic art is art which springs from
"hunger" rather than "superabundance," "impoverishment"
rather than "over-fullness of life" (*GS* 370). This is the psychic

condition which underlies life-hatred. As we saw in chapter 4 (sec. 19), the person of impoverished psychic energy is someone who is dissatisfied with, afraid of, life. Such a person fears, in particular, the future. ("But those spirits of a classical and those of a romantic bent – these two species exist at all times – entertain a vision of the future: but the former do so out of a *strength* of their age, the latter out of its *weakness*" [*HH* IIb, 217].) Hating and being afraid of life, the sick, romantic personality seeks simultaneous compensation for and revenge against it by making some other world into the focus of everything good, a world that may be located either in a metaphysical, transcendent domain or in the distant past (*WP* 419).

20 Thus far, Nietzsche's criterion of romanticism in art appears to be psychological: romanticism is alienation from the given, the actual; yearning for, affirmation of, that which is not. Thought of in this way, the romantic has as her antipodes the person who is psychologically assimilated to, "at home" in, the actual.

The situation is complicated, however, by the fact that Nietzsche also employs a second criterion of romanticism, a criterion that is not psychological but rather formal or stylistic. According to this, romanticism is understood as the antithesis not of anything like assimilation to the actual but of, rather, *classicism* (or "the grand style" [*WP* 842]), where the latter is understood – very much as it was during Nietzsche's "positivistic" period – in terms of such expressions as "logical, simple, unambiguous, mathematics, *law*," the will to "master chaos," to compel "chaos to become form" (*WP* 842), "coldness, lucidity, hardness... hatred for feeling, heart, *esprit*, hatred for the manifold, uncertain, rambling, contempt for detail" (*WP* 849). Classicism, in other words, is conceived in Nietzsche's final period, as it was in the "positivistic" phase (see ch. 3, secs. 17–20), as the dominance of balanced and harmonious form over feeling and romanticism as the opposite, the dominance of form by feeling; romanticism values "passion, meaning disorder and immoderation, 'depth' meaning confusion, the profuse chaos of symbols" (*WP* 79) as Nietzsche unsympathetically puts it.

21 Since Nietzsche would not (presumably) *willingly* introduce an ambiguity into his concept of romanticism it must be supposed that he takes his two criteria of romanticism to be equivalent: that all and only those art-works which count as romantic according to the

psychological criterion count also as romantic according to the stylistic criterion. That Nietzsche does assume their equivalence manifests itself, I think, in a persistent tendency in his last, as in the "positivistic," period to equate good art with classical art. (If romantic art is bad, life-denying art then, according to the psychological criterion, good art is nonromantic, that is, according to the formal criterion, classical art.) In *The Case of Wagner*, for example, he writes that every age extols the values either of "ascending" or "declining" life: "Aesthetics is tied indissolubly to these biological presuppositions: there is an aesthetics of *decadence* and a *classical* aesthetics" (*CW*, Epilogue).

The trouble with this equation is not merely that it looks to be mere prejudice and bigotry dressed up as a philosophical thesis (a thesis which is obviously false), but also that it is inconsistent with many of the judgments Nietzsche himself wants to make about individual artists. The matter comes to a head in his attitude towards Rubens, whom he admires as a paradigm of the "art of apotheosis" (*WP* 846, 847). While Rubens evidently is such a paradigm, it is also evidently the case that his lusciously turbulent forms are very far removed from the classical ideal, something like the antithesis of Winckelmann's ideal of the containment of turbulence of feeling within an overall reposefulness of form (see ch. 3, sec. 17).[13] This is why, art-historically, Rubens is of course classified as an exponent, not of the classical but of the baroque. Evidently, then, some nonclassical art is life-affirming and therefore, in Nietzsche's own terms, good art. And conversely: one only has to call to mind Victorian or postmodernist neoclassicism in architecture to see that classical forms may easily express a retreat from the actual, a (psychologically) romantic yearning for a bygone "golden age." An intimation of this may be connected with Nietzsche's classification of Ingres – formally speaking a neoclassicist – as a romantic (*WP* 105).

In view of these difficulties section 370 of *The Gay Science* is a crucial passage. What Nietzsche says there in answer to the question "what is romanticism?" is that although it may at first sight seem appropriate to answer in terms of a distinction between "the desire to fix, to immortalize, the desire for being" – i.e. the ideal of classical form – on the one hand, and "the desire for *destruction*, change and becoming" on the other, these desires are actually ambiguous in that each may be prompted by *either* love or hatred of life. Therefore, says Nietzsche, the "main distinction" is to be made not in terms of a dichotomy between the ideal of classical order and the denial of that ideal but in terms, rather, of the question: "Is it hunger [i.e. 'impoverishment of life,' of energy] or superabundance that has here become creative?" What this amounts to is the affirmation that the psychological conception of romanticism is fundamental, that romantic alienation may find expression in anticlassical but also in classical forms, and, conversely, that the spirit of life-affirmation may inhabit any form. Classicism, conceived in terms of form, disappears as the antithesis of romanticism.

But why then, having seen this as early as 1885–6 (the crucial part of section 370 of *The Gay Science* is identical with section 846 of *The Will to Power*, which was written then) does he still persist in opposing romanticism to classicism in the way we have seen him do – "there is an aesthetics of *decadence* and a classical aesthetics" – in his final year?

The answer, I think, lies in a view Nietzsche sometimes seduces himself into, the view that *nearly* all European art that is life-affirming comes from the classical or Renaissance period in European history and *nearly* all art that does not (e.g. the medieval art of "genuine Christianity") is life-denying. In line with this school-boyish thesis – a thesis which manifests Nietzsche's disposition to a simple-minded dichotomy of historical periods into pagan (life-affirming, good) and Christian (life-denying, bad) – the classical–romantic dichotomy comes to be used in a *third* way: neither psychological nor stylistic but rather *historical*. According to the thesis, "life-affirming art is classical" is true in the sense that if an artwork is life-affirming then it exemplifies that stance towards life which was, paradigmatically, exemplified during the classical period. And, correspondingly, "life-denying art is romantic" is held to be true in the sense that life-denial is paradigmatically exemplified in the art of nonclassical periods. This is the use of the classical–romantic antithesis which finds expression in, for example, section 842 of *The Will to Power*: observing that modern European music "began to blossom only when the renaissance world had already attained its evening" Nietzsche draws the (absurd) conclusion that all "modern," post-Renaissance music is "romanticism," that is, "decadence."

Not only is the view of art history manifestly absurd, it is also, in Nietzsche's own (psychological) sense, *romantic*. (In one early [1885] passage Nietzsche virtually confesses his own romanticism:

German philosophy as a whole – Leibniz, Kant, Hegel, Schopenhauer to name the greatest – is the most fundamental form of *romanticism* and homesickness there has ever been: the longing for the best that has ever existed. One is no longer at home anywhere; at last one longs back for that place in which alone one can be at home, because it is the only place in which one would want to be at home: the *Greek* world. [*WP* 419]

Notice that the confessional use of the pronoun in this passage has the effect of adding Nietzsche's own name to the roll-call of German greats.) By the time of *The Gay Science* Nietzsche realizes that he himself is vulnerable to the charge of psychological romanticism and warns himself to guard against it: the higher type, he says, must overcome his time, its thoughts and values, but "not only his time but also his prior aversion and contradiction *against* this time, his suffering from this time, his untimeliness, his *romanticism*" (*GS* 380).

Comparisons between present and past, to the detriment of the former do not, of course, necessarily constitute romanticism. For the romantic is alienated not from the *present* but from *life*, from its present *and future*. Hellenism, therefore, the idealization of classical antiquity, *can* constitute a nonromantic stance: it does so if the way back is genuinely conceived as the way forward. Nietzsche often likes to portray himself as a constructive Hellenist of this kind. But at the end this is not part of his philosophy. He is ultimately and fundamentally, as I shall shortly emphasize, himself a romantic – as he confesses on occasion, a "decadent."

22 In the previous section I noted some of the confusions contained in Nietzsche's conception of romanticism. What is clear, however, is that the important conception is the psychological one: romantic art is art which is alienated from the actual and yearns for or affirms a "better world" located either nostalgically in the past or else in a realm "beyond space and time." The attempt to view classicism conceived either stylistically or historically as the antithesis of romanticism in this sense is simply a mistake.

The reason that the psychological conception is, from Nietzsche's perspective, fundamental is that it is only as thus conceived that the phenomenon of romanticism comes into even apparent conflict with the thesis of the life-affirming character of (good) art. Only, that is, insofar as certain kinds of art appear to "negate" this world do they call for a response from the standpoint of Nietzsche's central thesis. Only as such is Nietzsche required to reject romanticism as bad art.

Is it true that romantic art (I shall use the term exclusively in Nietzsche's psychological sense from now on) is bad art? Is it true that art in which "hunger," "impoverishment" of, alienation from, life "has become creative" (*GS* 370) is bad art? Eric Heller accuses Nietzsche of the genetic fallacy. In the most poetic of ways: "psychology... cannot *establish* the worth or unworth, the beauty or ugliness, the truth or untruth of what has grown from roots sunk deeply into the psyche as little as botany or soil analysis or meteorology or geology can prove or disprove the justification of the sense of autumnal glory one may have in the sight of a yellowing birch tree before one's window or of the play of sunlight on the rugged faces of the mountains that rise beyond it."[14] But this, I think, is a mistake. What Heller has overlooked is Nietzsche's axiom, as I have called it, that "the effect of works of art is to excite the state that creates art" (see sec. 4 above).

Nietzsche, that is, so it seems to me, is concerned, centrally, not with the causes but rather the *effects* of art. His whole conception of the good and bad in art is focused on the question of effects: the good is conceived as that which *stimulates*, acts as a *tonic* ("Bizet makes me fertile," "a better human being." "Whatever is good makes me fertile. I have no other gratitude, nor do I have any other *proof* for what is good" [*CW* 1]) and the bad, the ugly, is excluded from art because, remember, it *depresses*.

He is interested in causes only because, given his axiom, it is a way of being interested in effects. His real argument against romanticism, that is, has the following structure. Art excites the same kind of state as that which produces it. Hence art created out of "sick," "impoverished," life-alienated states causes and reinforces similar states in the audience. But good art is art which promotes health, is "the great stimulus to life" (*TI* IX, 24). Conversely, art which is harmful to health, is detrimental to our being-in-the-world, is bad art. Hence art created out of sick, alienated states, romanticism, is bad art.

23 It is possible to register doubts concerning the Nietzschean axiom. For there is a quite familiar discrepancy between the psychology of the artist and the character of his art effectively exploited in, for example, Peter Schaffer's *Amadeus*. The most glorious, life-deifying art may well spring from and compensate for the existence of a crippled, life-suffering personality. This, indeed, is

surely Nietzsche's own account of the impulse to Apollonian art: the dream of Apollonianism stands to reality as the beautiful vision of the tortured martyr to his suffering (*BT* 3).

Nonetheless, if we think of romanticism as defined in terms of the effects Nietzsche associates with it, then his criticism of the genre (as distinct from his views on which particular artists belong to it) seems well taken. If it really is true of a certain kind of art that, as Nietzsche claims of Wagner's music, it "corrupts our health" (*CW* 5), then it seems very hard to dissent from the view that it is bad art. Art which is bad for us is bad art.

The question remains, however, as to whether *Nietzsche* is entitled to raise this criticism against any artist. In the "positivistic" period he criticized other-worldliness, whether in the form of religion or art (in effect, romanticism), as a "narcoticizing" of our sensitivity to the pains of existence. The characterization of romanticism that we have looked at in this chapter is similar. Romanticism, he says, caters to "those who suffer from *impoverishment of life* and seek rest, stillness, calm seas, redemption from themselves through art...intoxication, convulsions, anaesthesia and madness" (*GS* 320).

What, however, it may be asked, is so wrong about satisfying, and thereby reinforcing, this impulse? In *Human, All-too-human* the objection was that to desensitize us to the pains of existence is to diminish our will to eliminate their causes. Romanticism, in short, damages our mode of inhabiting the world because it prevents us from *doing* something about that in the world which troubles us. In a different way the same objection lies behind the animus against romanticism expressed in the period of *The Gay Science* and *Zarathustra*. The proper response to the questionable and painful existence is not (so Nietzsche is prepared to say at least some of the time) its evasions but rather the creation of a self in which the past is redeemed and the willing of the eternal recurrence, an "honest" *amor fati* replaces self-dislike and resentment, alienation from one's self and world. In *The Gay Science* – at least for the *übermenschlich* – as in *Human, All-too-human*, there is something to be *done* about one's alienation from the world (though, of course, a very different kind of doing is proposed in the two works).

But in the last period there is nothing to be done. Precisely what Nietzsche *himself* offers is "redemption" from world and self, through either Apollonian "superficiality" or else through Dionysian illusion. Given that these are the alternatives, Nietzsche's objection to romanticism – that it reinforces rather than combats alienation – amounts to no more than a baseless preference for one form (more exactly, two) of escapist inauthenticity over another. In the Preface to *The Case of Wagner* Nietzsche describes himself as "no less than Wagner, a child of this time; that is a decadent." Or in other words, a *romantic*. He was right. Romantics, he says, are those who seek refuge from themselves in "intoxication, convulsions, anaesthesia and madness" (*GS* 370). In his last works he sought refuge in intoxication. He was shortly to find it in madness.

Epilogue

1   In the foregoing chapters we have followed the curve described by Nietzsche's philosophy of art. We have followed it from its Schopenhauerian beginnings in *The Birth of Tragedy*, through the science-affirming anti-artism of *Human, All-too-human*. We saw how, during the period of *The Gay Science* and *Zarathustra*, Nietzsche's scientism evaporates, leading to a renewed sense of the importance of art, of viewing life aesthetically. And we saw how, during this period, he attempts, or at least contemplates the possibility of, an "honest" confrontation with and acceptance of the reality of one's existence as an individual human being. But we saw in the last chapter how, in the end, Nietzsche returns to the inauthenticity, the illusionism of "that point from which I once went forth: *The Birth of Tragedy*" (*TI* x, 5). As in *The Birth* we are again offered a choice between the Apollonian and Dionysian solutions to the pain of existence. Nietzsche's identification with Dionysus – "Have I been understood? – *Dionysus versus the crucified*" is how his last book, *Ecce Homo*, ends – makes it plain that his ultimate preference remains for the Dionysian. But both, I have argued, constitute modes of illusion. The implication of this (whether Nietzsche allowed himself to see the implication is another matter) is that pessimism, the wisdom of Silenus, is regarded, ultimately, as true. Real life, the life of human individuality, is something it would be better we had never been born into. To the extent, therefore, that its main aim is to be the "antipode" to Schopenhauerianism, to "affirm life," Nietzsche's philosophy ends in failure.

2   How, exactly then, does Nietzsche's final philosophy stand in relation to Schopenhauer? Clearly, if my account has been correct, their assessments of the worth of human existence do not, in the end, diverge: though Schopenhauer takes vengeful relish in *emphasizing*

his pessimism while Nietzsche fights to avoid it, or at least to disguise its truth from both himself and others, the truth about human existence is, in the end, as "ugly" for Nietzsche as it is for Schopenhauer.

With regard, however, to their responses, their solutions to pessimism, the two philosophers do diverge. Nietzsche's Apollonian solution, first of all, the idea of "overcoming" Silenus' truth through the redemptive power of the beautiful illusion, is something of which there is no hint in Schopenhauer's philosophy. In a way, this is strange since no philosopher has emphasized more than Schopenhauer the role of illusion in human life. We have already observed his emphasis upon the idea that our conception of the outer world is constructed in the interests of the practical will rather than those of truth (ch. 1, secs. 1 and 6). And when it comes to the inner world, Schopenhauer again is deeply alive to the role of illusion, of repression and self-deception, in the *normal* functioning of the human psyche. Ignoble motives and desires, he says (in a passage acknowledged by Freud to anticipate his central postulations of repression and the unconscious), we quite typically deny admission to "clear consciousness" since "the good opinion we have of ourselves would inevitably suffer." In their place we substitute fictions, as we do, too, with respect to the gaps created in memory by the repression of past experiences too painful to be acknowledged (*WR* II, pp. 209–10, 399–402; *WR* I, pp. 192, 296).

But while *recording* the role of illusion in human life with unprecedented thoroughness, Schopenhauer's stance towards it is always Platonic – contemptuous. The cause of this is his philosopher's morality, his care for truth – the fact that, as Nietzsche would put it, possessing an "unconditional will to truth" he is "still pious" (*GS* 344). This prevents him from entertaining the distinctively Nietzschean idea that illusion, "art," is "'more divine' than truth," prevents him making the inference that since "we have need of lies in order to live," well then, let there then be lies (*WP* 853).

Nietzsche's Dionysian solution, too, is something not offered to us by Schopenhauer. Not that he did not, in effect, consider it. "Only small, trivial minds," he writes, "fear death as annihilation" (*WR* II, p. 475). And he speaks of the fact that the species survives the destruction of the individual as "nature's great doctrine of immortality" (*WR* II, p. 475), her intuitive proof of the "indestructibility of our inner nature" by death (*WR* II, p. 463). If, that is,

Schopenhauer suggests, one identifies oneself not with the suffering and mortal individual but with the metaphysical will-to-live, then "he would willingly give up his individuality, smile at the tenacity of his attachment thereto, and say: what does the loss [or pain] of this individuality matter to me? for I carry within myself the possibility of innumerable individualities" (*WR* II, 491). The idea that we can escape the horror and terror of individual existence by achieving a state of sublimity, a sense of a supraphenomenal existence, is strongly present in Schopenhauer. Such a state is indeed *achieved* by the Schopenhauerian altruist: she escapes the anxious care for the individual self by identifying with the will that manifests itself in all individuals (see ch. 1, sec. 5).

What takes Schopenhauer, however, beyond this position is once again morality. The "transition from virtue [altruism] to asceticism" (see ch. 1, sec. 5) is brought about by the altruist's coming to share in Schopenhauer's moral revulsion against the will which, as the ground of the world's sufferings, comes to be perceived as evil. Schopenhauer, because he is unable to adopt the Nietzschean stance beyond good and evil, looks, ultimately, for redemption in identification not with the will but with some still more fundamental entity "beyond the will."

What sets Schopenhauer apart from both Nietzsche's solutions (and what, one might well feel, makes him ultimately a more human, more attractive figure) is his morality. On the other hand, what is common to both Schopenhauer and Nietzsche is romanticism, "romantic pessimism" (*GS* 370). Both Schopenhauer and, at the end, Nietzsche, is caused by his "great dissatisfaction" with life, to "look away...from himself and from his world" (*WP* 844), to yearn for some better mode of being.

3 I have suggested that Nietzsche's philosophy of art, in the end, returns to its starting point and hence describes a circle. It may be felt, however, that this foisting of a circular philosophy upon the philosopher of the circle is altogether too neat. In particular, it might be suggested, in seeking to turn Nietzsche's career into a neatly aesthetic phenomenon I have suppressed an important element of that career; for what I have done is pretend that Nietzsche's work ends with *Twilight of the Idols*, whereas it in fact ends (discounting compilations from earlier works) with the philosophical autobiography, *Ecce Homo*. And what one finds here, it might be said, is

not just that Nietzsche *claims* his "inmost nature" to be *amor fati* (*EH* XII, 4), but also that the work "exemplifies this attitude" towards his whole life,[1] viewing it "under the aspect of *amor fati* and thus [coming] to affirm it in every part."[2] Hence, it might be suggested, Nietzsche's work ends not in failure, nor with a Schopenhauerian whimper, but rather with a triumphant and uniquely Nietzschean bang; the achievement of that *Übermenschlichkeit*, the willing of the eternal recurrence, described but not yet attained in *The Gay Science* and in *Zarathustra*.

4 Actually, however, *Ecce Homo* is not an exercise in *amor fati* at all, but rather (though it contains occasional passages as fine as anything Nietzsche wrote) a sad, self-deluding and self-contradicting exercise in its *parody*, "profound superficiality." A few examples: Nietzsche's entirely fictitious claim to Polish ancestry (*EH* I, 3), the point of which is to leave him free to abuse all things German; the claim that only one person ever bore him ill-will (*EH* I, 4); the claim never to have experienced resentment (*EH* I, 5); the claim never to have experienced religious difficulties and consequently to have no sense of sin (*EH* II, 1); the claim that "a trait of fanaticism will be sought in vain in my nature. At no moment in my life can I be shown to have adopted any kind of arrogant or pathetic posture" (*EH* II, 10); the self-deifying megalomania (arrogance) of the chapter headings "Why I am so wise," "so clever," and so on, and of "wherever I go, here in Turin for example, every face grows more cheerful and benevolent at the sight of me. Old market-women take great pains to select together for me the sweetest of their grapes" (*EH* III, 2); the claim that only *The Birth of Tragedy* made Wagner a symbol of cultural hope (*EH* IV, 1); the claim that neither Goethe, Shakespeare, nor Dante could have "for a moment known how to breathe in the tremendous passion" of *Zarathustra*; and the claim that the Vedantic poets are "not even worthy to unloose the latchet of the shoes of a Zarathustra" (*EH* IX, 6). Most striking of all, perhaps, is the following sentence, suppressed by Nietzsche's sister and rediscovered only in 1969 by M. Montinari, editor of the new edition of his works: "when I look for the deepest contrast to myself, the unimaginable baseness of instinct, I find always my mother and sister – to think of myself as related to such baseness would be a blasphemy against my godliness" (*KG* VI, 3, p. 266; my translation). These and the many other examples of megalomaniacal delusion in

Ecce Homo reveal how far removed is the work from that "honest" confrontation with reality which is the *sine qua non* of genuine *amor fati*. It needs to be said, too, that their character is continuous with that of the delusions experienced by Nietzsche after his explicit mental collapse, the general theme of many of which is belief in his own divinity. "I would much rather be a Basle professor than God," he wrote to Jacob Burckhardt, "but I have not dared to push my private egoism so far as to desist for its sake from the creation of the world." Other remarks concern the taking over of political authority in Europe – hence the "authority" behind the well-known remark, "I am just now having all anti-Semites shot" – the assumption of divine authority – "the old God has abdicated, I shall soon be ruling the world" – and the absence of coincidence: "there are no coincidences any more. I think of someone and immediately a letter comes politely through the door." It is reported that in the sanatorium to which Nietzsche was confined he apologized for the poor weather promising, however, to "prepare the loveliest weather tomorrow."

In *Ecce Homo*, in short, that which is affirmed is not at all Nietzsche's *life* but rather a fiction, a profoundly superficial substitute for it. The work represents yet another excursion into the beauties of Apollonian illusion, an excursion which, this time, borders on madness. Nietzsche's work in no way ends in *übermenschlich* triumph but with, rather, yet another manifestation of the afflictedness that links him to Schopenhauer and takes him, finally, to madness.

Notes

INTRODUCTION

1 Bernd Magnus "Nietzsche's philosophy in 1888: *The Will to Power* and the '*Übermensch*,'" *Journal of the History of Philosophy* 24 (January 1986), pp. 79–99.

1 SCHOPENHAUER

1 I have discussed Schopenhauer's biological route to idealism in detail in chapter 1, section 3, of my book *Willing and Unwilling: a Study in the Philosophy of Arthur Schopenhauer* (Dordrecht: Nijhoff, 1987).

2 In *Willing and Unwilling* (see especially ch. III) I have argued that Schopenhauer is most coherently read as not so much abandoning Kant's dualism between an ideal nature and a non-natural thing in itself but as, rather, dividing up the natural side of the duality into (1) the world as conceived in the common-sense image and (2) the world as conceived in an image constructed out of philosophical reflection upon the foundations of natural science. The result is a *tri*partite structure composed of the common-sense world, a deeper world of "will", and the non-natural world in itself: the second, though often *called* the thing in itself is, I suggest, ultimately distinct from it. Nietzsche, however, most often reads Schopenhauer as implicitly naturalizing the Kantian thing in itself, as offering a dichotomy between the ideal world of common sense and an *an sich* that is to be conceived in terms of the equivalent notions of "force," energy, or "will." In what follows, I shall present Schopenhauer in Nietzsche's rather than my own way.

3 Schopenhauer's argument for this (see ch. 4, sec. 2) is, in a nutshell, that since (1) the most ultimate entities posited by any scientific theory must possess causal powers in order to have explanatory value and (2) atomism is committed to grounding any power or disposition in atomic structure, it follows that the atomistic view is infinitely regressive, that it can never consistently claim to possess an account of ultimate reality. In chapter IV, section 3, of *Willing and Unwilling* I have shown that Schopenhauer's dynamism places him in a tradition that goes back via Kant to Joseph Priestley and ultimately to the eighteenth-century Jesuit

mathematician and physicist Roger Boscovich. Nietzsche too, in his Heraclitean affirmation of "becoming" over "being" – his well-known rejection of all permanencies, "things" or "substances," as "errors" and "lies" – belong to this same tradition. He explicitly acknowledges a debt to Boscovich: "Boscovich," he writes in section 12 of *Beyond Good and Evil*, "has taught us to abjure the belief in 'substance,' in 'matter,' in the earth residuum [material seat of a causal power] and particle atom."

4 Nietzsche, too, in his unpublished notes makes the same move: "A force," he writes, "we cannot imagine is an empty word and should be allowed no rights of citizenship in science" (*WP* 621). And again: "The victorious concept 'force' by means of which our physicists have created God and the world, still needs to be completed: an inner will must be assigned to it which I designate as 'will to power'" (*WP* 619).

5 This conception is not Schopenhauer's only, or his most prominent road to the contrast. But I am, as I have said, presenting him in the way in which Nietzsche took him.

6 Schopenhauer, in short, is not an *absolute* pessimist, not a nihilist, not one who holds, in Nietzsche's characterization of the view, that "there is only *one* world, and this is false, cruel, contradictory, ... without meaning" (*WP* 853). So at least I have argued in *Willing and Unwilling* (see especially, chs. III and IX). My argument essentially presupposes my *tri*partite reading of Schopenhauer's metaphysics (see n. 2 above). On a bipartite reading, where the will is evil, suffering, but also ultimately real, there can be no salvation from suffering save in the (dubiously possible) hope for absolute extinction or nothingness. That Schopenhauer is generally read in the bipartite way explains why he is generally read as a nihilist; but not, at least not always, by Nietzsche. He was at times aware (though not approving) of the mystical turn taken by Schopenhauer's philosophy at its end (see *GS* 99).

7 In section 5 above I suggested that Schopenhauer is genuinely committed to a domain, a locus of salvation, beyond suffering nature, beyond the will and is therefore not a nihilist. Notice how this account of tragedy together with Schopenhauer's general cognitivism about art confirms this suggestion.

8 Susanne K. Langer, *Feeling and Form* (London: Routledge and Kegan Paul, 1953).

9 This is not to deny that there may be problems *within* opera, the raising of difficult questions of priority as musical and dramatic desiderata come into conflict. But that is entirely different from the problem *of* opera, the question of its very right to exist as an art-form. That problems occur *in* a marriage does not entail that it should never have taken place.

2 *THE BIRTH OF TRAGEDY*

1 Another reasonably influential minimizer of the Schopenhauerian influence is Richard Schacht: see *Nietzsche* (London: Routledge and Kegan Paul, 1983), ch. VIII *passim*.

2 *Nietzsche: Philosopher, Psychologist, Antichrist*, 4th edn. (Princeton, N.J.: Princeton University Press 1974), p. 131; see also *Tragedy and Philosophy* (New York: Doubleday Anchor, 1969), ch. IX, sec. 58; also his Introduction to his translation of *The Birth* and various footnotes, especially p. 59, n. 3.

3 See M. S. Silk and J. P. Stern, *Nietzsche on Tragedy* (Cambridge: Cambridge University Press, 1981), ch. 5.

4 Nietzsche holds that to "feel profoundly the weight and burden of existence" is a mark of "the more nobly formed natures" (*BT* 18). For them, "cheerfulness," if possessed at all, is an achievement, a victory. "Vulgar" (*ibid.*) people and cultures may, for a time, at least, be cheerful too, but only because they lack the profundity to experience the challenge to cheerfulness. (Nietzsche is full of contempt for easy cheerfulness, for, in particular, the "senile and unproductive love of existence" (*BT* 17) which he sees as characterizing the Alexandrian, decaying stage of Greek civilization.) The "we" to whom *The Birth* is addressed are – Nietzsche flatters us – these nobler natures.

5 How does consciousness make the transition from the metaphysically Apollonian to the aesthetic? I do not believe Nietzsche ever satisfactorily answered this question until right at the end of his thought about art in *Twilight of the Idols*. There, his answer is given in terms of *Rausch*, intoxication (see ch. 5, sec. 7 below). But in *The Birth* this is an answer he is precluded from giving by the fact that, as we are about to see, *Rausch* is associated exclusively with the Dionysian.

6 Kaufmann's translation of "*Schein*" in this passage as not "appearance" but "illusion" has been aptly criticized by Charles Sen Taylor, in "Nietzsche's Schopenhauerianism," *Nietzsche-Studien* 17 (1988), pp. 45–73. In my view the same mistranslation of *Schein* occurs (twice) in the second paragraph on p. 50 of his translation.

7 Notice that Nietzsche never abandoned this view. That central theme of his later philosophy that "things," temporally persistent substances, are "errors" or "lies" (see, for example, the beginning of book III of *The Gay Science*) merely repeats in non-Schopenhauerian language the thesis of the merely apparent status of the world of the *principium individuationis*.

8 A feature brilliantly exemplified in the dream sequence of Woody Allen's *Another Woman*.

9 The suggestion that dreaming is always pleasurable runs into the problem of nightmares. Nietzsche must have been, as it is called, a "lucid dreamer," as indeed he indicates – "even when dream reality is most intense we still have, shimmering through it, the sensation that it is *mere* appearance" (*BT* 1) – to have been able to take pleasure in

nightmares: "perhaps many will, like myself, recall how amid the dangers and terrors of dreams they have said to themselves in self-encouragement and not without success: 'It is a dream! I will dream on'" (*BT* 1). Many people, for example Descartes, are not lucid dreamers. It is important for our attempt to understand the Apollonian solution to pessimism (secs. 11–12 below) to remember that it is the *lucid* dream, the dream one, as it were, spectates rather than lives, to which aesthetically Apollonian consciousness is compared.

10 Notice here the early appearance of a theme much in evidence in Nietzsche's later philosophy. Living well – which implies at least living a *civilized* life – depends, we have seen, upon the existence of the "laws" and "barriers" erected between one individual and another by the (metaphysically) Apollonian mind. These are to preserve us from the crudities and cruelties of *barbaric* Dionysianism. But these barbaric impulses are not to be *eradicated* (as Christianity would like) but rather *sublimated* or, as Nietzsche puts it, "spiritualized," transmuted into, for example, art. "Evil," the later Nietzsche insists, is something we need, is inseparable from "greatness."

11 The quotations, from Wagner's *Opera and Drama* are given in Carl Dahlhaus' fine essay "The two-fold truth in Wagner's aesthetics," the second essay in his book *Between Romanticism and Modernism*, tr. M. Whittall (Berkeley: University of California Press, 1980). Notice the harmony between the musical theory of the younger Wagner and the opera-friendly version of Schopenhauer's theory.

12 There is a temptation to insist that since music cannot be formless content, the Apollonian must be present even in absolute music. There are two comments to be made here. First, that which is demanded by form is a contribution from, as I have called it, the *metaphysically* Apollonian mind, the ordering, organizing "rational" mind which gives us the world of the *principium individuationis*. The birth-of-tragedy thesis, however, holds that great art must contain, as a component, Apollonian *art*, must, that is, be in part a product of the *aesthetically* Apollonian mind. Second, during the period of *The Birth* Nietzsche did *not* admit the claim that music must possess form, taking as paradigms of musical "composition" the rhapsodic emissions of the Dionysian reveler and the conceptually unintelligible choral hymns to Dionysus that punctuate Greek tragedy. Later, Nietzsche saw that art must communicate and that communication demands (conventionally understood) form (see ch. 3, sec. 24); but communication is *not* demanded of music in his early period. In the unpublished fragment "On music and words" reproduced in a Kaufmann translation in Dahlhaus' book (see n. 11 above) he writes, in a discussion of song, that

the individual who is in a state of Dionysian excitement has no *listeners* to whom he has anything to communicate any more than does an orgiastic crowd, [though] ... the epic narrator and, more generally, the Apollonian artist, does presuppose such a listener. It is of the essence of Dionysian art it does not know any consideration for a listener; the enthusiastic servant of Dionysus is understood only by his peers. (p. 114)

13 Nietzsche is, of course, the famous philosopher of the circle. But Schopenhauer preceded him in the use of the circle as an image for time (see *WR* I, pp. 380, 280).

14 The borrowing of his paradoxical conjunction from *The Gay Science* (Preface, 4) is apposite here for it captures Nietzsche's insistence in *The Birth* that the "cheerfulness" of the Greeks was the *solution to a problem*, was *achieved* in the face of a deep sensitivity to the horrors of life and was not, as the dominant nineteenth-century conception had it, due to a blithe ignorance of such horrors (see n. 4 above).

15 This extraordinary evocation of musical experience might be seen as constituting an answer to the criticism made in section 9 above that Nietzsche seems mistaken in demanding an Apollonian aspect of all great art given the undeniable greatness of many works of purely instrumental music. As an answer, however, this would only be effective were we really willing to grant to absolute music the power to threaten permanent psychological dislocation.

16 This is the reason that the famous assertion that only as aesthetic phenomenon is life and existence justified (see sec. 15 below), an assertion which would *appear* to be a natural bedfellow for the idea of the Apollonian triumph of beauty over suffering, is, in fact, associated only with Dionysian, never Apollonian art. The world is *not* justified by the Apollonian outlook but only *seems* so to its inhabitants. In a later echoing of the famous sentence that *is* connected with Apollonian art Nietzsche is careful to eliminate the notion of justification; "as an aesthetic phenomenon," he says, "existence is still *bearable* for us" (*GS* 107; Nietzsche's emphasis).

17 Nietzsche's condemnation of modern culture parallels his condemnation of the culture of the "new Attic Comedy" that succeeded the age of Greek tragedy as a culture that takes "womanish flight from seriousness and terror" into the "craven satisfaction and easy enjoyment" of "the passing moment" (*BT* 11).

18 See Nietzsche's comments on Heraclitus in "Philosophy in the tragic age of the Greeks," in *The Complete Works of Frederick Nietzsche*, ed. O. Levy (London: Foulds, 1911), vol. II, pp. 106–11.

19 Notice that the artist–god with whom we identify is an *Apollonian* artist (sculpture, remember, e.g. sand-sculpture, is a paradigm of Apollonian art), someone the object of whose consciousness is the *principium individuationis* raised to a state of beauty. Occasionally, Nietzsche makes the resemblance to the human Apollonian artist even closer by suggesting that the demiurge's motive for creation is to find an escape from the reality of its own "pain and contradiction" (*BT* 5). He refers back to this conception in *Zarathustra*:

At one time Zarathustra too cast his delusion beyond man, like all the

afterworldly. The work of a suffering and tortured god, the world then seemed
to me. A dream the world then seemed to me, and the fiction of a god: coloured
smoke before the eyes of a dissatisfied deity. Good and evil and joy and pain and
I and you – coloured smoke they seemed to me before creative eyes. The creator
wanted to look away from himself: so he created the world. (Z 1, 3)

This notion seems to me (1) inconsistent with the dominant conception
of the demiurge as a joyfully playful child whose existence is "powerful
and pleasurable," "happy" (*BT* 17), and (2) inconsistent with the idea
that identification with the primal unity constitutes a solution to the
pain of human existence. If the primal unity's mode of existence is a
copy of our own then identification with it is a transition, merely, from
the frying-pan into the fire. These inconsistencies come about, I think,
because Nietzsche wants to use the idea of the artist–god to perform two
functions: (1) to contribute an answer to the cosmological question of
why the world came into being; and (2) to figure in the Dionysian
solution to pessimism. The kind of answer he gives to (1) determines a
characterization of the demiurge inconsistent with that demanded by
(2).

20 As Petra von Morstein has suggested to me.
21 In *Ecce Homo* Nietzsche suggests that in *Wagner at Bayreuth* he uses
Wagner as Plato used Socrates "as a sign language for Plato" (*EH* v,
3).

3 *HUMAN, ALL-TOO-HUMAN*

1 Since Nietzsche wants to reduce matter to force, "motions," it would be
incorrect to treat "materialism" as a synonym for the "naturalism" to
which he subscribes. In section 5 he rejects mind–body dualism as a
primitive superstition. It seems, therefore, that Nietzsche's particular
form of naturalism is best described as "neutral monism."
2 See G. J. Stack's *Lange and Nietzsche* (Berlin: Walter de Gruyter, 1983),
pp. 226–7.
3 Mozart's "Jupiter" Symphony was, I believe, so called because it seems
to possess the effortless perfection of a god.
4 This conjunction between (Apollonian) art and the *unconditional* willing
of life seems to anticipate the theme of *The Gay Science* that (as we will
see in chapter 4) art helps us will the eternal recurrence.
5 On one occasion, Nietzsche acknowledges a cognitive value in art: in
Wagner at Bayreuth he suggests that art can provide a simplification of the
multiplicity of phenomena that reveals to us the "laws of life"
knowledge of which is essential to the adoption of a "spiritual–moral"
attitude towards it (*WB*, p. 213). But never again does he acknowledge
that it has this value. This is the most consistent deficiency in his
thought about art. Schopenhauer, in this respect, had a much better
understanding.
6 This picture of science as a value-neutral activity seems to me a myth.
Many values – truth, beauty, simplicity, interpersonal harmony, for

example – are written into the activity of science. The scientist *qua* scientist is committed to these values and does not need any outside agency to determine them for her.

7 This distinction between "spirit" and "soul" is an allusion, surely, to Plato's division between the "spirited" part of the psyche and "reason." In the *Republic* "justice" in the soul is defined as harmony between its various parts, under the leadership of "reason." There are various forms of "injustice" one of which, the "timocratic" soul, consists in the dominance of the rational soul by aggressive, ambitious, militaristic "spirit." This is what Nietzsche here seems to be rejecting.

8 Quoted in E. M. Butler *The Tyranny of Greece over Germany* (Cambridge: Cambridge University Press, 1935), p. 46.

9 See M. S. Silk and J. P. Stern, *Nietzsche on Tragedy* (Cambridge: Cambridge University Press, 1981), ch. 1, sec. 2.

10 In Nietzsche's mature philosophy, above all in *Zarathustra*, there is, of course, a very powerful anti-ant theme. The "great and beautiful soul" is conceived as a rare and isolated individual standing out from and in opposition to the multitude or "herd." But in *Opinions* there is no hint of this. Indeed the logic of the discussion precludes it, for if artists are to construct "improving" archetypes then, by definition, their audience or target is the multitude. The great individual who stands out against the herd must, of necessity (a theme which will become prominent in ch. 4), be a *self*-creator rather than a follower of other-determined archetypes.

11 Notice that Nietzsche's distinction between the classical and "baroque" is reminiscent of the Kant–Schopenhauerian distinction between the beautiful and the sublime and, of course, his own between the Apollonian and Dionysian.

12 In *The Birth* "Asia" is the home of "barbarism" that threatens always to engulf Greek (i.e. classical) civilization.

13 In *Opera and Drama* Wagner accuses Berlioz of by "purely mechanical means" creating "an unprecedented variety of... the most marvellous effects" the content of which, however, is "inartistic rubbish" (quoted in Carl Dahlhaus, "The two-fold truth in Wagner's aesthetics," in his *Between Romanticism and Modernism*, tr. M. Whittall [Berkeley: University of California Press, 1980], p. 9). Nietzsche's critique of Wagner is not intended to be novel. The intention is rather, I think, to hoist him with his own petard.

14 It seems appropriate to enter a protest against the implicit demand here that an artist should conquer the formal constraints of his art with an "illusion of ease and validity." Not only is this a highly subjective, and not particularly attractive, valuation, it also sits most uncomfortably with the suggestion in *Human*, that we should not be taken in by the artist's attempt to make his work seem the "casual improvisation of a god" (see sec. 10 above). Does Nietzsche wish to be ravished by the artist or does he not?

15 This is the first published appearance of "romantic" used, in Nietzsche's characteristic manner, as a pejorative expression.

16 Though Nietzsche would sometimes like to represent Wagner's "baroque" art as *both* of these things (see *HH* IIa, 144) they cannot possibly be simultaneously coinstantiated.

17 Another conception of the romantic would conceive of him as someone alienated from the given world not by incapacity to deal with the present and fear of the future but by the demand for more than is yielded by the present and impatience to realize it in the future. According to Nietzsche's (arbitrary) terminology, however, that person is not "romantic" but "Dionysian" ("Zarathustrian" or "Nietzschean") (see *GS* 370).

18 If this comparison is correct Nietzsche's relation to the *Gorgias* is a peculiar one. His moral philosophy, it is clear, is deeply indebted to Callicles, the ablest defender of the rhetoricians' way of life. Indeed Callicles' distinction between master and slave morality, his defense of the former and postulation of resentment as the source of the latter so closely anticipates Nietzsche's own *Genealogy of Morals* as to place the latter in some danger of sustaining a charge of plagiarism. On the other hand, if I am right, Nietzsche's objections to Wagner are influenced by Socrates' objections to rhetoric. Nietzsche, it seems, borrows from both sides in the debate which is the *Gorgias*.

4 *THE GAY SCIENCE*

1 "Nietzsche's *Gay Science*, or, how to naturalize cheerfully," in R. Solomon and K. Higgins (eds.), *Reading Nietzsche* (New York: Oxford University Press, 1988), p. 69.

2 In a letter to Franze Overbeck of 1884. See *Selected Letters of Friedrich Nietzsche*, ed. C. Middleton (Chicago: University of Chicago Press, 1969), p. 223.

3 And have been thus interpreted by Alexander Nehamas in *Nietzsche: Life as Literature* (Cambridge, Mass.: Harvard University Press, 1985), ch. 2. One of the major pieces of evidence cited by Nehamas in favor of his interpretation is the fact that at *GS* 354 Nietzsche disassociates the affirmation of perspectivism from the "opposition of 'thing in itself' and appearance." This, together with section IV of *Twilight of the Idols* ("How the 'true world' finally became a fable"), he sees as establishing that the mature Nietzsche abandoned the metaphysical contrast between thing in itself and appearance. I agree that he did. But to deny that a *thing in itself* lies behind our interpretations of the world is not at all the same as holding that *nothing* does. Two comments are in order here. First, Nietzsche typically uses "thing in itself" when he wants to evoke specifically Kantian overtones, so that to be a "thing in itself" something has to be a *non-natural* item of the kind demanded by religion, presupposed by morality, and intimated by art (see ch. 3, sec. 4, above).

It is *this* world, I think, that is denied in part IV of *Twilight of the Idols* and is probably uppermost in Nietzsche's mind at *GS* 354. Ultimate reality, as conceived by Nietzsche, is a *natural* reality. But it is also (as we are about to see) a "chaos" in which the order implicit in our concept of thinghood finds no application. Even, therefore, were one to naturalize the concept of the thing in itself Nietzsche would still, quite understandably, resist its application to reality as he conceives it.

A further criticism I have of Nehamas' (as it may be described, postmodernist) interpretation of perspectivism is that rather than introducing it in the natural way that I have – by reference to Nietzsche's *published* account of the doctrine – he chooses rather to do so by reference to the *unpublished* jotting in *The Will to Power* (sec. 481): "facts are precisely what there are not, only interpretations" (p. 42). This of course leads him to see perspectivism as deeply paradoxical and potentially self-undermining: if there are only interpretations then surely the view that there are only interpretations "is itself an interpretation and therefore possibly false" (p. 1). On my under-standing of perspectivism, however, Nietzsche is no more ensnared by paradoxes of self-references than is Kant.

Actually, even the paragraph from which Nehamas quotes is far from clear in its support for his interpretation when quoted in full: "Against positivism, which halts at phenomena – 'There are only *facts*' – I would say: No, facts is precisely what there is not, only interpretations. We cannot establish any fact 'in itself': perhaps it is folly to want to do such a thing." Naturally taken, the burden of this passage would seem to be *epistemological* rather than, as Nehamas wants to suggest, ontological. It is interesting that Kaufmann's classic *Nietzsche: Philosopher, Psychologist and Antichrist* contains no discussion at all of anything remotely resembling Nehamas' "perspectivism," a fact which reminds us of the ease with which the preoccupations of a particular age and writer are read into the history of philosophy.

4 In Plato's *Timaeus* the world that constitutes the material of God's, the Demiurge's, creative activity is described as exhibiting both chaos and necessity in that, while it fails to exhibit any of the patterns of the Forms which he will try to impose on it, it yet has, like the material with which any craftsman must work, an inalienable, "necessary," nature (disorderliness) which both limits the creative possibilities available to the demiurge and endows his handiwork with a permanent disposition to "disorderly motion," to throwing off the order into which he has "persuaded" it. It is surprising that Nehamas, a classical scholar, fails (see n. 3 above) to notice the allusion to the *Timaeus* in *GS* 109, the comparison between the demiurge and ourselves as imposters of order upon chaos.

5 *Nietzsche as Philosopher* (New York: Macmillan, 1965), p. 96.

6 There is the world of difference between believing in the religious interpretation of life because you have never confronted any alternative

and doing so in a chosen or "born again" manner. I use the image of scab-picking to capture Nietzsche' belief that modern religiosity is of the latter kind. On some level, Nietzsche believes, the modern person *knows* religious belief to be absurd but clings to it, in a self-deceiving way, out of fear of "incurable pessimism" (*BGE* 59). Modern consciousness, even that of "the people," is wounded consciousness, our various faiths at best scabs that conceal the wound.

7 Notice that though, like "the people," we have become innocent of the will to truth, we have become gayer, freer, lighter than they are, weighed down by their bourgeois conventions and responsibilities. One must, it seems, be either "heavier" or "lighter" than they; at all costs, never the same weight.

8 As in English, one can use the word *Held*, as Nietzsche does here, to indicate a (not *necessarily* heroic) central character: the hero of a novel.

9 Schopenhauer too discusses at length the problem of "style," or as he calls it "character," and he too uses aesthetic analogies (*WR* II, 35). Most people, he suggests, lack it, living confused "zigzag" lives (*WR* I, 303). For him, however, this is as a result of lack of self-knowledge; ignorance or real desires as a result of repression or ignorance (because it is very difficult to work out) of the relative strengths of one's various desires, values, and aspirations (see *Willing and Unwilling*, ch. v, secs. 5–6). The task, therefore, of achieving style is the task of self-*discovery*. For Nietzsche, however, as we will see, it is a task of self-*creation*. The contrast between the two is at this point very stark.

10 The self of the Dionysian solution cannot be authentic in a sense which implies uniqueness. For, as will become clearer, there are *many* "honest" constructions of the self.

11 See Kaufmann's translation of *The Gay Science* (New York: Vintage Press, 1974), "Translator's Introduction," sec. 3.

12 An interesting question is why this evocation of ecstasy was eliminated from the 1887 edition. Does this suggest, perhaps, an underlying darkness of mood in 1887 absent in 1882? See section 20 below.

13 Also (1) a practical and (2) a never-ending process. (1) Discovering a "personal providence" in one's life is, says Nietzsche, a matter of "practical and theoretical skill in interpreting and arranging events" (*GS* 277). The theoretical skill is the *construction* of that "artistic plan" which constitutes one's character, the practical skill is the disciplined adherence to that plan, the living of one's life *in* character. (2) As future moves into past the character of the fate that one is to love is constantly altering. This means that one's account of who one is must be fluid, flexible, open always to revision. On the title page of the second edition of *The Gay Science* Nietzsche replaces the quotation from Emerson with a new epigraph of his own composition: "I live in my own place,/ I have never copied nobody even half,/ and at any master who lacks the grace to laugh at himself – I laugh." This, in addition to the injunction to originality, contains an injunction to a degree of ironic self-

detachment, to not taking one's self-image too seriously. Otherwise the personality becomes ossified and defensive (middle-aged) – another form of inauthenticity. The life Nietzsche requires is, therefore, a difficult, dialectical combination of definiteness and openness, fixity and fluidity.

14 I have been alerted to the relevance of this term to the understanding of Nietzsche by Kathleen Higgins' lively and refreshing *Nietzsche's Zarathustra* (Philadelphia: Temple University Press, 1987). Higgins persuasively argues that a central aspect of *Zarathustra* is that it is a *Bildungsroman* (see ch. 4).

15 A very different account of why, in Nietzsche's view, one cannot will the recurrence of one's own life without willing the recurrence of world history is given by Alexander Nehamas (*Nietzsche*, ch. 5). My reasons for rejecting Nehamas' account will be given in section 20 below.

16 See note 21 below.

17 At *HH* IIb, 217, Nietzsche makes it explicit that fear of the future is what he regards as the fundamental ground of "romanticism": "Both those spirits of a classical and those of a romantic bent – these two species exist at all times – entertain a vision of the future: but the former do out of a *strength* of their age, the latter out of its *weakness*."

18 Kathleen Higgins observes pertinently that, as the title of the section indicates, we are dealing here with a "Drunken song," not a lecture in logic (*Nietzsche's Zarathustra*, p. 198).

19 An allusion, surely, to Faust's promise of his soul to Mephistopheles "Werd' ich zum Augenblicke sagen: verweile doch! Du bist so schön!" ("If I should ever say to the moment: abide! You are so beautiful").

20 Here I disagree with Kathleen Higgins who, worried that Nietzsche requires us to "love atrocities" (*Nietzsche's Zarathustra*, p. 197), represents Zarathustra as a "blues singer" who does not attempt to "white wash" the negative into the positive but who suggests, rather, that life as a whole is valuable even if some of its parts are "horrible or tragic" (pp. 198–9). I cannot find this interpretation to agree with either the letter or spirit of *amor fati*.

21 See Wittgenstein: "*How* things are in the world is a matter of complete indifference for what is higher. God does not reveal himself *in* the world. The facts all contribute only to setting the problem, not to its solution" (*Tractatus* 6.432). And: "To believe in God is to see that life has a meaning" i.e. "stops being problematic" (*Notebooks 1914–16*, ed. G. H. von Wright and G. E. M. Anscombe (Oxford: Blackwell, 1969), p. 74). "Belief in God," in other words, is a matter of seeing the "solution of the problem of life…in the vanishing of the problem" (*Tractatus* 6.521), seeing that "*The riddle* does not exist" (*Tractatus* 6.5). For further discussion see my "Wittgenstein, Kant, Schopenhauer and critical philosophy," *Theoria* 50, 2–3 (1984), 73–105. Wittgenstein's early thought on what it is to inhabit "the world of the happy person" (sec. 17 above) is close to and may have been influenced by Nietzsche's.

5 *TWILIGHT OF THE IDOLS*

1 The publication of *Nietzsche Contra Wagner* was motivated by a desire to "set the record straight": to prove that the attack on the (now dead) Wagner in *The Case of Wagner* was not the expression of a sudden fit of pique but was rather the continuation of a critique that had been sustained for over a decade. It follows that the views expressed in the work do not necessarily belong to 1888, that the compilation of the work in that year does not imply that the compiler necessarily endorsed everything it contains. I shall, accordingly, not consider the work in this chapter.

2 *Daybreak*, tr. R. J. Hollingdale with an introduction by M. Tanner (Cambridge: Cambridge University Press, 1982), pp. xiv–xv.

3 *Nietzsche* (London: Routledge and Kegan Paul, 1983), p. 508.

4 Insofar as we are discussing the "subjective" form of aesthetic pleasure (see ch. 1, sec. 6).

5 At *GM* iii, 6, Nietzsche observes correctly that Schopenhauer gives a particuar twist to Kant's association between disinterestedness and aesthetic pleasure. But his suggestion that for Schopenhauer, aesthetic pleasure is pleasure in being free of, specifically, the *sexual* will is indicative of his *own* rather than Schopenhauer's obsessions. It is, of course, willing *in general* from which, for Schopenhauer, we are delivered in aesthetic experience. Nietzsche further observes in the same section that Schopenhauer had a strong interest in achieving the aesthetic condition. This is true but is not, as Nietzsche seems to think, paradoxical. (Kant, too, believes that we can have [moral and theological] interests in achieving disinterestedness.)

6 Schopenhauer (see *WR* i, 185, 194; *WR* ii, 407–8) agrees with this assumption. The model that provides its basis is a picture of linguistic communication: the artist, like the speaker (1) is in a certain mental state she wishes to communicate, (2) selects, creates an appropriate vehicle of communication that, with luck, (3) succeeds in recreating a similar mental state in the spectator.

7 The substance in hops which accounts for their (and beer's) bitter taste. I have failed to discover any other reference to its supposed anti-aphrodisiacal power.

8 Nietzsche continues to think of "The painter, the sculptor, the epic poet" as Apollonian "visionaries par excellence" (*ibid.*). Why, then, is "representation, imitation, transfiguration, transformation" reckoned as an expression of *Dionysian Rausch*? The answer, I think, is that Dionysian representation he regards as a mere vehicle for the expression of emotion, and Apollonian representation as representation for its own sake. Had Nietzsche been acquainted with expressionism and abstract expressionism in painting he would, I think, have abandoned the unsustainable idea that, paradigmatically, the visual arts represent without expression.

9 Remember the Nietzschean axiom that the state which produces is the same as that produced by art.

10 See also section 12 below.

11 This passage of uncertain date is actually presented as a summary of the outlook of *The Birth of Tragedy*. It seems to me, however, that while in some respects seriously inaccurate as an account of *The Birth* ("The antithesis of a real and apparent world is lacking"!), it accurately expresses one of the two art solutions to the riddle of life offered by Nietzsche in his final year.

12 Goethe, for most of Nietzsche's life, was one of his supreme heroes. But in 1888 he seems to have turned against him. In addition to the above remark, consider: "I have no words, only a look for those who dare say the word Faust in the presence of [Byron's] Manfred. The Germans are incapable of any conception of greatness" (*EH* ii, 4).

13 The case of Rubens is symptomatic of a deeper tension. For if, as Nietzsche's metaphysics holds, reality is "flux," "becoming," from which all "being" is absent, and if, moreover, as Nietzsche sometimes holds, "honesty" in one's perception of the world is a value, then art too should be honest and should reflect the flux-ridden character of the world. But this means that art must be *non*classical since classical art is dedicated to the deification of reposeful being (see *GS* 370).

14 *The Importance of Nietzsche* (Chicago: University of Chicago Press, 1988), p. 166.

EPILOGUE

1 W. Kaufmann in his translation of *Ecce Homo* (*EH*, p. 258, fn.).

2 R. Hollingdale, *Nietzsche* (London: Routledge and Kegan Paul, 1973), p. 157.

17/3/92.

Texts and translations

For Nietzsche's texts I have used *Werke: Kritische Gesamtausgabe*, ed. G. Colli and M. Montinari, 30 vols. (Berlin: de Gruyter, 1967–78) and *Werke in drei Banden*, ed. K. Schlechta, 3rd edn. (Munich: Carl Hanser, 1965). For Schopenhauer's texts, the *Zürcher Ausgabe*, 10 vols. (Zurich: Diogenes, 1977). This is a paperback version of the *Sämtliche Werke*, ed. A. Hubscher (Wiesbaden: Brockhaus, 1946–50). The translations on which I have generally depended (significant emendations are accompanied by the German original) are the following:

The Antichrist, tr. W. Kaufmann, in *The Portable Nietzsche*, ed. W. Kaufmann (New York: Viking Press, 1954).

Beyond Good and Evil, tr. W. Kaufmann (New York: Vintage Press, 1966).

The Birth of Tragedy, tr. W. Kaufmann (New York: Vintage Press, 1966). This volume contains also *The Case of Wagner*, tr. W. Kaufmann.

Daybreak: Thoughts on the Prejudices of Morality, tr. R. Hollingdale (Cambridge: Cambridge University Press, 1982).

On the Genealogy of Morals, tr. W. Kaufmann and R. Hollingdale (New York: Vintage Press, 1968). This volume contains also *Ecce Homo*, tr. W. Kaufmann.

The Gay Science, tr. W. Kaufmann (New York: Vintage Press, 1974).

Human, All-too-human, tr. R. Hollingdale (Cambridge: Cambridge University Press, 1986). This volume contains also *Assorted Opinions and Maxims*, tr. R. Hollingdale, and *The Wanderer and his Shadow*, tr. R. Hollingdale.

Nietzsche Contra Wagner, tr. W. Kaufmann, in *The Portable Nietzsche*, which contains also *Twilight of the Idols*, tr. W. Kaufmann.

Richard Wagner at Bayreuth, the fourth of the *Untimely Meditations*, tr. R. Hollingdale (Cambridge: Cambridge University Press, 1983).

The Will to Power, tr. W. Kaufmann and R. Hollingdale (New York: Vintage Press, 1968).

Thus Spoke Zarathustra, tr. W. Kaufmann, in *The Portable Nietzsche*.

Index